Silvester O'Flynn OFM Cap

The Good News of
Matthew's Year

G000268947

CATHEDRAL BOOKS
Distributed to the trade by
THE COLUMBA PRESS

CATHEDRAL BOOKS
4 Sackville Place, Dublin 1.

Distributed to the trade by
THE COLUMBA PRESS
93 The Rise, Mount Merrion, Blackrock, Co Dublin, Ireland

First edition 1989
Reprinted 1992, and 1995
Cover designed by Niamh O'Gorman
Origination by The Columba Press
Printed in Ireland by
Betaprint Ltd, Dublin.

ISBN 0 948183 89 6

Nihil Obstat:
Patrick Muldoon DD
Censor Deputatus

Imprimatur:
✠ Séamus Hegarty
Bishop of Raphoe

Contents

Introduction

The hand of the scribe is our cover picture for Matthew, whose writing provides the gospel reading for most of the Sundays of Cycle A of the Roman Lectionary.

On the cover of the companion volume for Cycle C, *The Good News of Luke's Year*, the picture of hands breaking bread expressed Luke's warm portrait of how God sat down at the table of life with us. If Luke can be considered a portrait-painter, Matthew wrote more as a teacher in the fashion of Jewish scribes. In his gospel, Jesus is the preacher of the kingdom of heaven and the fulfilment of all the Law and the prophets.

As the Jewish scribes were trained in the Law of Moses, Matthew sees the ideal Christian as one thoroughly trained in the teaching of Jesus Christ. Matthew pictures the ideal disciple thus: 'Every scribe who becomes a disciple of the kingdom of heaven is like a householder who brings out from his storeroom things both old and new.'*(Mt 13:52)* It has been suggested that Matthew has here portrayed himself in the role of a Jewish scribe who has converted to Christianity. Hence our cover picture of the scribe's hand.

While Matthew provides the gospel for the majority of the Sundays of Cycle A, there are two important seasons during the year which use John's gospel. Lent has three stories from John which are used as a preparation for baptism. And the Sundays of Easter use John's gospel to highlight the new life of the followers of the Risen Lord.

This book of reflections is offered to all who wish to draw inspiration for prayer and lessons for life from the treasure-house of scripture and the storeroom of the liturgical year. I offer two reflections on each Sunday's gospel. The first reflection usually stays close to a commentary on the text, while the second takes the text into the world of today.

The companion volume for Cycle C happily proved very useful to groups who meet for prayer or discussion on a weekly basis. I have endeavoured to make the best insights of the scholars accessible to the ordinary reader who has had little chance of religious study.

While this is no attempt at a book of ready-made homilies, I trust that weekly preachers will find here something to stir their own thoughts towards making the homily's vital connection between the revealed word and the living experience of people. I have added a plan for preachers who may wish to follow a development of themes over a number of weeks. For instance, there are seven Sundays (18th to 24th) on different qualities of the Christian disciple. This block offers the preacher an opportunity to develop a worthwhile catechesis on qualities of faith. Another block (14th to 17th Sundays) offers the possibility of addressing oneself to contemporary secularism's hostility towards religion.

I wish to express my gratitude to my Capuchin brothers here at Ard Mhuire, County Donegal, for allowing me time for writing. My thanks also to Niamh O'Gorman, my niece, for her inspiring cover picture. And thanks also to Marie Blake and Finnola O'Beirne for their invaluable help in the task of typing the text.

The Good News of Jesus Christ stirred up a great belief in Matthew's mind that God is with us. Jesus Christ is Emmanuel, God promising to be with the disciples until the end of time.

My prayer for all who journey with Matthew this year is that you will know in your mind and heart that God is with us throughout the conflicts of our pilgrimage.

May God be with you.

Emmanuel.

Silvester O'Flynn OFM Cap.

Preaching in Cycle A

Preachers who must face the same audience Sunday after Sunday search for a comprehensive programme for the year, which will apply the wisdom of Scripture to the main areas of doctrine as well as matters of everyday morality. The following is an attempt to develop from the Sunday gospels some themes in a continuity.

Season of Advent

We have been through periods dominated in turn by the spirituality of Lent, Easter and Pentecost. In this age of cold secularism, the spirituality of Advent helps us face the winter and wilderness of life.

Sunday 1: On time and eternity: the circle of time.
Sunday 2: Facing the winter and wilderness of our lives.
Sunday 3: Tested in the darkness of faith (John the Baptist).
Sunday 4: Full of hope: Emmanuel.

Season of Christmas

As we prepare to welcome the third millenium of Christianity the Christmas season invites us to reflect on aspects of the incarnation and the meaning of redemption.

Christmas Day: God's gift to the poor.
Holy Family: Family support to our faith.
Epiphany: The divinity of Jesus Christ.
1st Sunday Ord. Time: Baptism of Jesus: entering the rivers of sin.
2nd Sunday Ord. Time: The Lamb who takes away the burden of guilt.

Season of Lent

Sunday 1: Desert schooling: our struggles and temptations.
Sunday 2: Listen to him: our moments of light on the mountain.
Three stories from John to prepare us for renewal of baptism at Easter:
Sunday 3: The well and waters of friendship, cleansing and life.
Sunday 4: Blind man: the inner light of faith.
Sunday 5: Lazarus: the rhythm of dying and rising with Christ.
Passion Sunday: The book of the cross.
Holy Thursday: The Covenant Meal.

Season of Easter

Easter Sunday: The call to new life.
Sunday 2: Belief in the Risen Lord.
Sunday 3: Celebrating the Risen Lord in word and meal.
Sunday 4: The call of the Lord's voice today.
Sunday 5: Jesus Christ is the only way to the Father.
Sunday 6: The dwelling of God within us.
Ascension: Glorification of Jesus and mission of the disciples.
Sunday 7: Going to our upper room (prayer).
Pentecost: Christ's mission of reconciliation in the Church.
Trinity: God as our Creator, Redeemer and Sanctifier.
Corpus Christi: Prayer before the Blessed Sacrament.

Sundays in Ordinary Time

We have placed the first two Sundays in the Christmas Season.
Sunday 3: Matthew introduces the key themes: Kingdom and Church.

Block A: Sermon on the Mount: Masterplan of the Kingdom.

Sunday 4: The attitudes and actions of kingdom-people.
Sunday 5: Light and salt to counteract our contemporary paganism.
Sunday 6: (i) Healing the energies of anger and lust.
Sunday 7: (ii) The healing of hatred.
Sunday 8: (iii) The healing of anxiety.
Sunday 9: Building life on sand or on rock.

Block B: Preparation of the Apostles

Sunday 10: Call of Matthew: a taker becomes a giver.
Sunday 11: The Apostles: call to move from disciple to apostle.
Sunday 12: The courage to be an apostle in the face of opposition.
Sunday 13: The cost of being an apostle.

Block C: The Kingdom grows amidst hostility.

Sunday 14: Although in pain, Jesus is full of praise and compassion.
Sunday 15: (i) Today's hostile climate (sower and seed).
Sunday 16: (ii) Welcoming hostility and opposition (darnel).
Sunday 17: (iii) In a catholic church (dragnet), there is room for our inner contradictions and tensions.

Block D: Life in the Christian community
Seven Sundays on various qualities of Christian discipleship.
Sunday 18: Fed by the Lord in mind and spirit, the disciple shares with others.
Sunday 19: Learning to believe and have courage in the storms of life.
Sunday 20: Faith shows persistence, humility and humour.
Sunday 21: Faith is a divine gift: Peter is 'Blessed'.
Sunday 22: Accepting God's plans ... even the cross.
Sunday 23: Trying to win back a straying member.
Sunday 24: Remembering hurts with forgiveness, not vindictiveness.

Block E: Final invitation and various responses.
Sunday 25: The noble and generous ways of God.
Sunday 26: Belonging to the kingdom as well as to the church.
Sunday 27: The invitation meets with the response of anger.
Sunday 28: The response of apathy.
Sunday 29: The sacred and the secular (religion and politics).
Sunday 30: A religion of love (love of oneself).
Sunday 31: The style of Christian leadership.
Sunday 32: Ready for the final call and invitation.
Sunday 33: Judgment and accountability.
Sunday 34 (Christ the King): Summary of the year on the kingdom.

First Sunday of Advent

The season of Advent centres on the idea of the coming of God to us. Eventually Advent will lead us into the celebration of the historical event of the coming of God to us at Christmas. But on this first Sunday our attention is drawn to the final coming of God at the end of time. Three times the phrase recurs, 'when the Son of Man comes.'

Matthew 24:37-44
Stay awake so that you may be ready

Jesus said to his disciples: 'As it was in Noah's day, so it will be when the Son of Man comes. For in those days before the Flood people were eating, drinking, taking wives, taking husbands, right up to the day Noah went into the ark, and they suspected nothing till the Flood came and swept all away. It will be like this when the Son of Man comes. Then of two men in the fields one is taken, one left; of two women at the millstone grinding, one is taken, one left.

'So stay awake, because you do not know the day when your master is coming. You may be quite sure of this that if the house-holder had known at what time of the night the burglar would come, he would have stayed awake and would not have allowed anyone to break through the wall of his house. Therefore, you too must stand ready because the Son of Man is coming at an hour you do not expect.'

Good News

Not only are our lives to be considered as journeying towards God, but the news of God in this passage is that God is ever coming to meet us.

First Reflection
Life is a Circle

It must seem odd that the Church's year should start with a gospel reading about the end of time. But time is considered as a circle, for we have come from God our Creator and are living out a journey back to God our soul's destiny. And the starting point of a circle is precisely the point of its completion.

The Advent wreath is a good expression of this circular journey of life, from God at the beginning to God at the end. The wreath is a circle of evergreen sprays, adorned with four candles, one for each week of the season.

As Advent follows November, the month of the dead, the image of the circle of time is very appropriate. Life in all its passing moments is caught up in the unending line of eternity. At death, 'life is changed, not ended."

Today's gospel brings three pictures of life before our minds: the flood hurtling down the valley towards the unsuspecting town; the unexpected disappearance of people from the company of their workmates and associates; the stealthy burglar picking his way through the security of the house.

Pictures to alarm us and fill the soul with terror?

Or is their mood not so much one of terror as a salutary tone to remind us that we must never settle down here as if we have 'made it' here for time unending? Life is always moving on.

It happens that not a month goes by without its headlines of un-expected catastrophe in earthquake or explosion, plane crash or rail disaster, famine or epidemic. Nearer home, someone we know is suddenly plucked from our midst. We are wise for the moment but very quickly forget the circular shape of time.

We continue to live as if on a straight line going away from our Creator. That is to forget that the line of life is a circle which starts and ends with God. And nothing is ultimately of value unless it serves our journey back to God.

On our way we have to let go of others in our partings, we must move on when all we have treasured is taken away, and keep going when the familiar ways are changed. Whoever lacks the eye of faith sees only an ending and a farewell. But whoever sees with the eye of God moves on into a new stage of the journey.

In the Advent wreath the evergreen foliage is a symbol of hope. In the bareness of our northern winter, nature has preserved the evergreen leaves to show us that hope need never die. The love of God is everlasting. When all around seems to die and fade away, the green leaf of God's love stays with us. And the candles which adorn the wreath express the flicker of light in the midst of life's darkest winter of the spirit. Even in pre-Christian times people expressed their yearning for light with festivals of fire and light in the middle of winter.

Our wreath has four candles, one for each week of Advent. The light increases as Advent leads into Christmas, the birth in time of the light of God.

As the first Sunday of Advent marks the beginning of the Church's year we are given the thought that the end of the journey is precisely where life started from: God. It is a journey coloured in evergreen hope because God's love is everlasting and unconditional. And it is a journey out of darkness towards increasing wisdom and light.

Second Reflection
The Son of Man is Coming

The liturgical year will carry us through all the moods and experiences of the pilgrimage of life. Sunday after Sunday we will be caught up in the memory of Jesus Christ in all its aspects.

The first Sunday of the year sets our sights on life's horizon to the coming of Christ to us at the end. We must know where the journey of life is going before we start on the way. At the end, the Son of Man is coming. Three times today's short passage speaks of his coming. So important is this belief that it is stated in the short proclamation of the faith: Christ has died, Christ is risen, Christ will come again.

Who is coming and what will it be like?

The title given here to the Lord is 'Son of Man.' Surely this echo of the humanity of Jesus Christ suggests to us that the final coming will bear many of the characteristics of his coming once in the flesh. In other words, if we want to know what the final coming will be like, we can learn it from the incarnation.

Then he came to us as light, love and life.

And these are the ways in which he will come again. Once he came as the light of the world. He was rejected by some, accepted by others: destined for the fall and the rising of many in Israel, for his light exposed many of the pretences and camouflages of life.

When he comes again his light of judgement will penetrate our barriers and strip away our masks. Then we will see ourselves in utter honesty and will be our own judges. We will know within ourselves whether we can leap towards the arms of the God who is coming, or whether we want to hide away in the darkness of guilt over what we have done to our own lives. 'On these grounds

11

is judgement pronounced: that though the light has come into the world men have shown they prefer darkness to the light because their deeds were evil. And indeed, everybody who does wrong hates the light and avoids it, for fear his actions should be exposed; but the man who lives by the truth comes out into the light, so that it may be plainly seen that what he does is done in God.' (Jn 3: 19-21).

Secondly, he came in love. God the Father so loved the world that he gave his only Son so that we might not be lost but might have eternal life. He came in love ... as a brother to embrace us ... and to serve us ... and to be our ransom. And that is how he will come again ... to draw us totally into his loving embrace.

But just as those who have rejected or surpressed all love in their lives cannot bide its mention, so at the end those who are hardened in the ways of hatred and evil will be unable to respond to his embrace of love. And hell is the searing pain of rejecting love.

Thirdly, he came that we might have life to the full. He spoke of the need to let go, even to die to self in order to grow into divine life. And his words were verified in deed as he passed through death unto the resurrection. When the Son of Man comes again and we must return the breath of life to the Father, it will be to invite us to share in the fulness of divine life. But if we have sold our birthright for a mess of pottage, then his invitation will be to our shame and embarrassment.

That he will come again is certain: for all surely die. The only uncertainty is when. Too easily we are so deafened by the clamours of the flesh and the noises of the streets of life that we fail to hear the rumble of the approaching flood down our valley. Or we are so comfortably ensconsed in the domesticity of self-centred living that we fail to hear the burglar breaking through the wall.

The message at the start of Advent is to stay awake... watch...for the Son of Man is coming. The manner of his coming will be in imitation of the thrust of light, love and light which entered the world in Jesus of Nazareth. And the manner of our acceptance of him will be the way that we are open today to the honesty of light, the calls of love and the challenges of life. For as we live, so shall we die.

Second Sunday of Advent

Today's gospel draws attention to John the Baptist. His mission was to prepare the way for the Saviour. This passage tells of how John appeared, that he preached repentance and opened up for people the prospect of a greater person who would come on a more critical mission.

Matthew 3:1-12
Repent, for the kingdom of heaven is close at hand.

In due course John the Baptist appeared; he preached in the wilderness of Judaea and this was his message: 'Repent, for the kingdom of heaven is close at hand.' This was the man the prophet Isaiah spoke of when he said:

A voice cries in the wilderness:
Prepare a way for the Lord,
make his paths straight.

This man John wore a garment made of camel-hair with a leather belt round his waist, and his food was locusts and wild honey. Then Jerusalem and all Judaea and the whole Jordan district made their way to him, and as they were baptised by him in the river Jordan they confessed their sins. But when he saw a number of Pharisees and Sadducees coming for baptism he said to them, 'Brood of vipers, who warned you to fly from the retribution that is coming? But if you are repentant, produce the appropriate fruit, and do not presume to tell yourselves, "We have Abraham for our father," because, I tell you, God can raise children for Abraham from these stones. Even now the axe is laid to the roots of the trees, so that any tree which fails to produce good fruit will be cut down and thrown on the fire. I baptise you in water for repentance, but the one who follows me is more powerful than I am, and I am not fit to carry his sandals; he will baptise you with the Holy Spirit and fire. His winnowing-fan is in his hand; he will clear his threshing-floor and gather his wheat into the barn; but the chaff he will burn in a fire that will never go out.'

Good News
The news here is of a God who comes. And the way to prepare a road for this coming of God into our hearts is repentance.

13

First Reflection
Desert Sunday

The second Sunday of Advent might well be called Desert Sunday. In all three years of the lectionary this Sunday is dominated by the challenging voice from the wilderness, John the Baptist. Matthew's presentation of the Baptist is sparing: bare as the desert itself. Nothing is said of his background. In due course he appeared. That's all. And his message is straight from the shoulder. No attempt to woo an audience or to sell himself: "Repent, for the kingdom of heaven is close at hand."

Repent ... sort out your life ... clear up your vision ... reassess your values in life. And then do something about improving.

In the run-up to Christmas we need a desert day.

A desert day to counteract the commercial pressures and the sentimental hype that make Christmas the season of materialism, gluttony, drunkenness and shallow entertainment. Take a sharp look at today's Sunday papers to see what they are saying about Christmas. What values are reflected there? The religious meaning of Christmas?

I've never been to the real desert. I rely on what others have written and I try to imagine the experience of living there. I fancy that the sheer struggle for survival would so dominate every other consideration that you'd quickly sort out the wheat from the chaff of life: the essential from the unnecessary: the things that last from the things that pass away.

I think that if you had companions in the desert you'd very quickly see through all the masks and pretences of life. You would know the sincere friend from the insincere. Others would see through you too. And you'd probably see yourself with stunning clarity for the first time ever.

I asked an Australian sister what her first experience of a northern winter and Advent meant to her. The discomfort of coldness and damp were too obvious to mention. She spoke of her new experience of light in the contrasts of winter twilight. And of the stark shape of trees as never seen before. And the sharp contour of housetop, hilltop and horizon.

Desert days ... winter twilights ... experiences that invite the mind to reflect on the essential thrust and shape of life, stripped of its adornments and masks.

14

To sort out the wheat from the chaff. To repent. To prepare a way for the Lord who daily reaches out to come into our hearts.

Second Reflection
Advent Spirituality (1)

For many years the mood which prevailed in spirituality was that of Lent: religion came clothed in the garb of penance.

Then in the 1960's, as society basked in the euphoria which accompanied the new age of Camelot revisited, we rediscovered the spirituality of Easter. To the fourteen stations on the way of the cross some added a fifteenth station, feeling that a meditation on the sufferings of Christ should always include the victory of the resurrection. Black vestments were consigned to the attic and the mournful "Dies Irae", a hymn about the day of wrathful judgment, was heard no more. A cloud of suspicion hung over many penitential practices which were regarded as psychologically unhealthy. People spoke of the need for the eighteen inch drop ... from the head into the heart. If we believed in Christ as Redeemer of the world, then the message should be sent up to our faces!

Easter spirituality prepared the way for the charismatic movement and the spirituality of Pentecost. This was in the early '70's when the mood of society had changed. The dream of Camelot evaporated in the aftermath of notable assassinations: flower power had now become the drug problem: and a petrol shortage rocked national economies. A spirituality was needed which would reach into the broken areas of life and offer a healing touch. We were ready for Pentecostal spirituality and charismatic healing.

Now, in the late 1980's, perhaps it is time to draw from the spiritual wealth of another liturgical season, Advent. Pope John Paul II has directed our thoughts towards the year 2000 A.D., the second Millennium of our Redeemer. The decade leading up to that event is an extended Advent. Our attention was directed towards Mary as "the one who in the night of Advent expectation began to shine as the true Morning Star." (*Redemptoris Mater*, 3)

Advent is the season which faces up to the winter and wilderness of life. Winter, cold and dark, stands for all that we dread in life and all the happenings which diminish us, stripping us bare as the branches.

The wilderness represents the wild, untamed forces that we meet in ourselves. To many people the worldwide scenario is a terrifying moral wilderness: rampant promiscuity, increasing breakdown of family life, aggression on faces and despair in hearts. Many too are oppressed by the fear that the technological monster we have constructed will not have the heart to preserve the world from self-destruction. Mention of Chernobyl sends a chilling tremor down the spine and there are dire predictions due to ozone holes and melting icepacks. In this wilderness of the spirit depression is commonplace and we all know people who no longer find the motivation to go on living.

Advent spirituality is relevant for this generation living with the cold of winter and the dread of the wilderness. The strength of Advent is in honestly facing and naming the problems, in the sureness that the God who comes is more powerful than sin. The Advent man, John the Baptist, cried out: "Repent, for the kingdom of God is close at hand."

To repent means to admit our sinful ways and to accept responsibility for our lives. It means to change direction and to start afresh. The power to do so is available to us from the God who comes to our assistance.

The wish of Pope John Paul II is that we would celebrate an Advent-decade of repentance to prepare for the Lord's coming. And then we will be ready to celebrate the second Millennium of the coming of the Redeemer in the year 2000 A.D.

Third Sunday of Advent

John the Baptist is the great figure of Advent repentance. We met him last Sunday in his open air preaching. In today's gospel this rugged man of the open spaces is cooped up in the dark confinement of prison. The dark cell which confined his body corresponds to the dim region of faith in which his soul is travelling. And yet, this struggling soul is praised by Jesus as the greatest child ever born of woman.

Matthew 11:2-11

Are you the one who is to come,
or have we got to wait for someone else?

John in his prison has heard what Christ was doing and he sent his disciples to ask him, 'Are you the one who is to come, or have we got to wait for someone else?' Jesus answered, 'Go back and tell John what you hear and see; the blind see again, and the lame walk, lepers are cleansed, and the deaf hear, and the dead are raised to life and the Good News is proclaimed to the poor; and happy is the man who does not lose faith in me.'

As the messengers were leaving, Jesus began to talk to the people about John: 'What did you go out into the wilderness to see? A reed swaying in the breeze? No? Then what did you go out to see? A man wearing fine clothes? Oh no, those who wear fine clothes are to be found in palaces. Then what did you go out for? To see a prophet? Yes, I tell you, and much more than a prophet: he is the one of whom scripture says: Look, I am going to send my messenger before you. I tell you solemnly, of all the children born of women, a greater than John the Baptist has never been seen; yet the least in the kingdom of heaven is greater than he is.'

Good News

Blessed are they who do not lose faith in Jesus in times of darkness: for when their own plans are shattered, they remain open to the challenge of God's plans.

First Reflection
The Greatness of John

John the Baptist was a great saint. Jesus praised him highly: of all the children born of women, no one greater had appeared.

John was no bending reed who would sway with every passing breeze or popular fancy. Nor was he one to court the influence of political patronage. People flocked to him because they recognised him as a prophet, that is a man of God whose message came from heaven. It was centuries since they had a real prophet, a sure spokesman of God's will.

What did Jesus recognise in this rugged cousin? He could see the saint in him: the willingness to let go of self whenever God called him forward.

The story of John's life might easily have been the recipe for neurotic loneliness rather than sanctity. He was born an only child to aged parents. In so far as we can piece his life together, he went at an early age into the wilderness *(Lk 1:80)*. This probably means that as a young boy he was sent to the Essene monastery near the Dead Sea. Anybody who experienced boarding school will have some appreciation of the loneliness of his lot.

John seems to have left this monastery to start his own ministry. His life was penitential and his message harsh: a ministry which might attract followers but not close friends. Again loneliness was his lot.

Once Jesus appeared on the scene, John handed over to him, utterly unselfish. "Look, there is the Lamb of God ... follow him." The motto of his life is given to us by the evangelist John: "He must grow greater and I must grow smaller." *(Jn 3:30)*. Again total unselfishness.

It was this unselfishness that gave him the moral courage to confront Herod over his scandalous marital affairs. The reward for his courage was a dark cell in the forbidding mountain fortress, Machaerus. Here he discovered a new depth of loneliness in the absence of his familiar companions ... the free wind, the fresh water, the pure honey and the open sky.

Was there anything else that God might strip him of before he must lay his head on the block?

Yes, there was. John had to endure his very dreams being shattered.

Jesus, the one he had handed over to, was not producing the promised axe or threshing flail. The dramatic day of judgment which John had visualised was not coming about. It was John himself who was left threshing in the maelstrom of faith's dimness. So he reached out for help and sent messengers to Jesus. Jesus was confident that John's great sanctity would carry him through the storm of faith. His answer is gentle and calculated to

18

draw John's mind back to the light of God's goodness. Works of healing are being performed: news of God is being proclaimed. 'Blessed is the one who does not lose faith in me.'

John, so highly praised as a man of God, measured up to the challenge. We can be sure that he let his own dreams die in order to be changed by God. 'He must grow greater and I must grow smaller.'

The liturgical calendar catches the counterpointing themes of Jesus and John. The birth of Jesus is celebrated in mid-winter as we mark the return of the unconquered sun. But the feast of John the Baptist is timed for midsummer day when the sun begins to wane. John was the unselfish light who was willing to hand over.

One thinks of the lines of C. Day Lewis as he reflects on the first significant steps towards independence shown by his young son. It was the beginning of God's lesson on:

"How selfhood begins with a walking away,
And love is proved in the letting go."

John the Baptist proved willing to let go of all that God would ask on the pilgrimage of faith.

A great prophet.

And a great saint.

Second Reflection
Advent Spirituality (2)

Advent Spirituality develops the strength to wait: to wait with patience: patience that is born out of hope.

Advent picks up the experience of winter. We yearn for light: we search for heat: the very earth is barren and asleep. And yet, soon the days will begin to lengthen with the sure stretch of a cock's step.

John the Baptist, a great saint, was experiencing a winter of the spirit. The mood was cold: the mind was dark: he was imprisoned.

Many highly spirited people have felt totally free in prison. Like Paul, who wrote his words of purest joy in a prison cell. But John was far from joy: all locked up within: still chained to his plan for God's work. He had never imagined that God's plan might possibly be different from what he had preached. John, with his limited understanding of what was to come, promised a dramatic ending to the old order of affairs.

But the work of Jesus was directed more towards the beginning of the new order. People were beginning to see afresh, to hear again, to wear a new skin, to experience a new life. And the poor were hearing the new word of faith ... that God was on their side.

Advent spirituality is relevant today to many saintly souls who are experiencing a winter coldness of faith in the changed climate of religious thought and practice.

John the Baptist exemplified how we can be imprisoned in our own perception of God's plan, our own schemes, our own memory of the golden past. We may be resisting the new order.

As John's preaching of coming judgment was bound up with a vision of the ending of affairs, our unmoved thoughts too may be moribund, heading for death and dissolution.

The presence of the Spirit, however, will always be shown in new life, fresh vitality and growth. But where is that evidence of the Spirit? Many can see the signs of spring already in the church. And in abundance. But others seem to be asked by God to stay some time longer in winter.

Winter's pain is felt as religious houses are closed: in the decrease in religious vocations: in the loss of a much loved religious practice: when we find that a traditional religious dress or lifestyle is now counterproductive.

When the ways of the past have lost their vitality and no longer attract the young ... we must wait.

When the present vision is very unclear and we feel very insecure ... we must wait.

When the way forward cannot be seen ... we must wait.

Advent spirituality develops the strength to wait: to wait with patience: patience that is born out of hope.

Today's second reading (James 5:7-10) brings us back to the land and how the farmer learns to be patient with the seasons. Who would expect to see summer's growing powers in the middle of winter?

The life of faith too has its cycle of winter.

Winter and Advent call on us to wait with patience.

And 'blessed are they who do not lose faith in me.'

Fourth Sunday of Advent

In the last week of our preparation for Christmas our attention is directed towards the two people whose lives were most drawn into the event ... Mary and Joseph. The more familiar story of the annunciation is found in Luke's gospel. But the story in today's Mass is Matthew's account of the message given to Joseph by an angel in a dream.

Matthew 1:18-24

Jesus is born of Mary who was betrothed to Joseph, son of David

This is how Jesus Christ came to be born. His mother Mary was betrothed to Joseph; but before they came to live together she was found to be with child through the Holy Spirit. Her husband, Joseph, being a man of honour and wanting to spare her publicity, decided to divorce her informally. He had made up his mind to do this when the angel of the Lord appeared to him in a dream, and said, 'Joseph son of David, do not be afraid to take Mary home as your wife, because she has conceived what is in her by the Holy Spirit. She will give birth to a son and you must name him Jesus, because he is the one who is to save his people from their sins.' Now all this took place to fulfil the words spoken by the Lord through the prophet:

The virgin will conceive and give birth to a son
and they will call him Emmanuel,

a name which means 'God-is-with-us'. When Joseph woke up he did what the angel of the Lord had told him: he took his wife to his home.

Good News

The wonderful news given to Joseph is that the power of the Holy Spirit is in Mary's child. He will take away the barrier of sin between us and God. And from this time on God is the One-who-is-with-us.

First Reflection

A Saviour, Emmanuel

One of the great intentions of the evangelists is to answer the question, "Who is Jesus?" Matthew's answer is written in such a way as to reach out in appeal to the Jewish mind to accept that Jesus is the fulfilment of the Old Testament hopes and strivings.

This story of the annunciation to Joseph draws out of the rich river of Jewish memory. Matthew uses Joseph as his link with many of the great Old Testament saints and the hopes that they represented.

As we read that Joseph had a dream we remember another Joseph who had dreams, one of which was about a technicolour coat. We are linked to the days of the patriarchs, for this Joseph was the great-grandson of Abraham ... Abraham, the first recipient of divine revelation, the holy father of believers.

Then we hear that this child of Mary will save his people from their sins, leading them out of slavery. Suggestions of a new Moses, surely!

And Joseph himself is addressed by the angel as son of David. What memories of David tumble out before us! David was a native of Bethlehem. He was but a boy-shepherd when the call of God entered his life to anoint him as the future king. He was revered in sacred story as the king who overcame the tribal rivalries and united the nation, who succeeded in liberating the land from foreign invaders and who established their capital city, Jerusalem. And Jerusalem became the holy city, site of the temple of God's presence upon earth.

Who then is this child soon to enter upon the stage of history?

Matthew is telling us that he is the new Abraham, source of divine revelation and faith for the people. He is the new Moses who will liberate his people from the slave-land of sin. He is the new David, shepherd and ideal king, leading his united people to the new Jerusalem, city of the presence of God.

The saints of the Old Testament drew their strength and consolation from the words of promise, "I will be with you." Now at the climax of history the promise is fulfilled. God is with us.

The slave-chains of sin have been broken: the barrier from God's presence knocked down: the cloud hiding the face of God has been removed. For the one who saves from sin has come to Mary's womb. Jesus is the fulfilment of every holy hope, need and expectation.

Jesus is the presence of God to our desert-emptiness,
power to our weakness, life to our dying,
bread to our hunger, water to our thirst,
companion to our loneliness, forgiveness in our sins.

Second Reflection

Two Names

Advent spirituality is most relevant to the world of today when so many people are experiencing a winter of the spirit and a wilderness where terrifying demons stalk the land. Advent spirituality hears the call of the Baptist to recognise that the source of our modern evils is sin. Advent spirituality encourages us to wait in hope and not to lose faith.

And in today's Mass the spirituality of Advent reaches a climax of hope. The victory over sin has already been won. Matthew brings us the story behind two names, Jesus and Emmanuel.

Jesus means God-is-salvation. The Holy Spirit has begun to invade the world and the child in Mary's womb will be the one to save his people from their sins.

Emmanuel is a name which says God-is-with-us. Centuries before, when Isaiah confronted the wavering king, Ahaz, the name Emmanuel was a sign that God was with his people and there was no need to enter into alliance with pagan powers.

Now Matthew brings up the name again. This is the first of many instances where he takes an Old Testament text to show how Jesus was the answer to Jewish expectations. And this belief that God is with us is so important to Matthew that he will close his gospel on that same theme: Jesus, about to ascend to the Father, promises to be with the disciples always, yes, to the end of time.

By bringing the two names Jesus and Emmanuel together in one event, Matthew expresses a gigantic step forward in human history from the age of sin to the presence of God's power on earth.

Yet here in Advent's desert starkness we know all too well how strong is the hold of sin upon us still: how brutish and destructive are the effects of sin upon society.

But we are invited to step forward in faith. Faith believes that in Jesus the victory over sin has been won. The Holy Spirit has invaded the world in a powerful advance against the enemy. The child in Mary's womb is Jesus, whose precious name proclaims that God can save from sin. All we have to do is lay claim to the victory already won: to come forward to receive the prize.

And we can rejoice even in the wilderness of sin for the power of the Spirit in Jesus is greater than sin. This is what we celebrate in Advent's sacrament of reconciliation.

Christmas Day

Advent's waiting is over, its expectation fulfilled. Into the soul's winter darkness the light of God has shone. A saviour has been born.

Luke 2:1-14
Today a saviour has been born to you

Caesar Augustus issued a decree for a census of the whole world to be taken. This census – the first – took place while Quirinius was governor of Syria, and everyone went to his own town to be registered. So Joseph set out from the town of Nazareth in Galilee and travelled up to Judaea, to the town of David called Bethlehem, since he was of David's house and line, in order to be registered along with Mary, his betrothed, who was with child. While they were there the time came for her to have her child, and she gave birth to a son, her first-born. She wrapped him in swaddling clothes, and laid him in a manger because there was no room for them at the inn. In the countryside close by there were shepherds who lived in the fields and took it in turns to watch their flocks during the night. The angel of the Lord appeared to them and the glory of the Lord shone around them. They were terrified, but the angel said, 'Do not be afraid. Listen, I bring you news of great joy, a joy to be shared by the whole people. Today in the town of David a saviour has been born to you; he is Christ the Lord. And here is a sign for you: you will find a baby wrapped in swaddling clothes and lying in a manger.' And suddenly with the angel there was a great throng of the heavenly host, praising God and singing:

'Glory to God in the highest heaven,
and peace to men who enjoy his favour.'

Good News

A saviour has been born to us. God has shown his tender mercy towards us and in compassion has come to meet us in our human condition.

First Reflection
Luke's Story

Christian faith accepts that at a certain moment in time God stepped into our history, clad in our flesh and blood, in order to heal our sinfulness and draw us to himself. St John expressed the mystery in one short sentence: 'The Word was made flesh and dwelt among us.'

But St Luke has fleshed out the mystery in a story of people and places. It is a story that children can understand. In fact, it is only the child in the soul that can appreciate it with proper wonder and the sense of being involved in the story. Luke's familiar story has given us the crib tableau and the script of that play which four year-olds perform for admiring parents on their theatrical debut. It has inspired the artists, poets and hymn writers of a thousand cultures. We see pictures based on the story on Christmas cards which range from the masters to the modern commercial mixture of biblical figures and winter symbols like holly, redbreasted robins and snow.

But the story needs a closer look because familiarity may have dulled the edge of appreciation.

Luke has a great sense of how God has put down the mighty from their high places and exalted the lowly in the reversal of human standards. He cites the names of places in an order of decreasing importance. Commencing with a decree that affects the whole world, the picture centres on the province of Syria before narrowing down to the unpretentious town of Nazareth in Galilee and the small Judaean town, Bethlehem. Luke is aware that the movement would be reversed and that from Bethlehem and Nazareth the message of life would spread throughout Syria and reach Rome, the capital of the world.

The same descending movement is attached to the houses and dynasties mentioned. The story begins in the imperial palace of Caesar Augustus. It reaches the ancient royal house of David. But where the divine child is born is not even a house. Luke's words are deliberate: 'there was no room for them at the inn.' Yet the divine reversal is hinted in the name Bethlehem, which means the house of bread. Again Luke is aware that no house can contain the divine one who has come: yet for our sake he chose to be present in the Eucharistic bread. And he who came to feed the world's spiritual hunger is first laid in the feeding trough of the dumb animals.

The people who are caught up in the story come to us in the same descending order. Luke begins with the emporer, Caesar Augustus. Next comes the govenor of Syria, Quirinius: then Joseph

25

and Mary, unknowns in the eyes of the world. Finally we meet the shepherds, poorly paid hirelings, commonly regarded as thieves and unwelcome at religious celebrations because of their smelly clothes and contraventions of religious hygiene.

Again Luke delights in the reversal of roles. Bethlehem had been the birthplace of David, who from the unlikely start of shepherd boy and youngest son became the nation's greatest king. Now, to the other Bethlehem shepherds, is given news of great joy for the whole world.

Into these humble places shines the light of glory. And unto such unimportant people comes the messenger angel and the great throng of the heavenly choir.

Luke always likes to follow up his description of action with a comment on the inner reactions of people to the event.

He reveals something of the inner life of Mary who treasured these things and pondered them in her heart. Not just weighed them up: but Luke's word indicates how Mary kept on connecting these happenings with later events.

About the shepherds, Luke notes that they responded to the happenings by glorifying and praising God.

Christmas is the time to find the saviour in the most unlikely place of all ... in my own sinful soul. And to discover the child in my own soul, capable of wonder and astonishment: willing to let go of self to rise into praise and glory.

Second Reflection
God's gift to the poor

Christmas is for all: and especially for the poor and lonely, for those who are weighed down by sin and for all who feel alienated from God or the church.

Christmas is the gift of God to all. It is the good news of a joy to be shared by the whole people. However, the commercial and social interpretations of Christmas have so usurped the mind that this news of religious joy cannot reach the hearts of many. Sadly, there are many people who hate the very thought of Christmas and dread the prospect. There is pressure on them to go through the motions of exchanging greetings of happy Christmas: but every smile is a pain and their words echo in silent loneliness within.

The commercial exploitation of Christmas alienates those who do not have the money to be caught up in the shopping orgy. It is the season of deepest pain for those children who have no Santa to answer their dreams. It means bitterness in the hearts of those who feel they cannot visit relatives because they would have to go emptyhanded.

The social merry-making associated with Christmas grates on the nerves of those who are lonely whenever they notice the empty chair at home. And the season of peace will be a week of war in those homes which are wrecked by the selfish abuse of drink. All this commercial exploitation and social expectation make it difficult for the soul to hear the good news.

Maybe if we had less fuss about exchanging gifts with one another we might have a better appreciation of God's gift to us which is the heart of the celebration.

The song of the angels celebrated the two dimensions of Christmas: glory ascending from earth to God on high; and peace of soul to all on earth who are now the recipients of God's gift.

For years we were familiar with the translation 'and peace to men of good will.' It left us with the impression that peace was for the good people. Almost as if their goodness had deserved it. St Paul, however, makes it very clear that God's gift was not due to any righteous actions we might have done: 'it was for no reason except his own compassion that he saved us.' *(Titus 3:5, a text used in the Dawn Mass.)*

The stupendous gift of God is a saviour to a sinful world: a shepherd to lost sheep: a light to those in darkness: the healing of God for our wounds: the side-by-side companionship of God for all of us on the road of life.

Luke intentionally highlights the involvement of unknown people and unfashionable places in the story of God's gift. Not even the poorest of the poor can feel alienated when they hear how the divine child came into a no-room beginning.

Would the powerful Caesar Augustus or the governor, Quirinius, have appreciated the angel's message as much as the low class shepherds?

Would the event have drawn in people of every age had the birth occurred in the imperial palace rather than the bare cave?

I think the well-off people would have regarded it as a reward for their imagined goodness.

But Mary, Joseph and the shepherds knew that it was purely God's gift. They were simply astonished and full of wonder at the news.

Christmas is the news of God's compassion towards us in our poverty and pain, our loneliness and alienation, our sinfulness and straying.

'I bring you news of great joy, a joy to be shared by the whole people.'

A gift especially for the poor and lonely, the guilt-ridden and the alienated.

Feast of the Holy Family

From Bethlehem and the tableau around the divine child in the crib, we are drawn forward into the early years of Jesus. Today's feast sets up the holy family of Jesus, Mary and Joseph as a model for every Christian family.

The first two readings – from Ecclesiasticus and Colossians – offer very practical suggestions about family life. The reading from Matthew's gospel, however, opens up thoughts on quite a different level. Matthew, in his endeavour to make Jesus acceptable to the Jewish mind, tells the story of the early years of Jesus in a manner that re-echoes the entire history of God's redeeming work for their nation.

Matthew 2:13-15.19-23
Take the child and his mother and escape into Egypt

After the wise men had left, the angel of the Lord appeared to Joseph in a dream and said, 'Get up, take the child and his mother with you, and escape into Egypt, and stay there until I tell you, because Herod intends to search for the child and do away with him.' So Joseph got up and, taking the child and his mother with him, left that night for Egypt, where he stayed until Herod was dead. This was to fulfil what the Lord had spoken through the prophet: I called my son out of Egypt.

After Herod's death, the angel of the Lord appeared in a dream to Joseph in Egypt and said, 'Get up, take the child and his mother with you and go back to the land of Israel, for those who wanted to kill the child are dead.' So Joseph got up and, taking the child and his mother with him, went back to the land of Israel. But when he learnt that Archelaus had succeeded his father Herod as ruler of Judaea he was afraid to go there, and being warned in a dream he left for the region of Galilee. There he settled in a town called Nazareth. In this way the words spoken through the prophets were to be fulfilled:

He will be called a Nazarene.

Good News

The mighty and merciful work of God throughout the history of the Old Testament people has reached a climax in the story of Jesus.

First Reflection
Two journeys

We read of two journeys: the hurried escape into Egypt; and then the return to the land of Israel, eventually to Nazareth.

The journey into Egypt was a flight to safety out of danger. In the mind of Jewish history Egypt was associated with refuge for those who were fleeing persecution. Jacob once found refuge in Egypt. Later, his son Joseph found safety there from his jealous brothers, who, in turn, were driven there in search of food.

At the time of Matthew's writing, after the destruction of Jerusalem by the Roman armies, Egypt had become the abode of many of the dispersed Jews. Indeed, there are reports that one city alone, Alexandria, housed as many as one million Jewish exiles. The journey out of Egypt made a significant connection with the story of Moses. It was out of Egypt that Moses led the people in the long trek of exodus until their eventual entry into a land of their own, Israel. From being a motley band of downtrodden slaves God had chosen them and formed them into a nation with a home of their own. This was the first act of the great drama of salvation.

Matthew rejoices in applying to Jesus the same words which had expressed the saving call of the nation, Israel: 'I called my son out of Egypt.'

The second journey of Jesus eventually reaches Nazareth, where the family settled. Matthew takes poetic liberty with words in his effort to find an Old Testament echo in the name Nazareth. One explanation links the word 'Nararene' with the word for a branch. And this is enough for Matthew to hear the echo of Isaiah as he promised a blessed king in the house of David, a new branch from the old roots. *(cf. Is 11:1)*

Matthew, then, invites his readers to see in Jesus all that Moses and David stood for. In him the entire story of God's saving work reaches a fulfilment. As the new Moses or law-giver, Jesus would bring the law to its inner meaning and fulfilment. And he would be the leader of the sin-enslaved people across the waters of baptism into the heritage of the Father's kingdom.

As the new David, Jesus would be the shepherd of the people and the king to overcome tribal differences in the reconciliation of all nations.

From a different perspective one can see further levels of meaning in the two journeys. Egypt represents how Jesus visited us in our exile to lead us home as chosen children of the Father. Egypt, as the place of refuge, shows the mission of Jesus to be among the innocent victims of injustice, exploitation and persecution. Egypt, associated with fleshpots and sinful ways, represents the outreach of God to us by coming to meet us in our sinfulness.

The second journey represents quite a different experience of life. The family settled at Nazareth. Nazareth was an unpretentious town which had no associations with religious history. It may very well have been a town which expanded with the influx of labourers and tradesmen who were involved in Herod's great building projects. Nazareth, the labourers' town, represents the coming of God to meet us in the ordinary affairs of workaday life.

Who is Jesus? He is the one who raises up the entire Old Testament story to a new level of meaning. He is the Saviour come to meet us in our exile: in our experiences of injustice and violence: and even in our sinfulness. And he is the divine one, now fully human, who settled into ordinary family affairs and invested our everyday world with new sacredness.

Second Reflection
The Hidden Life
Eventually the family of Joseph, Mary and Jesus settled in Nazareth. This unpretentious town was a fitting location for the growing years of Jesus which were conspicuous for the lack of extraordinary happenings. It was a hidden life.

According to Luke, Jesus lived under the parental authority of Joseph and Mary. He advanced in wisdom, grew in physical stature and matured in his relationship with God and people. *(cf.Luke 2:51-52)*

Later, when Jesus began his public ministry, the people of Nazareth were taken aback at his new career. They could not accept the preaching of one whom they knew as the carpenter's son (and probably a carpenter himself too). They knew all his relations. And these same relations, so Mark tells us, thought that the excitement around Jesus had gone too far, so 'they set out to take charge of him, convinced he was out of his mind.' *(Mark 3:21)* The inner greatness of Jesus was indeed hidden under the extraordinarily ordinary circumstances of life.

The same pattern of hidden inner greatness of soul applied to Joseph and Mary. Matthew's stories present Joseph as a spiritually sensitive soul who was capable of hearing the word of God in dreams. Everybody dreams but not everybody is in touch with what the dreams tell us. Mary, in Luke's story of the annunciation, is deeply attentive to God's spiritual messenger and is totally open to whatever God will have done to her.

Mary and Joseph go forward in life, totally submissive and obedient to God's will. This attitude makes them models in the pilgrimage of faith.

In his letter for the Marian Year, Pople John Paul ll wrote of the faith of Mary in terms of how she abandoned herself to the truth of the word of the living God, knowing and humbly recognising how unsearchable are his judgments and how inscrutable his ways. *(Redemptoris Mater, 14)*

The pilgrimage of faith is a lifelong journey through experiences which correspond to the clear light of day and our dim peering through the dark of night.

Faith casts daytime light on many of life's questions and pursuits. But the journey of faith is not totally in clear light. Otherwise it would be called sight, not faith. The journey goes into the soul's experience of the desert in dryness of heart and darkness of mind: it leads into areas beyond our understanding: into the 'silence beyond words'.

The papal letter reflects on the dim light of faith in Mary's life as she (and Joseph too) freely accepted with an open heart everything that was decreed in the divine plan ... the prospect of the sword of sorrow that would pierce her heart, enforced exile, being subject to the changing winds of political powers.

Mary and Joseph were on this journey together. They were each strongly supportive to the other. And that is a very important part of the pilgrimage of faith

Our journey in faith is never on a road that is travelled alone. And we can invent all manner of problems when we fail to remember those who travel with us.

Our very first steps in faith were taken upon hearing the

word from another. The support that we receive from a believing society around us is incalculable. But the erosion of faith in an unsupporting atmosphere is also immeasurable.

For better or for worse, the most influential people in our lives are those with whom we live. The greatest support or barrier to the development of faith comes from the quality of family life in our formative years. Which is the reason why recent popes have referred to the Christian family as the domestic church or the little church.

Hidden in the ordinary, everyday journey of family life, the inner greatness of faith develops. The model is the home at Nazareth where Jesus, living under the authority of Joseph and Mary, 'increased in wisdom, in stature, and in favour with God and men.' *(Luke 2:52)*

Solemnity of Mary, Mother of God

On New Year's Day we are asked to pray for a year of peace throughout the world. Liturgically the focus is on Mary under the highest of her titles, Mother of God. The gospel of the day refers to the eighth day, when the child was circumcised and given the name Jesus.

Lk 2:16-21
The shepherds found Mary and Joseph, and the baby ...

When the eighth day came they gave him the name of Jesus

The shepherds hurried away to Bethlehem and found Mary and Joseph, and the baby lying in the manger. When they saw the child, they repeated what they had been told about him, and everyone who heard it was astonished at what the shepherds had to say. As for Mary, she treasured all these things and pondered them in her heart. And the shepherds went back glorifying and praising God for all they had heard and seen; it was exactly as they had been told.

When the eighth day came and the child was to be circumcised, they gave him the name Jesus, the name the angel had given him before his conception.

Good News
Christmas is more than some winter feast, celebrated for a few days, and then forgotten. It is to be treasured and pondered every day, for it is the news that God has entered the world as our saviour, known to us as Jesus.

First Reflection
Mary Treasured and Pondered

'How did you get over the Christmas?'

'It was very quiet this year, wasn't it? Not like long ago.'

'Wasn't the television hopeless! Never saw anything like it!'

Jaded comments, typical of a week after Christmas.

Christmas is not just a few days for getting sentimental about the figure of a baby lying in a manger before we get on with the serious business of real life for the rest of the year. The message of the coming of God to us in our human flesh is vitally relevant to every day and every moment of the year we are commencing. It is a year which is numbered from the first Christmas, *Anno Domini*, a year of the Lord.

The shepherds went back to their fields glorifying and praising God for all that they had heard and seen. Were they still full of the prayer of praise a week later ... a month later?

We do not know. But what we are told is that Mary stayed with the message and it enlightened her life every day from there on. Luke tells us that 'she treasured all these things and pondered them in her heart'.

Mary so treasured the Bethlehem experience that she carried it through into everything that happened down the years. That is exactly what is meant by a contemplative attitude toward life. Contemplation is to do with measuring.

The root of the word is the Greek word for cutting a notch in a measuring rod. So we speak of temperature as the measurement of heat, temperance as the virtue of knowing your measure and so on. Contemplation is an attitude that measures life in the light of religious experience.

Every day of the rest of Mary's life would be measured by the Bethlehem experience which she treasured and never could forget. That was the source of her strength in a pilgrimage of faith that certainly had its joys but also had the dark nights of suffering.

Christmas is more than a passing diversion to break up the pains of winter. It is a feast to bring us the experience of God's compassion, so loving the world that he gave his only Son that we might not be lost but might have eternal life.

If we have celebrated Christmas as God's saving love which seeks to embrace and unite all the human family, and, if like Mary we treasure that experience, then we will walk through the coming year in the light of God's love. Everything will be measured under divine light.

And if we mentally connect every encounter and event with God, we will necessarily be building the fabric of peace for the year. It is when contemplation fails that the diabolical works of disharmony, division and destruction take place.

Mary, contemplative woman, treasuring and pondering, pray for us.

Mary, contemplative saint, sustained through darkness and suffering, pray for us.

Mary, contemplative mother, at peace even on Calvary, pray for us.

Second Reflection
The Name Jesus

New Year's Day is the eighth day of Christmas. On the eighth day the child was circumcised, according to the law of the covenant made with Abraham. And he was given the name Jesus, the name announced by the angel. Yet this sacred name is the subject of irreverent abuse every day of the week.

The name Jesus means that God is salvation. It is a name that expresses our hope for salvation. Without hearing the name Jesus we would still be lost in our sins and cut off from heaven. This sacred name expresses the redeeming love of God which sought us out as the good shepherd seeks the straying sheep to bring it home.

There is divine power in the name Jesus. There is an incident in the Acts of the Apostles where a cripple at the temple gate begged alms of Peter and John. Peter's answer is beautiful: 'I have neither silver nor gold, but I will give you what I have; in the name of Jesus Christ the Nazarene, walk!' *(Acts 3:5)* The name of saviour is a name of power. All the prayers in liturgy are directed to God the Father in the name of Jesus Christ. For Jesus promised: 'Anything you ask for from the Father he will grant in my name.' *(Jn 16:23)*

It is a name to be revered. Since Jesus Christ is raised to the Father's glory, the name Jesus is to be given the same reverence due to the very name of God. 'All beings in the heavens, on earth, and in the underworld, should bend the knee at the name of Jesus ... and every tongue should acclaim Jesus Christ as Lord.' *(Phil 2:10)* The early act of faith said 'Jesus is Lord', expressing belief in his divinity. We can imagine what the name Jesus must have meant to Mary in the years after the Ascension. She was one who treasured memories and worked with them.

The name Jesus would have been a total prayer experience to her. May it be for us also.

Blessed be the name of Jesus, name of hope, without which we would be lost and left with no hope.

Blessed be the name of Jesus, name of divine power, the name under which our prayers reach to the Father.

Blessed be the name of Jesus, raised to the Father's glory, Jesus the Lord.

Second Sunday After Christmas

Today's Mass is an invitation to enter into a deeper appreciation of the birth of our saviour. St John raises the mind beyond the historical happening at Bethlehem unto the theological meaning of the event. Christmas is more than the commemoration of one day in the year. It belongs to all time: and to beyond-time, eternity.

John 1:1-5.9-14
The Word was made flesh, and lived among us
In the beginning was the Word:
the Word was with God
and the Word was God.
He was with God in the beginning.
Through him all things came to be,
not one thing had its being but through him.
All that came to be had life in him
and that life was the light of men,
a light that shines in the dark,
a light that darkness could not overpower.

The Word was the true light
that enlightens all men;
and he was coming into the world.
He was in the world
that had its being through him,
and the world did not know him.
He came to his own domain
and his own people did not accept him.
But to all who did accept him
he gave power to become children of God,
to all who believe in the name of him
who was born not out of human stock
or urge of the flesh
or will of man
but of God himself.
The Word was made flesh,
he lived among us,
and we saw his glory,
the glory that is his as the only Son of the Father,
full of grace and truth.

Good News

God, in a new act of creation, has reached down into the flesh and blood of our lives. He has spoken his word to us: shines his light for us: and shares his life with us.

First Reflection
Our Divine Adoption

Christmas is the celebration of birth. The infant in the crib recalls the birthday of Jesus Christ in the flesh. But it is also about our birth as children of God, chosen to share in divine life.

Christmas marks the beginning of the new creation. And that is the reason why John opens his gospel with a clear echo of the opening page of Genesis and the story of creation. 'In the beginning God created the heavens and the earth.' On each of the six 'days' of creation the power to create is in a word of God. On each day 'God said'. Every created thing is word of God.

The perfect mind of the Father needs but the one Word to express everything. But in the imperfection of our thoughts we grapple with many words in an attempt to express ourselves. The Son is the perfect expression of the Father. 'He is the radiant light of God's glory and the perfect copy of his nature.' *(Heb 1:3)* Everything that has ever been created was already contained in the one perfect Word of God.

'Through him all things came to be,

not one thing had its being but through him.

All that came to be had life in him.' *(Jn 1:2-3)*

The great Easter story of the new creation began at the moment when the word of God came to us in our own flesh and blood

At a particular moment in time, on a special day in history, the Word was made flesh and dwelt among us. And to all who accepted him 'he gave power to become children of God.'

The new creation means that we are called to a higher level of life, nothing less than a sharing in divine life. Indeed, in today's second reading, St Paul returns praise and thanks for the blessings of this new creation. He rejoices that God has chosen us and determined that we should become his adopted children. He lists three ways in which the divine life within us ought to be expressed:

- a life free from sin, 'holy and spotless':
- a life lovingly aware of God's presence, 'to live through love in his presence':
- a life which celebrates God, 'to make us praise the glory of his grace.'

In a famous Christmas sermon, St Leo, a pope in the fifth century, reflected on the new life offered to us: 'O Christian, be aware of your nobility for it is God's nature that you share; do not then, by an ignoble life, fall back into your own weaknesses.'

Our Christian nobility originates in the new life we are given as the adopted children of God. It is expressed in a life that is 'holy and spotless', striving 'to live through love in his presence' and 'praising the glory of his grace.'

In the beginning of time God spoke the word of creation and things were created in their natural life. On a day in time God spoke the Word in our flesh and so began the new history of the human race, now created anew with divine life.

Christmas is our birthday in God, through divine adoption.

Second Reflection
Advent-Christmas Spirituality
God spoke his word into our silence.
He shone his light into our darkness.
And he shared his own life with us in our dying.
The spirituality of Advent led us into Christmas.

Throughout Advent we were making the point that it is the season with a spirituality most in touch with the needs of the soul in these last years of the twentieth century.

This is a time when the experience of many people is a winter of the spirit. It is hard to have hope in the face of rampant promiscuity and the breakdown in standards of behaviour. It is hard to cope with the fear that our technology has created a monster beyond our mastery, in the use of nuclear power, in the rape of the environment, in the breakdown of communities, in the alienation of so many from the institutions of religion. It is hard to find a way through the darkness of those who see no reason for living and have never known a reason to celebrate.

Pope John Paul II is very close to the pulse of life today. The first encyclical letter of any pope is a statement of his vision and policy for the church in his time. John Paul II's first encyclical was entitled *Redeemer of the Human Race*. He asks people to admit our human helplessness in the midst of our fears and darkness and to recognise our need for the divine redeemer of our race, Jesus Christ.

In keeping with this concentration on the need for a redeemer, the Marian Year had a distinct Advent character to it as part of our preparation for the second Millennium of our redeemer.

Pope John Paul II is asking us to get in touch with Advent's longing for a saviour, so that when Christmas of the year 2000 A.D. comes, we will truly celebrate what the coming of the redeemer means.

Christmas is the answer to Advent's longing. God came down to us in the flesh of Jesus Christ in order to lift us up.

But the work of that redemption is a gradual process, not an instant removal of every problem. So, when the Word was made flesh, he came unto his own and his own people did not accept him, though some did.

The redemption of each individual is a lifelong journey of responding to God's call. As St John puts it: 'Indeed, from his fulness we have, all of us, received – yes, grace in return for grace.' The work of redemption has been set in motion.

The Word was made flesh.

He came as the true light to enlighten all people.

He gives the power to become children of God.

The Epiphany of the Lord

The Epiphany means the manifestation of the divinity of Jesus. The feast celebrates the coming of the gentile nations to faith and to the adoration of God.

Matthew 2:1-12

We have come from the East to worship the king

After Jesus had been born at Bethlehem in Judaea during the reign of King Herod, some wise men came to Jerusalem from the east. "Where is the infant king of the Jews?" they asked. "We saw his star as it rose and have come to do him homage."

When King Herod heard this he was perturbed, and so was the whole of Jerusalem. He called together all the chief priests and the scribes of the people, and enquired of them where the Christ was to be born. "At Bethlehem in Judaea," they told him, "for this is what the prophet wrote:

And you, Bethlehem, in the land of Judah, you are by no means least among the leaders of Judah, for out of you will come a leader who will shepherd my people Israel."

Then Herod summoned the wise men to see him privately. He asked them the exact date on which the star had appeared, and sent them on to Bethlehem. "Go and find out all about the child," he said, "and when you have found him, let me know, so that I too may go and do him homage." Having listened to what the king had to say they set out. And there in front of them was the star they had seen rising; it went forward and halted over the place where the child was.

The sight of the star filled them with delight, and going into the house they saw the child with his mother Mary, and falling to their knees they did him homage. Then, opening their treasures, they offered him gifts of gold and frankincense and myrrh.

But they were warned in a dream not to go back to Herod, and returned to their own country by a different way.

Good News

Who is this child born of Mary at Bethlehem? Gold for a king hints at his future work in setting up the kingdom of heaven upon earth. Frankincense suggests the true priest who alone mediates between heaven and earth in his own right. Myrrh, which was used in anointing, suggests the suffering servant who would take the sins and death of the people upon himself.

First Reflection
Epiphany

We believe that Jesus Christ was truly human and divine.

The liturgy of Christmas up to this point has emphasised the humanity of Jesus. We were drawn in mind to see the helpless infant in the crib. St Luke stressed the human themes of poverty and humility through the Christmas story. Then we were taken forward some years to reflect on the holy family at Nazareth. These were the hidden years when Jesus was so ordinarily human that those who knew him at Nazareth would not accept him later as a preacher.

The Epiphany, by contrast, emphasises the divinity of Jesus Christ. The Greek word, epiphany, could be applied to the triumphant entry of a king into a town to the cheers of public acclaim. Nowadays we might think of the victorious team bringing home the cup to the strains of the local bands, the mayor reading the citation of greatness and the cheering thousands responding in thunderous acclamation.

As the gospels tell the human story of the ministry of Jesus, the theme of his divinity constantly works its way into the narrative. There are several episodes which specifically manifest his divine power and glory. Technically these are called epiphany stories: epiphany here meaning the outward showing of the inner, divine greatness.

Remember the day on the mountain when Jesus was transfigured in awesome light. And the day of his baptism when the voice from heaven testified to his identity as the Beloved Son of the Father. His miracles also manifested the power of Jesus. The story of the miracle at the wedding at Cana was developed by John unto this conclusion: 'He let his glory be seen, and his disciples believed in him.' (*Jn 2:11*)

The event we most associate with epiphany is today's story of the coming of the wise men who knelt in homage before the infant king and offered appropriate, symbolic gifts. This story is like a summary of the entire life of Jesus. His birth was like a new star rising in the skies to guide people on their pilgrimage of life. He was recognised and followed by all who genuinely sought wisdom. But many of his own nation rejected him for various reasons.

The political leaders of the Jews, represented by Herod and the Jerusalem set, were perturbed. They felt threatened by a child. The chief priests and scribes had access to all the right texts. But they stayed there peering into their texts and did not step out on the road of faith. The wise men, however, continued their journey forward. They found the house and went into it.

It represents the house of faith.

The gift of gold expressed the inner significance of kingship; the use of incense was an outer manifestation of priesthood; and myrrh suggested the Messiah as the Suffering Servant.

At the time of his writing Matthew had seen how the Jews had by and large rejected the Christian preachers. But the gentile nations had come forward to belief and were entering the house of faith, the church. That was something which thrilled the heart of St Paul. In today's second reading he rejoices that 'the pagans now share the same inheritance, that they are part of the same body, and that the same promise is made to them, in Christ Jesus, through the gospel.' (Eph 3:5-6)

The epiphany stories are rich in their inner significance. The outer details of the stories point to the mystery of divinity hidden in Jesus Christ. The feast of the Epiphany celebrates his divinity and calls on all people to follow his star and to walk in his light.

O Light of God, rising for us at the birth of Jesus, shine powerfully through the darkness of this age and guide us in the ways of wisdom.

O Light of God, resplendent in the teaching of Jesus, may we grow in faith and experience the delight of walking in your paths.

O Light of God, implanted in our hearts by the Spirit of Jesus, may we experience what it is to fall on our knees in adoration.

Second Reflection
Matthew Explains

With the benefit of hindsight I can see now that I was too subtle with some of these stories about the infancy of Jesus. But how could I have anticipated that my writing would reach people so far removed from our Jewish culture in miles and centuries?

People who do not appreciate the subtlety of our Jewish literature have picked up the incidental details of my story but missed the truth of what I wrote. Talk about seeing the trees and missing the forest!

How much energy has been spent and ink used in the outer details of the story while the inner meaning has been neglected!

What star or conjunction of stars, they ask. But, tell me, how could a star travel south from Jerusalem to Bethlehem when the nightly journey of every star is from east to west?

And the three kings ... where did they come from? As a matter of accuracy, I did not say they were kings. Nor did I say they were three. I suppose three gifts were taken to indicate three donors.

What was I trying to say in this story of the visit of the wise men? This story was part of the introduction to my book on the inauguration of the kingdom of heaven on earth by Jesus Christ. What Jesus did was the fulfilment of the saving work of God throughout Jewish history. But the majority of my fellow Jews would not accept this claim. They had made it impossible for us to continue as Jews. I wrote in a heartfelt appeal to their teachers and leaders to reconsider the claims of Jesus.

I wrote with the ink of Jewish history in the hope that they might read the signs. For instance, the oracle of Balaam had foreseen the star of Jacob that would arise to lead the people. I was suggesting that the birth of Jesus was the rising of this star. But as this same Balaam could not move his donkey forward on the road, neither did the star of Bethlehem move those who were in Jerusalem. Only the true seekers of wisdom followed this star. I ventured into the world of dreams and stars in an attempt to open up their closed minds.

Bethlehem was important in the story because it was the birthplace of King David from whose line the messiah was expected to come. Herod represented the secular leaders who rejected Jesus as they felt threatened by him. His behaviour resembled that of the Pharaoh at the time when Moses was born. The scribes had all the necessary knowledge but they did not move one step to follow it through into action. Their hypocrisy disgusted me.

Along came the outsiders who were led by the star of wisdom and they recognised Jesus in faith. They entered the house of faith and worshipped. That's how it stood at the time of my writing. The Jewish leaders, secular and religious, had rejected Jesus. The gentile nations were accepting him and entering the church.

I wrote of gifts which would recall the visit of the Queen of Sheeba to Solomon in recognition of his great wisdom. The gift of gold stands for kingship: the whole thrust of the work of Jesus was to establish the kingdom of heaven upon earth. Frankincense gives off a sweet-scented cloud to accompany prayers rising up to God: in the story it symbolizes the priestly linking of heaven and earth through Jesus. The myrrh of anointing represents him as messiah in the manner of Isaiah's Suffering Servant who would heal in his woundedness.

Nothing can ever be the same again for someone who has visited the house of faith and who has known what it is to worship God. So, the wise men returned home by a different way since the old ways were no longer adequate.

Our Jewish mind is subtle. Any story we tell draws more from the deep well of memory than from the face value of the word. Little wonder then that people of different times and training tend to misunderstand our stories.

The Baptism of the Lord

The story of the baptism of Jesus is a most important epiphany, that is, a revelation of his divine nature. Mark, Matthew and Luke tell of the baptism but each one has a particular point of emphasis. Matthew alone relates the exchange between Jesus and John. The reason why Jesus subjects himself to the ministry of John is for the sake of righteousness. Jesus, entered the river of life to associate with all sinners and set them at rights with God

This episode at the Jordan establishes for Matthew's readers the divine identity of Jesus and sets the tone for the ministry which he is about to commence.

Matthew 3:13-17
As soon as Jesus was baptised
he saw the Spirit of God coming down on him

Jesus came from Galilee to the Jordan to be baptised by John. John tried to dissuade him. 'It is I who need baptism from you,' he said, 'and yet you come to me!' But Jesus replied, 'Leave it like this for the time being; it is fitting that we should, in this way, do all that righteousness demands.' At this, John gave in to him.

As soon as Jesus was baptised he came up from the water, and suddenly the heavens opened and he saw the Spirit of God descending like a dove and coming down on him. And a voice spoke from heaven, 'This is my Son, the Beloved; my favour rests on him.'

Good News
Who is Jesus? He is the Beloved Son of the Father. What did he do? He entered the muddy waters of the human condition to save us from drowning in sinfulness.

First Reflection
What Righteousness Demands
Righteousness is not a very happy word. It can suggest the hypocritical, better -than-thou attitude of the self-righteous.

Or it is a terrifying word when it conjures up the picture of a very strict God who is angry with us when we break his law. This righteous God would never let his face smile on us or let us go out to play on Sunday.

When religion is dominated by the concept of a strict, exacting God it drives people to insane fanaticism, morbid depression or gnawing self-hatred. God is then feared but not loved: and religion is very correct but also very cold.

The good news is that Jesus did not wait on the bank of the Jordan until the sinners were perfectly washed. He went into the river, anxious to be at one with them. He fully entered the muddy waters of human existence. He is true to his name, Jesus: saviour of the sinner: not a messiah sent to gather the perfect people into an elite club.

Then occurred the extraordinary revelations from heaven. The cry of the prophet was answered as God tore the heavens open and the Spirit descended upon Jesus.

Matthew knows that this day was important not only for Jesus but for all of us. Where Mark and Luke tell us that Jesus heard the words from heaven, Matthew writes as if all are to hear it said: 'This is my Son, the Beloved; my favour rests on him.' What is said of Jesus that day is to be echoed in every Christian baptism.

Matthew is fond of a first and last trick in writing (what the scholars call inclusion). Something he wants to stress is mentioned at the start and end of a story or episode. So it is with baptism. The first appearance of the adult Jesus is on the day of his baptism: and at his last appearance, on the mountain in Galilee, he tells his disciples to baptise all nations 'in the name of the Father and of the Son and of the Holy Spirit.' *(Matt 28:19)*

The first is the model of the last. The baptism of Jesus is seen as the model of Christian baptism. The revelation of God at the baptism of Jesus enlightens us about the effects of Christian baptism. It establishes a person on a new level of relationship with Father, Son and Holy Spirit. The baptised person enters the family of God as a beloved child of the Father, now entitled to pray 'Abba, Father!' Under the waters of baptism we are embraced in the cleansing and healing love of the Son, who entered the rivers of human life to be one with us.

And the Spirit of God descends upon the baptised soul, igniting the first spark of God's fire, which we are asked to fan into a consuming passion of love.

The way to righteousness, then, is not in some exacting programme of perfection in which we prove our worthiness. No, righteousness is a gift that God wants to give us.

All we have to do is to let God be God: and to be aware of
- the Father's love for us as his beloved children:
- the Son's association with us in the waters of human life:
- the Spirit's desire to set our hearts aflame with the fires of divine love.

Second Reflection
The Crushed Reed and Wavering Flame

Jesus came for the crushed reed and for the sake of the wavering flame.

At the start of his public career, the evangelists use the story of his baptism to establish his divine identity firmly in the reader's mind and to set the tone of the mission of Jesus. To catch the full impact of the passage, the best commentary is today's first reading, Isaiah 42:1-4, 6-7. Matthew surely had one eye resting on Isaiah as he wrote.

Jesus is identified as the chosen servant in whom the Father's soul delights. He is endowed with the divine Spirit as he embarks on the mission of divine justice to all the nations of the world.

The approach of Jesus will be in gentleness rather than violence; more interest in restoring than in condemning: healing rather than destroying.

'He does not break the crushed reed
nor quench the wavering flame.' *(Is 42:3)*

He entered the river with sinners for he would witness to the power of goodness and truth from within the pains and pressures of the human condition. In this way his ministry would open the eyes of the blind, free captives from prison and those who live in darkness from the dungeon.

It would be a mission of enlightenment and liberation.

This Christian approach is exemplified in the life of Pope John XXIII. He was visiting the prison, Regina Coeli in Rome. But when he saw the line of broken humanity in front of him he felt a large lump in his throat and was unable to deliver the prepared speech. Eventually he began to speak, straight from the heart.

'Men,' he began, 'I have come here today to put my eyes into your eyes.'

It had an extraordinary, deep effect on the prisoners. After the pope's death, one of these prisoners recounted on television how he had been interiorly liberated that day. Pope John had stepped into the river of the prisoners' condition and had shown them that the real sources of imprisonment are the chains within us which restrict our growth and freedom.

'Stone walls do not a prison make
Nor iron bars a cage ...' (Richard Lovelace)

The day of the baptism of Jesus marked the beginning of his public mission. He began by entering into the river with sinners. He would not preach condemnatory sermons from a distance: the last thing a sinner needs to hear is a further blow to his self-worth.

Jesus would be a victim of the human condition, suffering from misunderstanding, opposition and eventually persecution unto death. But he would witness to the power of goodness and love from within the waters of pain and pressure. In this way he would open the eyes of the blind and free people from all sorts of inner captivity.

His programme would not be to condemn but rather to enlighten and restore.

He came to bind up the bruised reed and to fan the wavering flame into a consuming fire.

Note: The text for next Sunday, the Second Sunday in Ordinary Time, is to be found on page 121.

First Sunday of Lent

The forty days of Lent are a preparation for Easter, when we renew our baptismal commitment. The first Sunday of the season recalls the forty days fasting of Jesus and the story of his temptations in the wilderness. For us, these temptations represent the struggles of our earthly pilgrimage before our total entry into the glory of the Lord's resurrection.

Matthew 4:1-11
Jesus fasted for forty days and nights.

Jesus was led by the Spirit out into the wilderness to be tempted by the devil. He fasted for forty days and forty nights, after which he was very hungry, and the tempter came and said to him, "If you are the Son of God, tell these stones to turn into loaves." But he replied, "Scripture says:

Man does not live on bread alone but on every word that comes from the mouth of God."

The devil then took him to the holy city and made him stand on the parapet of the Temple. "If you are the Son of God," he said, "throw yourself down; for scripture says: He will put you in his angels' charge, and they will support you on their hands in case you hurt your foot against a stone."

Jesus said to him, "Scripture also says: You must not put the Lord your God to the test."

Next, taking him to a very high mountain, the devil showed him all the kingdoms of the world and their splendour. "I will give you all of these," he said, "if you fall at my feet and worship me."

Then Jesus replied, "Be off, Satan! For scripture says: You must worship the Lord your God, and serve him alone."

Then the devil left him, and the angels appeared and looked after him.

Good News

We draw hope and strength for our times of struggle from the remembrance that Jesus is with us in the wilderness: that the Holy Spirit is leading the whole process: and that the comforting angels of God are close at hand.

First Reflection
Temptations Old and New

The experience of Jesus in the wilderness reached back into the time when the Chosen People, under Moses, spent forty years in the wilderness before entering into the promised land. The three temptations open up areas where the Israelites proved weak in their faith but where Jesus is totally faithful, trustful and obedient to the Father.

The story of the temptations also reaches forward as it relates to our lives in areas where our faith and confidence in God are tested.

'Turn these stones into loaves of bread.'

The first temptation is to trust no longer in God's providence. The Israelites began to doubt in God's ability to feed them. Had God led them out to inevitable starvation and destruction? They doubted and complained loudly. But then God gave them manna from heaven.

Manna means 'what is this?' It was something unknown and strange. It proved that a surprising and unexpected answer is not impossible to God. One should never doubt God.

Where is the manna today, we ask, when every two seconds a child is dying from hunger? Close to 40,000 children each day. Not to mention adults.

Pagans of old placated their gods with child sacrifice. And so do the pagans who worship the gods of today in Star War Programmes, Defence Systems, Market Protection and so on.

The manna has been given but the stronger people hoard it to their own advantage. They regard it as their own to sell or loan at a crippling rate of interest. Every Lent a pitiable gesture is made to quieten the voice of conscience. But even as we read of it the children are dying in sacrifice to the gods.

The policies which run our first world countries remind one of the little parable of the two men on a desert island. One had a loaf of bread while the other had none. The one who hoarded his loaf did not sleep that night.

We may have hoarded the manna by the million but we still need security. For man does not live on bread alone. Ultimate security is found only in believing that God is to be trusted.

The second temptation is about putting God to the test.

51

The Israelites began to doubt God's plan for them. Were they not better off in Egypt despite their problems there? They wanted more signs than the manna. Jesus too was to find a people who saw many signs but still called for more. How about a sensational jump off the temple wall into the invisible safety net of angels arms! Can we ever have enough signs?

Our baptismal life is a sharing in the dying and rising of Jesus Christ, and our temptation is to want more signs of the resurrection and fewer traces of the crucifixion.

We put God to the test if we doubt the presence of God close by us in our experiences of the cross. His comforting angels are near us even when we are struggling with our weaknesses, obsessions and compulsions: when we come face to face with our fears: when we have to live with failure: when we are deeply anxious over loved ones: when others treat us very badly.

The third temptation is to compromise on the unique place of God in our worship. The Israelites wavered in their loyalty to God when they fashioned a calf of gold, which they worshipped with sacrifices. Jesus was tempted with the bait of the kingdoms of this world and their splendour: power and the trappings of power. Few of us are offered the trappings of power and prestige. But eveyone is faced with situations of compromise: to give God less than 100% of our worship.

We compromise on truth when we slip into white lies of excuse or exaggeration. We compromise on charity when we avoid people, fail to listen to them, or pretend that we do not know their needs. We compromise on justice if we do not work conscientiously or if we are tardy in paying our debts. We compromise on prayer if we are skimpy in the time we make available to it. Are we prepared to spend as much time in the Lord's affairs as we do with television? God surely deserves more than the compromised response of the half-hearted effort. 'You must worship the Lord your God and serve him alone.'

The times of testing showed up the Israelites as wavering in their faith and confidence, and openly disobedient to God. In contrast, Jesus faithfully stands by the word of scripture and totally dismisses any suggestions of compromising on the unique worship due to God alone. Lent offers us a time to reflect on our fidelity to the life of Jesus, which is the ideal of our baptism.

Second Reflection
Desert Schooling

Matthew writes that Jesus was lead by the Spirit. Where? Out into the wilderness. Why? To be tempted by the devil.

It happened immediately before Jesus embarked on his public ministry. This was the Holy Spirit's idea of a preparatory course. Hardly the sort of course we would devise before a ministry among people! But the Spirit's reasoning was that whoever is in touch with the inner heart of his own being will also be in touch with the inner heart of others.

Today we might call it inculturation. That is how missionaries and business people prepare before a foreign assignment. They know that they must listen before they speak to their potential customers. So they learn what they can of the culture of the people before they travel.

Jesus enrolled in the school called wilderness. The teachers there were solitude and emptiness, vastness and space, necessity and frugality. The subject of the course was knowledge of the human heart.

The bareness of the desert quickly sorts out the authentic from the hypocritical. There are no audiences to be impressed with outward show. Nobody to be deceived by the roles we adopt or the games we play. Nobody to blame.

One must face oneself. And whoever comes to an honest acceptance of his own inner centre with its strengths and weaknesses has reached a knowledge of the human condition which will benefit everybody else.

As Evagrius Ponticus, in the fourth century, wrote of the desert fathers: 'The monk is one who lives separated from everyone and united to everyone.' Understanding the ways of one's own heart is the key to the knowledge of all hearts.

In the school of wilderness Jesus grew in understanding through experience of the human condition.

The first lesson was about bread and hunger; or, on a broader scale, about our appetites and how we respond to them. Bread is the symbol of all that is needed for a healthy life. People live on bread in its many forms: but not on bread alone. The struggle is unending to achieve the balance between attending to the appetites of the body and the call of the spiritual life.

The second lesson comes from the suggestion of a sensational stunt. Right in the centre of religion, the temple area, perform this amazing jump. Sensationalise religion!

We find that the human mind today is struggling to come to any point of depth because of the distracting attention demanded by all that is superficial and sensational, by the utterly trivial or whatever is passing popular this week. The standards of evaluation prize what is newest or latest, trendiest or most fashionable, the number one best-seller and the Oscar winner. When the mind is preoccupied with such superficialities it is very difficult to reach any depth in one's inner life.

The third temptation is to settle for a kingdom here and now. To do so one must sell one's soul to Satan, the diabolical power.

Diabolical literally means divisive energies. To acquire the divisive, diabolical kingdom one must grow hard-hearted, tough-minded, prepared to trample competitors underfoot.

Forty days of solitude and fasting brought Jesus to a clear perception of the struggles, camouflages and temptations that are part of every human heart. We need not set out for a distant Sahara to find the desert experience. The desert comes to us in any experience that strips away our blinkers or peels off our layers of camouflage. Bereavement, illness or an unexpected handicap will open up the shallowness or depths of our inner strength.

Times of failure and criticism are precious opportunities. Like the exodus experience they are given 'to humble you, to test you and know your inmost heart.' *(Deut 8:2)*

Ageing is nature's own way of weakening our physical potential so as to deepen our discernment between the passing and the eternal.

The desert is a school favoured by the Spirit for the soul's education. 'Learn from this that Yahweh your God was training you as a man trains his child.' *(Deut 8:5)*

Words I heard, but whose source I cannot trace, express the richness of the tested life:

'Where people have lived with inwardness
The air is charged with blessedness and does bless.'

Second Sunday of Lent

Through baptism we are drawn into the contrasting experiences of the death and resurrection of the Lord. Last Sunday's liturgy drew us into the testing school of the desert with the Lord. Today is the contrasting experience on the mountain of meeting, where all is light and wonder in an awesome sense of God's glory.

Matthew 17:1-9
His face shone like the sun

Jesus took with him Peter and James and his brother John and led them up a high mountain where they could be alone. There in their presence he was transfigured: his face shone like the sun and his clothes became as white as the light. Suddenly Moses and Elijah appeared to them; they were talking with him.

Then Peter spoke to Jesus. "Lord," he said, "it is wonderful for us to be here; if you wish, I will make three tents here, one for you, one for Moses and one for Elijah." He was still speaking when suddenly a bright cloud covered them with shadow, and from the cloud there came a voice which said, "This is my Son, the Beloved; he enjoys my favour. Listen to him." When they heard this, the disciples fell on their faces, overcome with fear. But Jesus came up and touched them. "Stand up," he said, "do not be afraid." And when they raised their eyes they saw no one but only Jesus.

As they came down from the mountain Jesus gave them this order, "Tell no one about the vision until the Son of Man has risen from the dead."

Good News

Jesus is the Beloved Son of the Father. Although we cannot see God directly, yet if we listen to Jesus we will be led up the mountain to meet with God.

First Reflection
Listen to Him

No mortal person could see the face of God and live. Why, we cannot even look at the sun directly but we would damage our eyesight.

But God has accommodated the divine glory to our human

limitations. The Word of God has come to us in human flesh. And if we desire to meet God we are told to listen to Jesus: 'Listen to him.'

Our sense of hearing has been specially sanctified through baptism. Recalling how Jesus cured the man who could neither hear nor talk, the celebrant touches the ears and mouth of the newly baptised as he prays: 'The Lord Jesus made the deaf hear and the dumb speak. May he soon touch your ears to receive his word, and your mouth to proclaim his faith, to the praise and glory of God the Father.'

A practical ideal for Lent might be to check up on our use of these sanctified ears!

The traditional works of penitence are fasting (self-control), almsgiving (towards others) and prayer (towards God). We tend to jump into some active programme of what I will do for God. We take on acts of self-denial or saving for the third world or more prayers, like a do-it-yourself kit for holiness. Why not consider fasting, almsgiving and prayer as three ways in which we can 'listen to him'? We need to fast from noise. In this technological age the mind is assualted by noise. For most people who desire to develop a prayer-life the first step is to train the mind to attend to sounds which are heard but are normally excluded from our awareness. We need to fast from compulsive radio and obsessive television. It can be a lenten programme to sit and listen to sighing windows and creaking radiators, to birds and dogs, to ticking clocks and distant murmurs. Or to walk in quietness in a spring garden or under a star ry night.

For alms, we might give our ears and attention to people. Paying attention to somebody is the first work of love. The challenge of Lent might be to spend more time at home: to avoid the newspaper at meals: to sit with people: to visit and to listen.

Most of us complain of our problem in finding time. But busy-ness is usually of our own making. Our ideal must be to make time available for listening to others.

A very busy teacher described how the birth of her children contributed to her development in prayer. The demands of the children on her time made her change her pace and simplify her preoccupations. Life obtained a new meaning for her. She learned to listen ... and to pray.

Fasting from superfluous noise and learning how to listen will prepare us for the third work of Lent, prayer: especially prayer as listening to God.

One tried and tested way of listening to God is with the words of Scripture. We come to God humbly begging for his word. We seek his word as a lamp for our steps and a light for our darkness. We mull over the passage. We wait with it until some word or phrase or picture stirs up the heart. We stay with it, like a boat on sea, our souls floating with the living words. At baptism our ears were sanctified to receive his word. Lent prepares us for the renewal of our baptism. It calls for us to shun the destructive word, the trivial news-mongering and blaring sensationalism in order to give time and space to the word of God.

Today's opening prayer at Mass is appropriate:

God our Father, help us to hear your Son.

Enlighten us with your word,

that we may find the way to your glory.

Second Reflection
The Bright Cloud

That day on the mountain was one when the three disciples experienced wonder, awe and fear. When the bright cloud covered them with shadow and when they heard the divine voice from the cloud, they fell on their faces, overcome with fear.

To a great extent we have lost all fear of God today. It was no harm to lose that soul-terror which was linked to a punitive concept of God. But the healthy fear of God, that gift of the Holy Spirit, is also hard to find. There is a distinct absence of awe and a conspicuous lack of due reverence to God and due respect for the things of God.

The Lord's name is a common part of everyday vocabulary: worse again, it is used as a curse word.

The Lord's day is no longer sacred for many. The ease with which people trip up to receive the Eucharist and the apparent lack of private thanksgiving make one suspect a lack of awe and reverence.

Some people say that the 'new liturgy' is responsible! An over-simplification of a complex change surely, but there may be a certain amount of truth there.

Changing from Latin to the everyday language brought great advances in participation. But language is no mere matter of sounds. It is deeply rooted in the cultural mentality which has grown in years that number in hundreds or thousands.

The use of the vernacular can take away the sense of mystery if it creates the expectation that all this ceremony can now be understood. Words are taken on their own value without pointing beyond themselves to the inexpressible mystery of God. We use too many flat words which never help people climb the mountain to meet the bright light of God.

A spate of words sweep over us without space or silence. Three readings, a psalm, a homily, profession of faith and prayers of the faithful, at least. There may be further words of introduction as long as the readings themselves!

So many words in full spate that we are lucky if we receive one word we can hold on to. We have reached the stage described by T.S.Eliot in 'Choruses From the Rock' when we have

'Knowledge of speech but not of silence;
Knowledge of words, and ignorance of the Word.'

In the absence of mystery and awe, people complain that the liturgy is boring! It's some achievement to make God appear boring but we have managed it.

In many bible stories the writers picture a bright cloud to convey a moment of meeting with God.

One cannot look directly into the sun, much less meet God face to face. But through the filter of a cloud one can gaze heavenwards. And though clouds are dark by nature, the cloud of revelation is bright because of the intensity of light within it. The cloud conceals God but his brightness reveals him.

The mistake made by the word-obsessed mind is to look at the cloud and see only a cloud. Instead of inviting one to a deep experience of God, now the cloud of words only gets in the way. And without the deep experience of God people will never fall prostrate in adoration.

Awe and reverential fear are rare in this age of flat words. One word on the mountain is sufficient.

'This is my Son, the Beloved; he enjoys my favour. Listen to him.'

Third Sunday of Lent

During Lent we prepare for the renewal of our baptismal promises around the pascal light of the risen Lord. The lectionary invites us to explore the richness of baptism through reflection on stories from John's gospel over the course of three Sundays.

John 5-15, 19-26, 39, 40-42
The water that I shall give will turn into a spring of eternal life

Jesus had come to the Samaritan town called Sychar, near the land that Jacob gave to his son Joseph. Joseph's well is there and Jesus, tired by the journey, sat straight down by the well. It was about the sixth hour.

When a Samaritan woman came to draw water, Jesus said to her, "Give me a drink." His disciples had gone into town to buy food. The Samaritan woman said to him, "What? You are a Jew and you ask me, a Samaritan, for a drink?" — Jews in fact, do not associate with Samaritans. Jesus replied : "If you only knew what God is offering and who it is that is saying to you: Give me a drink, you would have been the one to ask, and he would have given you living water." "You have no bucket, sir," she answered, "and the well is deep; how could you get this living water? Are you a greater man than our father Jacob who gave us this well and drank from it himself with his sons and his cattle?" Jesus replied: "Whoever drinks this water will get thirsty again; but anyone who drinks the water that I shall give will never be thirsty again: the water that I shall give will turn into a spring inside him, welling up to eternal life." "Sir," said the woman, "give me some of that water, so that I may never get thirsty and never have to come here again to draw water. I see you are a prophet, sir. Our fathers worshipped on this mountain, while you say that Jerusalem is the place where one ought to worship." Jesus said: "Believe me, woman, the hour is coming when you will worship the Father neither on this mountain nor in Jerusalem. You worship what you do not know, we worship what we do know; for salvation comes from the Jews. But the hour will come — in fact it is here already — when true worshippers will worship the Father in spirit and truth: that is the kind of worshipper the Father wants. God is spirit, and those who worship must worship in spirit and truth."

The woman said to him, "I know that Messiah—that is, Christ — is coming, and when he comes he will tell us everything." "I who am speaking to you," said Jesus, "I am he."

Many Samaritans of that town had believed in him on the strength of the woman's testimony so, when the Samaritans came up to him, they begged him to stay with them. He stayed for two days, and when he spoke to them many more came to believe; and they said to the woman, "Now we no longer believe because of what you told us; we have heard him ourselves and we know that he really is the saviour of the world."

Good News
At the well of baptism Jesus invites us to drink of his friendship: to be cleansed in his forgiveness: and to let the spring of divine life flow within us.

First Reflection
A Story About Baptism (1)
'If you only knew what God is offering,' said Jesus to the woman at the well. If we could only appreciate what God has offered us at the well of baptism!

In this story John uses the symbol of water to express several aspects of the soul's thirst for God.

(i) John opens the narrative with a very human picture of Jesus, tired and thirsty, flopping down beside a well, waiting on somebody to come with a bucket. We immediately feel that we can relate to this frail and needy person. He does not threaten us.

Jesus surprises the woman when he speaks to her for in so doing he is breaking through the dividing barrier between Jew and Samaritan and the second barrier which forbade a man to associate with a woman in public. We note how the disciples, on returning, are surprised to see them talking to one another. Dr Erich Fromm, in his book, *The Art of Loving*, (Unwin 1970), asserts that the deepest need of the human being is to overcome one's separateness, to be liberated from the prison of aloneness. The absolute failure to accomplish this spells insanity.

The village well was normally the centre for meeting and gossip. But this woman came alone: and at a most unusual time, the sixth hour, which was the height of the midday sun. Only the pale sun-worshippers of Northern Europe would venture out at that hour! It seems likely that she came alone because she was victimised in the village on account of her marital history. To this isolated person Jesus reaches out, disregarding the social barriers.

At the well of baptism our first level of contact with Jesus Christ is this invitation to come to him in our deep need for companionship. 'Oh, come to the water all you who are thirsty; though you have no money, come!' (Is 55:1)

Jesus is the Friend we relate to in prayer. He is waiting there for us. He needs something that I alone can bring, the empty bucket of my heart. Sadly, many baptised people never seem to break through to the point where they are comfortable in one-to-one prayer with Jesus. They never learn how fresh and invigorating is the 'living water' of prayer. They settle for the stale, stagnant waters of the mechanical formula and the words of another which they have never made their own.

(ii) Once her relationship with Jesus has begun, the woman's moral thirst comes to light. Her life is in a mess. She thirsts at a deep level for the moral righteousness that comes with forgiveness. She has suffered the pain of the break-up of five marriages. Her present alliance is with no husband; only a live-in boyfriend. She is someone to be found in any street of today. Deeply hurt inside, she has lost the ability to promise fidelity.

But as she speaks with Jesus, something about him lights up the spark of hope again. What he is offering contrasts with all the untruthfulness and the infidelities that she has known. She yearns for that fresh water that will cleanse her past and restore her vitality and pride. 'Give me some of that water, so that I may never get thirsty again and never have to come here again to draw water.'

She reaches the point where she comes to terms with herself. 'I have no husband ... I've been through so much that I've lost the ability to sustain a relationship.' Jesus remarks: 'You spoke the truth there.' And the truth sets her free.

When she goes back into the town she says of Jesus, 'he told me everything I ever did.' Everything? At least she has the feeling that he understood everything. And what a blessed relief to feel understood and accepted even as she was. She is released from her guilt, washed clean, able to face her neighbours.

Our baptismal union with Jesus releases us from the clutches of sin. St Paul loved to explain that going down into the water of the baptismal pool was entering into the tomb with Jesus:

'You must consider yourself to be dead to sin but alive for God in Christ Jesus.' *(Rom 6:11)*

Yet our daily struggle with sin continues. The clouds of guilt, fear and anxiety still tend to obscure the light of God from us. But when we grow in our relationship with Jesus we learn how to let go of the chains. For, as the people of the town recognised, he is the saviour of the world.

(iii) The water which Jesus offers has satisfied her thirst for acceptance and forgiveness. But the heart has yet deeper needs. Jesus leads her to recognise her thirst for the unending, unchanging and eternal. As Augustine discovered, the heart is made for God and will find no ultimate rest until it rests in him. The ultimate repose of all energy and the end of all striving is in the worship of God.

But the woman has a question: 'Where is this worship?' On Jewish hill or Samaritan mountain, in Latin or vernacular, with beads or mantra, old way or new way? Jesus answers that the externals are no longer of any importance. The only place that matters now is worship in the Spirit. The only language is the divine Word, the truth incarnate. True worship is to render all honour and glory to the Father, through the Son, in the power of the Holy Spirit.

Water, pouring at baptism, is a symbol of how 'the love of God has been poured into our hearts by the Holy Spirit which has been given us.' *(Rom 5:5)* The in-flow of God's Spirit is that water which Jesus promised '... a spring of water inside, welling up to eternal life.'

At the well of baptism we are invited to slake our thirst for friendship in the companionship of Jesus. We are cleansed of sin's clutching grasp. And we receive the first spring of divine life, destined to become totally immersed in the eternal ocean of the Holy Trinity.

Second Reflection
Rising Thoughts

Every story in John's gospel is an invitation to believe. At the end of the gospel he writes: 'These signs are recorded so that you may believe that Jesus is the Christ, the Son of God, and that believing this you may have life through his name.'

John's style of writing is an invitation to raise up our thoughts and perspective to ever higher levels.

He writes as the skylark sings, circling over the one area but on ever higher levels of song. He begins this story with a very ordinary request for a drink of water and his song rises up through higher levels of thirst unto the belief that the Spirit of God is to be found poured into our inner souls.

In the woman's relationship with Jesus there is an ascending scale in the manner in which she addresses him.

Jesus is introduced to us in human frailty, tired and thirsty, dependent on the favour of another. The woman first calls him a Jew, but her tone of contempt is softened by a certain curiosity in her voice: 'What are you doing asking me, a Samaritan, for a drink?'

Soon she is growing in respect and she calls him 'Sir'. Then there is room for the question whether he is a greater man than Jacob, who gave them that well. At this stage she recognises that he, the beggar initially, is really the one who has something to give. So she begs the living water of him.

When her own life is revealed, she recognises that she is in the presence of a prophet, one who reveals God. Eventually she raises the possibility that he is the Messiah, the Christ, the promised, Anointed One. The answer of Jesus, 'I am he', is heavily weighted with the memory of God's name as revealed to Moses: 'I am'.

The titles have ascended from the initial mixture of contempt and curiosity to divine mystery. The woman's response is partial faith: 'I wonder if he is the Christ.' But even this partial faith is enough to make her want to share it with others. At the end of the story the people say of Jesus: 'He really is the saviour of the world.'

Elsewhere in the gospel John draws up our thoughts

around the idea of wind (when speaking with Nicodemus), bread, light and life. His style suggests a simple way of contemplative prayer, a ladder ascending from earth to heaven.

Take some common, everyday object like bread, a stone, a flower, a leaf, a tree, a newspaper, an old shoe ... anything. Let it tell its own story to you. Savour its properties in touch, colour, smell, shape, usefulness, fragility or solidity. Bring it to Jesus. Listen to him explain how this object of creation is his: for everything that exists is a word of the creating Father; and every word is contained in the Word. Invite Jesus to develop a parable especially for your life around this object.

'The kingdom of heaven is like ... this stone ... old shoe ...'

John is the skylark who sings over one small area, but rises ever higher on the warm current of air. If you learn from him how to let your thoughts rise up in contemplation you will discover the meaning of Jesus's words:

'The water that I shall give will turn into a spring of water inside him, welling up to eternal life.'

Fourth Sunday of Lent

The cure of the blind man is the second story taken from John to prepare us for the renewal of our baptismal promises at Easter. In the second reading, St Paul expands on the theme of light to exhort Christians to live according to the ethical values of their baptismal enlightenment.

John 9:1. 6-9. 13-17. 34-38.
*The blind man went off and washed himself
and came away with his sight restored.*

As Jesus went along, he saw a man who had been blind from birth. He spat on the ground, made a paste with the spittle, put this over the eyes of the blind man and said to him, "Go and wash in the Pool of Siloam" (a name that means "sent"). So the blind man went off and washed himself, and came away with his sight restored. His neighbours and people who earlier had seen him begging said, "Isn't this the man who used to sit and beg?" Some said, "Yes, it is the same one." Others said, "No, he only looks like him." The man himself said, "I am the man."

They brought the man who had been blind to the Pharisees. It had been a sabbath day when Jesus made the paste and opened the man's eyes, so when the Pharisees asked him how he had come to see, he said, "He put a paste on my eyes, and I washed, and I can see." Then some of the Pharisees said, "This man cannot be from God; he does not keep the sabbath." Others said, "How could a sinner produce signs like this?" And there was disagreement among them. So they spoke to the blind man again, "What have you to say about him yourself, now that he has opened your eyes?" "He is a prophet," replied the man. "Are you trying to teach us," they replied, "and you a sinner through and through, since you were born!" And they drove him away.

Jesus heard they had driven him away, and when he found him he said to him, "Do you believe in the Son of Man?" "Sir," the man replied, "tell me who he is so that I may believe in him." Jesus said, "You are looking at him; he is speaking to you." The man said, "Lord, I believe," and worshipped him.

Good News
Jesus Christ, sent by the Father, is the light of the world. He opens up the eyes of the soul in the new light of faith.

65

First Reflection
A Story About Baptism (2)

In the early centuries of the church a favourite name for baptism was Illumination or Enlightenment. In early Christian art and writings the cure of the blind man was regularly used to express the light of Christ which is given in baptism. The symbol of light is still retained in the sacrament and in the renewal of baptism around the light of the paschal candle during the Easter Vigil.

The minister of baptism lights a candle from the paschal candle and gives it to the newly baptised (or parent/sponsor), saying: 'Receive the light of Christ.'

The parents and godparents are addressed on their responsibility to keep that flame burning brightly. The candle represents the flame of faith which will be expressed in a life of faith rather than darkness. The minister prays that this light will be kept burning brightly until the end of life. Then may the light-bearer be as the wise virgins, ready to go out to meet the Lord on his return.

The cure of the blind man is not narrated as an instantaneous cure in the fashion of most of the gospel miracles. The actions of Jesus are deliberate and the slow development of the story is weighted with meaning. Jesus daubed the blind eyes with a paste made from spittle and dust of the earth. It recalls the story of the creation of Adam from dust of the earth. In baptism we are created anew on a higher level of life: we are adopted into the life of God. The man is told to go and wash in the pool of Siloam. The evangelist explains that Siloam means sent. This deep well inside the walls of Jerusalem contained the water which was sent through a conduit which has been cut through 400 metres of rock. This superb feat of engineering provided the pool which would be the life-line of Jerusalem in time of siege. John sees this pool of sent water as representing Jesus, who was sent by the Father. It links this story with another baptismal story, the woman at the well.

The man who had been born blind received new sight at the washing. But as the story develops we learn how this new gift of light had to grow. The life that is given in baptism is as yet only a tiny plant which must be given favourable environment and the chance to grow.

As in the story of the woman at the well, John invites us to raise our thoughts to higher levels of faith in Christ. The once blind man rises to new levels of understanding, as is indicated in the ways he re fers to Jesus.

Initially, when he replies to the neighbours and onlookers about who cured him, he refers to 'the man called Jesus'. Later, the Pharisees interrogate him: 'What do you have to say about him?' Now the man is ready to reply: 'He is a prophet.' The story reaches its climax when the man attains to faith in the Son of Man. Who is this Son of Man? 'You are looking at him; he is speaking to you.' He then addresses Jesus as Lord. And he worships him.

His vision of Jesus has risen from man to prophet to Lord.

The ascending levels of the story suggest that growth in our baptismal life is through knowing Jesus as man, as prophet or teacher and as Lord. We grow in our knowledge of Jesus as man by increasing our familiarity with the gospel. As St Jerome said: to be ignorant of the gospel is to be ignorant of Christ. It is through steeping ourselves in the gospel that we learn more about the character of Jesus, how he acted towards people and how he reacted in all sorts of situations. We must first know Jesus if we are to follow in his way. 'I have given you an example so that you may copy what I have done to you.' *(Jn 13:15)* But how can we follow that example unless we are familiar with the gospel?

Our faith deepens as we listen more to Jesus as our prophet and teacher. Increasingly we view life through the eyes of Jesus. The more he is our teacher the more Christ-like will be our daily thought patterns. As St Paul said to the Philippians, appealing to them to be less conceited and divided: 'In your minds you must be the same as Christ Jesus.' *(Phil 2:5)* As we grow in faith, the mind of Jesus increasingly becomes the light in which we judge everything. 'I live now not with my own life but with the life of Christ who lives in me.' *(Gal 2:20)*

At the third level of faith, the man who had received new sight acknowledges Jesus as Lord and worships him. Worship is the ultimate act of faith. The believer hands over everything to the transcendent God. It is an anticipation of the blessed contemplation of God which is heaven.

Today's liturgy for the preparation of catechumens for baptism has this beautiful prayer which we can make our own:

Father of mercy, you helped the man born blind to believe in

your Son and through that faith to reach the light of your kingdom. Free your chosen ones from the falsehoods that surround them and blind them.
Let truth be the foundation of their lives.
May they live in your light for ever.
Through Christ, Our Lord.

Second Reflection
In Your Light We See Light
A woman who has been blind, but whose sight returned after an accidental fall one night, spoke of her hours of quiet ecstasy gazing at her sleeping husband and child for the first time. To have light and vision restored to life must be exciting beyond words. Yet John's story of this blind man is remarkable for the absence of any excitement on the part of the man or his parents. The reason for this understatement is that John is concentrating more on the inner vision, or faith.

The restoration of physical sight is but the outer shell of the miracle. The kernel of the story is the inner vision which has been woken up. A very early Christian hymn celebrates this awakening in baptism:

'Wake from your sleep, rise from the dead, and Christ will shine on you.' *(Quoted by St Paul in Eph 5:14)*

It reminds me of how one man felt at the end of a very intensive three-day retreat. 'I am very tired now,' he said, 'but for the first time in my life I am awake.' His inner eyes had been opened. He would appreciate the lines of the American poet e.e. cummings:

'now the ears of my ears awake and
now the eyes of my eyes are opened.'

The effects of this new way of seeing are indicated by St Paul in today's second reading: 'Be like children of the light, for the effects of the light are seen in complete goodness and right living and truth.' *(Eph 5:9)*

These three effects of the light of Christ are worth pondering. The first sure sign that one is seeing with the eyes of Christ is the ability to see goodness and beauty in the most unlikely places. The famous lines of Frederick Langbridge express the power of one's subjective view:

'Two men look out through the same bars:
One sees the mud, the one the stars.'

Jesus had a rare talent for sensing the hidden goodness in people who were notorious sinners or compromised tax-collectors, in a hot tempered fisherman and the sons of thunder, in zealous nationalists or a rich but unhappy young man.

In contrast to the eye of Jesus who saw goodness, everything looks a sickly yellow to the jaundiced eye. Our prejudices are so influential that we use our eyes more as a filtering inlet than as windows of objectivity. The Pharisees had already judged Jesus so all they can now see is the breaking of the Sabbath. In their blindness they cannot see any goodness. Today, bad news has mesmerised the media of communication. This preoccupation has so eaten into people's minds that now we need a special ministry of affirmation. Criticism has come to mean fault finding and nothing else.

Blame is more common than praise. But whoever has eyes that see with the light of Christ has the ability to see goodness, to appreciate effort, to pay compliments and to praise. In the words of the psalmist: 'In your light we see light.' *(Ps 35)*

The second effect of the light of Christ in the soul is right living or a concern for justice. The unenlightened mind operates on the purely selfish level. Self-interest is the primary motivating force. But the mind enlightened by faith operates out of Christ's vision. And its motivating power is charity.

The third effect of Christ's light is what St Paul calls truth. With the light of Christ one is no longer afraid to come out in honesty and openness. Even sin can be faced and truthfully admitted because the true light of Christ shows a merciful love that is greater than sin.

By contrast, the works of darkness are secretive and undercover, full of shady dealings and underhand practices, blinded by prejudices and limited by selfishness. Guilt is not admitted but one hides behind the screen of euphemisms or tries to offload blame towards someone else.

Lord, Jesus Christ, you are the light of the Father. Like the waters sent into the well, you were sent to be our light. With the clay of new creation you open up our inner eyes to goodness, right living and truth. Light of the world, wake us from our slumbers so that in your light we might see light.

Fifth Sunday of Lent

The raising of Lazarus is the third story of John used in our Lenten programme of exploring the riches of baptism. The miracle is a sign that Jesus has power over death and life. Through the sacraments we are called, like Lazarus, to leave the tomb of death and to come alive in the freedom of the children of God.

Today's other readings, Ezechiel 37:12.14 and Romans 8:8-11, form a unity with the gospel on the theme of rebirth from a situation of death, in the power of the Spirit.

John 11:3-7, 17, 20-27, 33-45
I am the resurrection and the life

The sisters Martha and Mary sent this message to Jesus, "Lord, the man you love is ill." On receiving the message, Jesus said, "This sickness will end, not in death but in God's glory, and through it the Son of God will be glorified."

Jesus loved Martha and her sister and Lazarus, yet when he heard that Lazarus was ill he stayed where he was for two more days before saying to the disciples, "Let us go to Judaea."

On arriving, Jesus found that Lazarus had been in the tomb for four days already. When Martha heard that Jesus had come she went to meet him. Mary remained sitting in the house. Martha said to Jesus, "If you had been here, my brother would not have died, but I know that, even now, whatever you ask of God, he will grant you." "Your brother," said Jesus to her, "will rise again." Martha said, "I know he will rise again at the resurrection on the last day." Jesus said: "I am the resurrection. If anyone believes in me, even though he dies he will live, and whoever lives and believes in me will never die. Do you believe this?" "Yes, Lord," she said, "I believe that you are the Christ, the Son of God, the one who was to come into this world." Jesus said in great distress, with a sigh that came straight from the heart, "Where have you put him?" They said, "See how much he loved him!" But there were some who remarked, "He opened the eyes of the blind man, could he not have prevented this man's death?" Still sighing, Jesus reached the tomb: it was a cave with a stone to close the opening. Jesus said, "Take the stone away." Martha said to him, "Lord, by now he will smell; this is the fourth day." Jesus replied, "Have

I not told you that if you believe you will see the glory of God?" So they took away the stone.

Then Jesus lifted up his eyes and said: "Father, I thank you for hearing my prayer. I knew indeed that you always hear me, but I speak for the sake of all these who stand round me, so that they may believe it was you who sent me."

When he had said this, he cried in a loud voice, "Lazarus, here! Come out!" The dead man came out, his feet and hands bound with bands of stuff and a cloth round his face. Jesus said to them, "Unbind him, let him go free."

Many of the Jews who had come to visit Mary and had seen what he did believed in him.

Good News
I am the resurrection and the life.
If anyone believes in me, even though he dies he will live;
and whoever lives and believes in me will never die.

First Reflection
A Story About Baptism (3)
The story of the raising of Lazarus is used in the liturgy of Lent because it illustrates baptism as a dying and rising with Christ. The Easter Vigil, which is only two weeks away, will celebrate the glorious aspect of new life with Christ, so it is fitting that as we prepare for it we should reflect on baptism's demand that we should first die with Christ.

When Jesus first hears of the illness of Lazarus his behaviour is puzzling. He is in no rush to go to the sick person's bedside. He stays where he is for two more days and then he announces that he is going.

Lazarus is dead. But Jesus tells the disciples: 'For your sake I am glad I was not there because now you will believe.'

It seems that Jesus permits the death of Lazarus so that the significance of restoring him miraculously will be all the greater. Curing a sick person would be one thing: but to raise someone to life after three days in the tomb is an incontrovertible sign. The death of Lazarus, then, is a necessary part of the sign. Just as the death of Jesus was a necessary part of God's plan of redemption: and death unto sin is part of our baptism.

To celebrate Easter Sunday without mention of Good Friday would lead to an unbalanced religion. Any excitement about the resurrection which would obscure the need of dying with Christ would be a dangerous euphoria. There is no shortcut to sanctity. The glory of sharing in Christ's resurrection involves the process of daily dying to sin and selfishness. Masters of the Christian life have always insisted on the need for the purgative stage before the illuminative and unitive. Christianity is a religion of death and life, of taking up the cross and following Christ.

No writer has ever been so conscious of the Christian rhythm of dying and rising with Christ as St Paul. Some of his key texts are worth repeating.

Rom 6: 1-11 is the classical statement of the double symbolism of baptismal water, meaning both death and life. *'You have been taught that when we were baptised in Christ Jesus we were baptised into his death; in other words, when we were baptised we went into the tomb with him and joined him in death, so that as Christ was raised from the dead by the Father's glory, we too might live a new life.'* (Rom 6:3-4)

Phil 3: 10-11 is an expression of the deepest longing of Paul's life to be totally absorbed in the life and death of the Lord. *'All I want is to know Christ and the power of his resurrection and to share his sufferings by reproducing the pattern of his death.'* Paul believed that whoever enjoyed the power of the resurrection should also participate in the sufferings of the Lord.

2 Cor 4: 10-11: here Paul explains how he sees the problems, opposition and persecutions of life as his chance to live out his dying with Christ. For him, baptism is a sacrament that is lived out every day. *'Always, wherever we may be, we carry with us in our body the death of Jesus, so that the life of Jesus, too, may always be seen in our body. Indeed, while we are still alive, we are consigned to our death every day, for the sake of Jesus, so that in our mortal flesh the life of Jesus, too, may be openly shown.'* Every day we experience some diminishments of life through malice or mistakes, through deliberate opposition or bad luck, through our partings and bereavements, through sickness and ageing. Paul's ideal is to see these experiences as our daily living out of baptism's dying with Christ.

Col 1: 24 opens up the possibility of seeing our sufferings as sharing in the redemptive sufferings of Christ. *'It makes me happy to suffer for you, as I am suffering now, and in my own body to do what I can to make up all that has still to be undergone by Christ for the sake of his body, the Church.'*

The risen Lord explained to the disciples on the road to Emmaus how it was necessary that the Christ should suffer and so enter into his glory. The death of Lazarus was necessary in its own way that the glory of God might be seen in his restoration. And it is necessary too for the Christian to die daily to sin and selfishness so as to live towards God in complete love.

The climax of our participation in the Easter Vigil will be the renewal of our baptism around the candle of the risen Lord. This renewal should be a conscious, deliberate 'Yes' to Christ who died and rose to life. When we say 'Yes' to the resurrection we also say 'Yes' to the cross.

Second Reflection
Head And Heart

We sometimes feel very mixed up when our faith tells us one thing but our feelings go the other way. But it is consoling to see how Jesus, too, experiences the conflict between the pain that prevails in the heart even as the head makes clear statements of faith.

In this story John accords a remarkable amount of human emotion to Jesus. He is so competent in handling the divinity of Jesus that he can afford to show the fragile side of his nature too. The Preface of today's Mass expresses the duality:

'As a man like us, Jesus wept for Lazarus his friend.

As the eternal God, he raised Lazarus from the dead.'

Several times in the story our attention is drawn to the love that Jesus felt towards his friend, Lazarus, and his sisters, Martha and Mary.

Human love exposes the heart to pain and sorrow. Simon and Garfunkel sang that 'a rock feels no pain, an island never cries.' But the heart which loves is tender and sensitive and it bleeds in the suffering of the loved one. So, when Jesus sees the tears of Mary and of the other mourners, his heart is deeply distressed. John has caught a moment of deep emotion in writing of 'a sigh that came straight from the heart.' And then, 'Jesus wept.' The shortest verse in the bible: two words: needing no comment.

What is most remarkable about this human frailty of Jesus is how it exists alongside the clear statements of divine faith. At the start of the story Jesus announces that the sickness would end, not in death, but in God's glory. At the centre of the story comes the great divine claim of Jesus: 'I am the ressurection and the life.'

And towards the end of the story Jesus thanks the Father for hearing his prayer: 'I knew indeed that you always hear me.' The point is repeatedly made that the believing head cohabits with the distressed heart. This experience of conflicting emotion is one that we recognise in our own lives.

For instance, at a time of bereavement our mind can be accepting the consoling doctrines of faith even as the heart's distress moves us to tears.

Or we are faced with worry and anxiety about the wayward behaviour of someone we love. We pray and pray but see no improvement.

We must appreciate how deep trust in God co-exists with our anxiety and the sleepless nights of worry.

Or again, we are taking up some challenge for Christ's sake. We are confident that God is calling us here and will be with us in the venture: but our knees knock and our hearts flutter with nervousness at the same moment.

In this experience of conflict between the divine faith of the mind and the frailty of human feelings, we are not alone. Our consolation is in knowing that Jesus, too, experienced how the believing head co-exists with the distressed heart.

Passion Sunday

Today is known as Passion Sunday and as Palm Sunday. These two titles express contrasting themes. The reading of the passion draws attention to the human suffering and death-agony of Jesus. But the palm expresses the triumphal entry of Jesus into Jerusalem. The two titles remind us that the events of Holy Week form a story which must be read on the two levels of human suffering and divine triumph.

Matthew 26:14 - 27:66

Because of the length of this passage the reader is requested to take it directly from the lectionary or bible.

Good News

The Good News in Matthew's passion is brought out in the royal dignity with which Jesus suffers. His death is the sacrifice of the new covenant and his blood is shed to ratify this covenant.

First Reflection

The New Covenant in My Blood

Whenever we celebrate the Eucharist we remember the passion, death and glorification of Jesus Christ. Matthew, in common with the other evangelists and St Paul, understood the last supper as a covenant meal. It was there at the last supper that Jesus interpreted the human drama of his suffering and death on a divine level. The bloodstained events of that week acquire a new meaning when understood in terms of divine sacrifice. And because of this divine meaning, the events of that one week in history belong to the living memory of every age. So, St Paul could say: 'Until the Lord comes, therefore, every time you eat this bread and drink this cup, you are proclaiming his death ...' *(1 Cor 11:26)*

A covenant is an agreement or a pact between two parties, with obligations undertaken by both sides. The entire bible is the story of two covenants or testaments between God and his people.

The old testament is the story of the relationship between God and his chosen people. This relationship was clarified and deepened through three great covenants. The first covenant was made with Noah after the flood. God promised never to destroy the earth again: the people's part was to end murder and the destruction of life.

The second stage of covenant was made with Abraham. Abraham must accept the unique position of Yahweh as the one true God. In return, he is to become the father of many nations. The old covenant was finally completed with Moses. In this, God, who had led them out of the slavery of Egypt, promised to be their God, leader and protector. The people were obliged to be God's people by observing the laws of worship and morality which were set out in the commandments.

In the minds of people two actions were associated with covenants: the shedding of blood and a meal.

Blood was understood as the carrier of life. The shedding of blood in sacrifice was a way of saying how the promises one was making were guaranteed on one's very life. 'Upon this blood, symbol of my life, I make this solemn promise.' Moses sprinkled the people with the blood of the sacrificial animals as a sign of the ratification of the covenant. 'This is the blood of the Covenant that Yahweh has made with you, containing all these rules.' *(Ex 24:8)*

The second action associated with any covenant was the meal which celebrated the new relationship between the parties. Sharing the same food expressed the new unity in life between the parties. It was an act of the deepest betrayal to turn against any party with whom one had shared a covenant meal.

From the time of Moses onwards, God remained ever faithful and loyal to his side of the covenant , but the people were so unfaithful that the various prophets spoke of the need for a new covenant.

Now, at the last supper, the time had come for this new covenant to be set up. Jesus had ministered among the people with the message of the kingdom. Matthew has portrayed Jesus as the new Moses: he has the authority to deepen and fulfil the Mosaic covenant. 'You have heard it said of old ... but I say to you.' A new covenant is being enacted.

The law of this new covenant will not be an external code on tablets of stone that religious lawyers can tamper with. The new law is the universal, unrestricted law of love, written on the fleshy tablet of the heart. The ratification of this covenant is not in the blood of lambs or goats but in the blood of Jesus 'which is poured out for many for the forgiveness of sins.' *(Matt 26:28)* The passion and death of Jesus are understood in terms of divine sacrifice.

The last supper is the covenant meal which celebrates the new relationship set up between God and his people. Jesus, taking the bread, says: 'Take it and eat; this is my body.' And of the wine: 'Drink all of you from this for this is my blood, the blood of the covenant, which is to be poured out for many for the forgiveness of sins.' The relationship set up in this new covenant is a sharing in divine life. To eat the body and drink the blood of Jesus is to share in the life of God. By this food we deepen our union with God and grow in divine likeness. As St Augustine so beautifully explained, this divine food is not digested as ordinary food to become part of us, but by it we are changed to become more truly a part of Christ.

Matthew introduces a dramatic, apocalyptic passage to express what happened on Calvary. 'The veil of the Temple was torn in two from top to bottom; the earth quaked; the rocks were split.' The drama is the ending of the old covenant and the inauguration of the new. Tombs were opened and holy men rose from the dead, for this dramatic moment is the day of release from all captivity, even death. Jesus, the new Moses, has released his people.

Christians assemble in faith to remember and proclaim what the Lord Jesus did. 'The blessing-cup that we bless is a communion with the body of Christ ... Every time you eat this bread and drink this cup, you are proclaiming his death.' (1 Cor 10:16. 11:26)

Second Reflection
The book of the Cross
When the early followers of St Francis asked him to teach them about prayer, he spoke to them about the book of the cross. He felt that all the lessons they would ever need could be read on the cross of Jesus Christ. Countless meditations in every age have developed lessons from the school of Christ's passion. Here we will follow one of the earliest passion meditations as given to us in the First Epistle of Peter, 2: 21-24.

(1) The first word that we read on the cross is love: the love of Christ for us and his love for the Father's will. In the words of Peter: 'Christ suffered for you.'

In contrast to the other characters of the drama who are enslaved by their political fears, ambitions and venality, Jesus strides through the events with a noble freedom of choice. His motivation is love. He makes the free choice to follow through the Father's will unto the very end.

'No one takes my life from me; I lay it down of my own free will ... and this is the command I have been given by my Father.' *(Jn 10: 17-18)* As his young life faces the imminent reality of death he is torn asunder in mind and heart. His companions are drowsy after too many cups of wine and they offer him no support. He suffers alone but reaches into a depth of soul where he finds that loving loyalty to the Father's will overcomes all human loneliness.

His love for the Father's will is accompanied by his loving outreach to embrace all sinners in this saving grace. St John deliberately opens up his account of the passion by calling our attention to Christ's love. 'He had always loved those who were his in the world, but now he showed how perfect his love was.' *(Jn 13:1)* The greatest test of love is to lay down one's life for the other: 'A man can have no greater love than to lay down his life for his friends.' *(Jn 15:13)*

The noble freedom of Jesus throughout the passion is born out of his love for the Father's will and for us, sinners.

2) The second lesson in the book is the example of Jesus in how to suffer without bitterness. St Peter tells us that Christ 'left an example for you to follow the way he took. He had not done anything wrong, and there had been no perjury in his mouth. He was insulted and did not retaliate with insults.'

Jesus did not seek suffering in any masochistic way. He prayed earnestly to avoid it if possible. But once he accepted its necessity, he displayed exemplary calmness and patience. He showed how suffering can be borne with love rather than in bitterness. As he had once preached on turning the other cheek, now he gave the example of not retaliating against extreme provocation.

He must have been sorely distressed when one who had shared the covenant meal with him, Judas, walked out of his friendship to betray him. He was disappointed at the weakness of Peter: disgusted at the moral cowardice of Pilate and his hypocritical washing hands of responsibility: angry at the perversion of justice in the juridical charades and trumped-up charges he had to face: saddened by the insensitive mockery of the soldiers.

'But Jesus was silent.'

One short sentence portrays his noble strength of character. In the sermon on the mount he spoke of a love that is greater than the hurts that one has to bear: a love that pushes forward through all obstacles: a love that refuses to be poisoned by the evil it encounters.

Jesus showed how to suffer with love and dignity. He would not retaliate or be dragged down to the pits of evil reaction. And as Luke records, his love found a reason to forgive his persecutors: 'Father, forgive them; they do not know what they are doing.' (23:34) Jesus suffered with love and not in bitterness.

St Peter continues his lesson: 'When he was tortured he made no threats but he put his trust in the righteous judge.' In his suffering he did not lose the dignity of hope. Though everyone around him seemed to be in the feverish grip of evil, he did not lose his belief that God is in charge of the world and all will be well.

Our temptation is to despair of God's control of events. If we react in anger and take vengeance into our own hands, it shows that we have despaired of God. Jesus all the time put his trust in the Father, the righteous one. He suffered with the dignity of trust rather than in the undignified reactions that accompany despair.

3) The third word that we read on the cross is sin. St Peter points to our faults: 'He was bearing our faults in his body on the cross, so that we might die to our faults and live for holiness.'

The wounded, torn and lacerated body of Jesus vividly shows the death-dealing stabs of sin. Every lash of the whip, every piercing thorn, every graze from his falls is a glaring statement of the ugliness of sin. 'Ours were the sufferings he bore, ours the sorrows he carried. He was pierced through for our faults, crushed for our sins.' (Is 53: 4-5)

To become a follower of Christ one enters the baptismal process of dying to all sinful passions. The wounded body of Jesus on the cross states more loudly than words how seriously we must take the Christian programme of dying to sin.

4) The fourth word that we read on the cross is hope: for Jesus is our healer, our shepherd and the guardian of our souls.

'Through his wounds you have been healed. You had gone

astray like sheep but now you have come back to the shepherd and guardian of your souls.'

The wounds and anguish suffered by Jesus show the depth of his compassion towards us and his solidarity with us in our brokenness and pain. When we contemplate his anguish in Gethsemane and hear his loud cries of prayer in pain, then we know that he is near us in our conflicts and darkness. He has reached down to the lowest pits of human woundedness to heal our worst brokenness. He is our wounded healer.

He is the shepherd who loves the straying one with an everlasting love that makes him wander the hills to cry out for the return of a soul.

He is the guardian, protector and keeper of our souls through all the storms of life.

Holy Week brings us face to face with the passion of Jesus. But it is right to commence the week with waving palms to mark the triumphal entry of the Messiah-King into Jerusalem.

Through his death he conquered death
and the tree of death became the tree of life.

Easter Sunday

Easter is the celebration of what Pope Paul V1 described as 'the unique and sensational event on which the whole of human history turns.'

Scripture has no account of the actual happening of the resurrection of Jesus. We are told of the discovery of the empty tomb and of the appearance of the risen Lord to various disciples. By means of these appearances the diciples are led into making the huge step of faith from following the man, Jesus of Nazareth, to believing that he was the Son of God who triumphed over death.

It was as if somebody who could walk suddenly found the ability to fly. Resurrection life is as much (and more) above ordinary, earthly life as flying is above walking. Faith is such a leap forward from the human level of life to participation in divine life.

Matthew 28:1-10
He has risen from the dead and now he is going before you to Galilee

After the sabbath, and toward dawn on the first day of the week, Mary of Magdala and the other Mary went to visit the sepulchre. And all at once there was a violent earthquake, for the angel of the Lord, descending from heaven, came and rolled away the stone and sat on it. His face was like lightning, his robe white as snow. The guards were so shaken, so frightened of him, that they were like dead men.

But the angel spoke, and he said to the women, "There is no need for you to be afraid. I know you are looking for Jesus, who was crucified. He is not here, for he has risen, as he said he would. Come and see the place where he lay, then go quickly and tell his disciples, 'He has risen from the dead and now he is going before you to Galilee; it is there you will see him.' Now I have told you." Filled with awe and great joy the women came quickly away from the tomb and ran to tell the disciples.

And there, coming to meet them, was Jesus. "Greetings," he said. And the women came up to him and, falling down before him, clasped his feet. Then Jesus said to them, "Do not be afraid; go and tell my brothers that they must leave for Galilee; they will see me there."

Good News

The tomb is empty: Jesus Christ is risen: and the story of humanity will never be the same again.

First Reflection

Resurrection, not Resuscitation

The tomb was empty. What happened? Was it the same as happened to Lazarus or the daughter of Jairus or the widow's son? These people were revived, resuscitated. They resumed their old life after a period of interruption.

John gives a detailed account of the exact whereabouts of the linen binding cloths, all of them still in the tomb. By contrast, when Lazarus came forth from the tomb he was still bound in the cloths. The evangelist intends the reader to see the difference between the return of Lazarus and the rising of Jesus.

The resurrection of Jesus was not the same as resuscitation. It was not a matter of now returning to his old manner of life after a three-day interruption. Resurrection means new life. The evangelist intends the reader to catch the significance of 'the first day of the week'. It was the dawning of the first day of the new creation. This new creation is a level of life beyond our human experience, or categories of thought and speech. However the evangelists offer us signs and hints through the various stories of the apparitions of the risen Lord which invite us to conjecture what this new life means.

In three of the apparition stories, various disciples did not recognise Jesus until some sign was given. Mary Magdalen did not recognise the risen Lord and thought she was speaking with the gardener until she heard him call her by name.

The seven disciples who had gone back fishing, at least five of whom were apostles, did not recognise the risen Lord either by sight or by voice until they saw the huge catch of fish as a sign. And in the story of the two disciples on the road to Emmaus, Luke tells us that something prevented them from recognising him. It all adds up to the conclusion that the appearance of Jesus was very different to what they had known.

On the other hand, the physical reality of Christ's risen body is established in the way that he cooked food, ate food and invited disciples to touch him and identify the wounds in his hands and feet: 'Yes, it is I indeed. Touch and see for yourselves; a ghost has no flesh and bones as you can see I have.' *(Lk 24:39)* The Lord rose in the same identifiable body as had received the wounds of crucifixion, but in a new condition. The risen body is no longer supported by the laws and energies of physical life but lives now by the energies of divine life.

The risen body is the same, but different. It is the same body but in a different condition. Whereas in the cases of Lazarus, the widow's son and Jairus' daughter, they returned on the same level of life they had previously experienced.

Resurrection means a new level of life. Jesus is glorified. He has returned to the glory of the Father's countenance after his period of 'emptied' life within the limitations of human flesh.

The hugely significant fact for us is that the resurrection is a story that involves us. In the risen body of Jesus, all human life is invited to transcend the grave and share in divine life. Through baptism we die and rise with Christ. We enter the tomb and rise from the tomb with him. Our eternal destiny is to go through death to be totally one with Christ in the glory of the Father.

Even now, in the days of our earthly life, the call to heavenly life has begun. That is why St Paul calls on the Colossians to die to the ways of sin and to live out of the belief that one already has a foot in heaven. The magnificent passage, Colossians 3:1-17, deserves time on its own.

Easter is more than a mere historical remembrance. It is the celebration of the raising up of humanity to a sharing in divine life with Christ. The risen Lord now lives in us, through baptism, and leads us through our earthly life to the full experience of divine adoption in heaven. In the resurrection of Jesus Christ a new level of life has been opened up to humanity. Truly, as Pope Paul VI said in his Easter Sunday address (1972):

'the resurrection of Jesus Christ is the unique and sensational event on which the whole of human history turns.'

Second Reflection
Your Empty Tomb

There is a very puzzling line in the old translation of the Apostles' Creed: 'He descended into hell.'

It is a phrase that locates Jesus on that Sabbath between the dying and the rising.

The word 'hell' in this instance is not a reference to the state of eternal damnation. The word originally meant a hiding place. Later it acquired a more precise application to the hidden abode of the dead. The phrase in the creed expresses the belief that Jesus liberated the souls of the just who had died before his time.

In an apocalyptic reflection on the death of Jesus, Matthew's gospel states: 'The rocks were split; the tombs opened and the bodies of many holy men rose from the dead, and these, after his resurrection, came out of the tombs, entered the Holy City and appeared to a number of people.' (27: 52-53)

The notion of Jesus opening up the hiding places of the dead is relevant to all the caves of darkness where we hid in pain from the fulness of light and life. In his dying he destroyed our death: by his wounds he heals our wounds: by his lying in the tomb he has visited all our private tombs.

We descend into the tomb of darkness whenever the reality of life is too painful for us to endure. The quality of our living is diminished, we are emotionally crippled and mentally stagnated.

Is your cave of darkness due to the pain of bereavement? Then reflect on the fulness of life released for us by the victory of Jesus. And remember how he experienced the pain of family farewell as his mother's heart was pierced by the sword of sorrow.

If your dark cave is due to experiences of misunderstanding, misrepresentation, or malicious conspiracy, just remember that Jesus was in there before you. He was the victim of religious envy, a political pawn and he was betrayed by one who had shared the covenant meal with him.

His suffering was of a physical nature in the hundred inventions of cruelty unleashed upon him: he suffered intense mental anguish: and he even visited the dark realm of spiritual suffering.

He was condemned in court to hang with convicted criminals, mocked in ungrateful tribute to his works of healing, and stripped bare of the very garments of human dignity. Is there any form of private hell he did not visit?

Whatever your tomb, your hiding place,
your private hell,
come out of it this Easter day.
In the light and power of the risen Christ, leave behind you an empty tomb.

Second Sunday of Easter

This gospel passage rises in three stages.
First, the risen Lord shares his divine mission with the disciples and bestows on them the power of the Holy Spirit.
Then the wellknown story of the hesitation of Thomas leads to the crescendo of his act of faith.
Finally, the evangelist tells us that the purpose of his writing was to lead people to faith in Jesus as the Son of God, that we might have life in his name.

John 20:19-31
After eight days Jesus came in and stood among them

In the evening of that same day, the first day of the week, the doors were closed in the room where the disciples were, for fear of the authorities. Jesus came and stood among them. He said to them, "Peace be with you," and showed them his hands and his side. The disciples were filled with joy when they saw the Lord, and he said to them again, "Peace be with you. As the Father sent me, so am l sending you." After saying this he breathed on them and said: "Receive the Holy Spirit. For those whose sins you forgive, they are forgiven; for those whose sins you retain, they are retained."

Thomas, called the Twin, who was one of the Twelve, was not with them when Jesus came. When the disciples said, "We have seen the Lord," he answered, "Unless I see the holes that the nails made in his hands and can put my finger into the holes they made, and unless I can put my hand into his side, I refuse to believe." Eight days later the disciples were in the house again and Thomas was with them. The doors were closed but Jesus came in and stood among them. "Peace be with you," he said. Then he spoke to Thomas, "Put your finger here; look, here are my hands. Give me your hand; put it into my side. Doubt no longer but believe." Thomas replied, "My Lord and my God!" Jesus said to him: "You believe because you can see me. Happy are those who have not seen and yet believe."

There were many other signs that Jesus worked and the disciples saw, but they are not recorded in this book. These are recorded so that you may believe that Jesus is the Christ, the Son of God, and that believing this you may have life through his name.

Good News

The Lord is risen from the dead in newness of life. His mission of reconciliation continues through the lives of those who have been blessed in the power of the Holy Spirit.

First Reflection
The Closed Doors

There is an old Irish proverb that the help of God is nearer to us than the closed door.

In the room where the disciples were the doors were closed for fear of the temple guards and Roman soldiers. Human prudence might say that there was every reason for fear because whenever tyrants taste blood, arrests rarely stop at one.

The closed doors vividly express the mental condition of the disciples. As a group they were without leadership, purpose or direction. And as individuals each one cowered in a private little hell of lostness, guilt, sadness, fear or anxiety. The message of the empty tomb had not registered with them yet.

Then the risen Lord came and stood among them. The atmosphere changed immediately. He greeted them with 'Peace'. They were filled with joy.

He invited them to come out of their caves of darkness and to discover new life. He gave them a new breath; divine breath. Breath, to their thinking, was the principle of life: that invisible thing without which one ceased to live.

They remembered the Genesis text of God breathing life into the first man: and Ezechiel's vision of the breath of life entering the bones in the valley of the dead. Now the risen Lord was breathing into them the new breath of divine life. 'Receive the Holy Spirit.' They were being given a new life: life on a higher level than ever previously experienced in human history.

In this new life they were being called to share in the mission of Jesus. He spoke to them of two sendings: two divine missions.

The first mission was when the Father sent Jesus into the world. And in the second mission, the risen Jesus was now sending out the disciples, in the power of the Holy Spirit, to continue his work of healing the world through forgiveness and reconciliation.

They were now commissioned to bring the divine love in a forgiveness which was greater than anything sin could do.

With the power of the Holy Spirit in them, there would be no more closed doors, but only the open highway to the four ends of the earth. And no more caves of darkness for wallowing in fear and self-pity. They were called forward to leave the tombs empty behind them.

One of the apostles was absent. As providence would have it, the missing one was Thomas, who by nature was cautious in the extreme. We know from meeting him elsewhere how he would see the full cost of every commitment, but for all that he would be loyal to the last. Thomas, cautious but loyal, was surely chosen for the sake of all who hesitate. If Thomas could believe, anybody could!

All he needed was time. So, after a week of growing with the idea, he was ready. And the evangelist, John, honours Thomas by placing onto his lips the highest act of faith reached in the gospel: 'My Lord and my God.'

This is the final crescendo of faith in the rising thoughts of John's gospel. Having reached this crowning moment, the evangelist adds a final summary of his writing. The purpose of his work was to invite people to believe that Jesus is the Christ, the Son of God. And those who believe this have life in his name.

And what life! Nothing less than a sharing in the life of God, in the power of the Holy Spirit.

O risen Lord, in the power of the Holy Spirit call us to come out from behind the closed doors of life. Call us out of the tomb of guilt unto full belief in the Church's divine power for forgiveness. Call us out of the dark cave of fear into the light of faith in your presence with us. Call us out from the claustrophobia of anxious fretting into the open air of full trust in your care for us. Risen Lord, bring us to fulness of life.

Second Reflection
Blessed are you who help others to see

The familiar saying goes: 'Seeing is believing.' But seeing is not sufficient for believing. For seeing only touches the outer, physical evidence, whereas believing belongs to the interior, invisible areas of life.

A tale is told of the Jewish Rabbi who asked his servant every morning if the Messiah had come. The servant went to the window and observed the people who passed by on the street. Every morning he returned to the Rabbi with the news that on the evidence of what he had seen in people, his conclusion was that the Messiah had not come.

First there was one preacher of the kingdom: Jesus, sent by the Father. And then, in the time of the resurrection, the one became many when the church was born: the risen Lord sent out the disciples in the power of the Holy Spirit.

The Spirit, in time, inspired four evangelists to write down the church's memory of Jesus Christ for teaching all ages.

Four gospels, one for each point of the compass, N,E,W and S. But even four gospels are not enough to convince people that the Messiah has come. A fifth gospel is needed: the gospel written by you and me in the evidence of our lives.

Was this why Thomas needed time? Cautious Thomas was sceptical of words alone. He would wait to observe the behaviour of those who were speaking so excitedly of the appearance of the Lord to them.

Pope Paul VI, in his letter on evangelisation, stresses the point that the first means of evangelisation is the witness of an authentic Christian life. 'Modern man listens more willingly to witnesses than to teachers, and if he does listen to teachers, it is because they are witnesses.'

The number of believers multiplied rapidly in response to the witness of the early Christian community. They were 'faithful to the teaching of the apostles, to the brotherhood, to the breaking of bread and to the prayers.' Today's first reading portrays the life of the community.

Down the years of history the witness of people like Francis and Dominic, Clare and Therese, stirred up the faith of people more effectively than libraries of learned books. People are moved to believe when they meet the risen Lord in authentic people of grace.

Easter is only a lifeless fossil of ceremony if it does not send you out from the dead way of life which knows no love, joy or peace, no forgiveness, hope or trust.

Easter is to hear the risen Lord say to you: 'I am sending you out.'
To easter with him is to rise into...
believing that you are loved by God,
and daring to hope and trust in his presence and power.
In the power of the Spirit let there be...
new life in your heart,
new light on your face,
and new joy in your believing.
The Messiah has been sent by the Father.
And he has sent you, baptised Christian, to win the world from
the darkness of sin.
Blessed are you whose life enables others to see and to believe.

Third Sunday of Easter

This is the only Sunday of the present liturgical year when the gospel is from Luke. The Emmaus Road is a story which shows his outstanding literary ability with its polished composition, his sensitivity to the inner feelings of the characters, and his deft use of irony which enables the audience to know more than the characters on the stage. And the episode is sprinkled with memorable phrases like 'We had hoped'... 'Was it not ordained that the Christ should suffer' ... 'It is nearly evening'... 'Did not our hearts burn within us'... 'the breaking of the bread.'

Luke 24:13-35
They had recognised him at the breaking of the bread

Two of the disciples of Jesus were on their way to a village called Emmaus, seven miles from Jerusalem, and they were talking together about all that had happened. Now as they talked this over, Jesus himself came up and walked by their side, but something prevented them from recognising him. He said to them, "What matters are you discussing as you walk along?" They stopped short, their faces downcast.

Then one of them, called Cleopas, answered him, "You must be the only person staying in Jerusalem who does not know the things that have been happening there these last few days." "What things?" he asked. "All about Jesus of Nazareth," they answered, "who proved he was a great prophet by the things he said and did in the sight of God and of the whole people; and how our chief priests and our leaders handed him over to be sentenced to death, and had him crucified.

"Our own hope had been that he would be the one to set Israel free. And this is not all: two whole days have gone by since it all happened; and some women from our group have astounded us: they went to the tomb in the early morning, and when they did not find the body, they came back to tell us they had seen a vision of angels who declared he was alive. Some of our friends went to the tomb and found everything exactly as the women had reported but of him they saw nothing."

Then he said to them, "You foolish men! So slow to believe the full message of the prophets! Was it not ordained that the Christ should suffer and so enter into his glory?" Then, starting with Moses and going through all the prophets, he explained to

90

them the passages throughout the scriptures that were about himself.

When they drew near to the village to which they were going, he made as if to go on; but they pressed him to stay with them. "It is nearly evening," they said, "and the day is almost over." So he went in to stay with them.

Now while he was with them at table, he took the bread and said the blessing; then he broke it and handed it to them. And their eyes were opened and they recognised him; but he had vanished from their sight. Then they said to each other, "Did not our hearts burn within us as he talked to us on the road and explained the scriptures to us?"

They set out that instant and returned to Jerusalem. There they found the Eleven assembled together with their companions, who said to them, "Yes, it is true. The Lord has risen and has appeared to Simon." Then they told their story of what had happened on the road and how they had recognised him at the breaking of bread.

Good News

The risen Lord is with us on our road with his heartwarming word and his bread of service. He had to suffer, his bread must be broken, because he is Christ the Servant at our table of life.

First Reflection
The People, the Word, the Meal

The story of the risen Lord on the Emmaus road reads like a dramatisation of the Eucharistic celebration. The three necessary elements for Eucharist are highlighted in turn – the assembly of people, the lessons of the word and the sharing of the meal.

The People

Ever before the word is proclaimed or the meal shared, there is the assembly of God's People.Those who journey together in the dim light of faith on life's pilgrimage gather in the memory of Jesus, who died and rose again. Cleopas and his companion were talking out of their memory of 'all that had happened' to Jesus.

The celebration commences with a confession of sinfulness. Believers do not wait to be perfect before they assemble: pilgrims know that they have not arrived: those who assemble for Eucharist know they are still sinners.

The two disciples unwittingly confess their sins. They have lost their hope in Jesus. They have turned their backs on Jerusalem, which is the city of life's pilgrimage in Luke's gospel. Their faces are downcast, their eyes devoid of purpose. The more they talk, the more their sinfulness is admitted. Not only had they lost hope in Jesus but also their belief in what their friends reported about the empty tomb.

And as for taking seriously the evidence of the women! Luke lets their sinful dismissal of the feminine speak for itself.

As Christians assemble in the memory of Jesus Christ, they recognise their weakness, their wavering and their sinfulness. They know that they must be fed in mind and in soul. They are ready to listen to the word.

The Word

The risen Lord responded to the foolishness of the disciples. He drew their minds back to the wisdom of the scriptures where they would find the divine light for life. Later they admitted that their hearts were burning within them as he talked to them on the road and explained the scriptures to them.

In the dimness of our faith our prayer needs the constant enlightenment of the sacred word. Through the intricate paths of daily life our conscience needs the guiding light of God's own teaching. In the cold darkness of a secularistic society we need to experience our hearts burning within us at the good news of God's self-giving love for us.

The Meal

The eucharistic liturgy advances from the table of the word to the table of the bread. Those who have heard the good news now need to celebrate. And celebration, for Luke, means a table. 'Stay with us Lord,' is the heartfelt cry of the disciple. The Lord has heard this cry and answers us in the wonder of the real presence.

Luke deliberately echoes the four Eucharistic actions of the Lord. He took ... he blessed ... he broke ... and he gave. The actions done on the bread apply also to the disciple. Those who assemble are the chosen or taken people who have received the gift of faith.

Out of all the loaves of bread in the world today, this one loaf is taken. Out of all the billions of people who exist or have existed, this assembly is now called together by God.

God is blessed and praised and thanked for all he has given. The great hymn of Glory to God rises from the people. They lift up their hearts to give thanks and praise: that is what eucharist means. Through Christ, with him and in him, by the power of the Holy Spirit, all honour and glory is returned to the Father of all giving. And the assembled believers loudly acclaim: 'Amen'.

Then the Sacred Bread is broken. It must be broken before it can be shared. The broken bread is a symbol of the Servant Christ who had to suffer and so enter into his glory.

And as the disciples contemplate this plan of God, they learn how God is with them in their woundings, breakings and dying. Selfishness and sin are progressively broken by God, so that the disciple may increasingly conform to Christ the Servant who loved his own unto the end.

As he handed the broken bread to them their eyes were opened and they recognised him. Those who eat the Sacred Bread are changed. They become more alive with Christ's life: more like him.

Ordinary food is changed into our energy. But in Christ's Bread, those who eat are changed into his energy.

Conclusion

The two disciples are no longer tired and downcast. In this new energy of Christ they set out that instant on the road. Their faces are glowing, their eyes full of light and purpose. Their pilgrimage of faith has recovered its direction ... back towards the Holy City.

And they tell their story to the world: not so much their own story as the story of God's word and God's bread.

That is why, when the Mass is ended, the assembled people, who have received the fire of the word and the energy of the bread, are sent out to 'love and serve the Lord'.

Second Reflection
Programme for a Journey

The encounter of the risen Lord with the two disciples on the road is told in three stages. He is first a fellow traveller on the road with them: then he explains the scriptures to them: and finally he goes in with them to sit at their table.

These three stages of the story correspond to the vital parts of a Christian life. By reflecting on them we can highlight a programme for Christian life. Spiritual writers have traditionally pictured the tripod which requires the balance of action, study and prayer.

In the first stage of the story the risen Lord was their fellow traveller on the road. But they did not recognise him. Nor do we, without the light of grace, recognise the presence of God in those who travel the road of life with us. It is only the light of faith that can raise our eyes above that limited vision in which we can hate people, envy them, focus on their faults, be irritated by their quirks and foibles.

Faith reveals how the other person is a creature of the Father's love, is loved unto the cross by Christ the Son, and is a sanctified temple of the Holy Spirit. Perhaps the greatest gift one can give to others is to help them recognise who they are in the loving eyes of the Triune God.

When we begin to glimpse the divine worth in other people we will act in love towards them. Christianity has always been a religion of loving action.

In the second stage of the journey, Jesus set their hearts on fire as he explained the scriptures to them. This corresponds to the second leg of the tripod: study. Adult study of religion has been a serious weakness in Catholicism.

The Emmaus disciples were downcast and without hope in God or trust in others until their hearts were warmed by the explanation of the scriptures. If a person's mental intake is chiefly from the bad news which the mass media sensationalise, is it any wonder that there is so much sadness, depression and inability to cope with the pressures of life?

The third leg of the tripod is prayer. The Emmaus story proceeds to a table. And for Luke, tables are his favourite symbolic setting to express the experience of prayer. He went in to stay with them, and this particular table expresses the prayer of eucharist.

'Stay with us, Lord.'

The risen Lord is with us on the road to our Jerusalem.

We reach out to him through the people who journey with us.

We listen to him through study of the scriptures.

We celebrate his living memory at the Eucharistic table.

Fourth Sunday of Easter

The gospel for the fourth Sunday of Easter in all three years of the lectionary is about Christ as the Good Shepherd. These words of Jesus acquire a rich meaning when we apply them to the Risen Christ.

The idea of the shepherd calling his flock is the basis for choosing this Sunday as Vocations Sunday.

John 10:1-10
I am the gate of the sheepfold

Jesus said: "I tell you most solemnly, anyone who does not enter the sheepfold through the gate, but gets in some other way is a thief and a brigand. The one who enters through the gate is the shepherd of the flock; the gatekeeper lets him in, the sheep hear his voice, one by one he calls his own sheep and leads them out. When he has brought out his flock, he goes ahead of them, and the sheep follow because they know his voice. They never follow a stranger but run away from him: they do not recognise the voice of strangers."

Jesus told them this parable but they failed to understand what he meant by telling it to them. So Jesus spoke to them again: "I tell you most solemnly, I am the gate of the sheepfold. All others who have come are thieves and brigands; but the sheep took no notice of them. I am the gate. Anyone who enters through me will be safe: he will go freely in and out and be sure of finding pasture. The thief comes only to steal and kill and destroy. I have come so that they may have life and have it to the full."

Good News
The risen Lord calls us to the fulness of life. He is the only gate of entrance to the divine life.

First Reflection
I am the gate

The evangelist John liked to group important happenings in groups of seven. There are seven great 'I am' texts. Each of these texts is a claim to divine life on the part of Jesus; and they express some aspect of his relationship with us.

The words 'I am' on the lips of Jesus are a claim to divine life. They echo the name of God revealed to Moses when he received his call to lead the oppressed Hebrew people out of Egypt (Ex 3:14) Yahweh, who called him, was not to be thought of as one local god among others. 'I am', and there's no more to be said. 'I am', beyond words. One true God, the eternal being, before all creation, and in everything that exists. The beginning, the middle and end of all things.

As Jesus echoes that name there is an invitation to all who have ears to hear, to believe that he is God.

I am the gate of the sheepfold

Flocks of sheep are protected from the wild animals of the night in an area surrounded by a sound wall. There is no gate as such into this sheepfold. The shepherd acts as gate. Sheep pass into the fold through his hands as he examines each one in turn, applies healing olive oil to any scratches or bruises, and gives each one a drink of cool water. Dry, dusty eyes are soothed in a cup that is overflowing. When all have passed through, the shepherd lies across the entrance to become the protecting gate which shuts out all prowling predators.

In this text the risen Lord speaks to my soul. As the shepherd calls the sheep by name, so he has called me to share in divine life through baptism. He is the only gate to the fulness of life. No one can go to the Father except through him.

As the shepherd examines each sheep, I feel my life being examined in the light of his teaching. He shows up my bruises and hurts in order to heal me. He offers me the delight of prayer if I end each day by drinking from the overflowing cup of his presence.

Anyone who enters through me will be safe

He offers me the care and security which enable me to enjoy true freedom. He alone can raise us up, in the power of his rising, to divine life.

By human effort we can work towards physical wellbeing, intellectual development and emotional balance. But it is only in the call of Christ to the soul that we can sense the divine energy of his life within us. He came that we might have life ... and have it to the full. And fulness of life is reached only when we let God's presence within us be expressed to others, through our thoughts, attitudes and actions.

The risen Lord calls me to pass through his gate. In response to this invitation, I must resolve not to go anywhere except through Jesus; not to be involved in any activity unless Jesus can be there.

O my soul, rest in the Lord. He is my shepherd who calls me on the road to fulness of life. He is the only gate into the fulness of life. He is the protecting gate which offers me security and freedom.

Second Reflection
Vocation Sunday

The gospel picture of the Good Shepherd calling his flock has inspired the Church to focus attention this Sunday each year on vocations. The flock of Jesus Christ will always need the leadership of people who make commitment to Christ and his gospel their professed way of life. In a very special way, priests are called to be the mediators who bring people to God and bring God to the people. Through the liturgical action of the Church they act as 'stewards entrusted with the mysteries of God'. (1 Cor 4:1)

A vocation to the religious life is a call to commit oneself to the service of God and the Church through the profession of a gospel-based way of life. What is being highlighted today is the vast but untapped vocation of all the baptised to serve the cause of the gospel. Perhaps the most serious aspect of the critical shortage of vocations is the failure to call forth the potential of the laity. Too much emphasis on a clerical model of the Church has left us with an impoverished legacy of neglecting the apostolic charisms of baptism and confirmation.

We are living at a crossroads period in the history of the Church. At the close of the second Christian millenium, society in many traditionally Christian countries is seriously tempted to forsake the inspiration of the gospel and take on secularistic ways of thinking and evaluating.

For the past four hundred years, the Church was confronted chiefly by doctrinal heresies. It was the age of theologians and priests. Nowadays the chief arena of debate is in secular society. And that's the world of the Christian laity. This is the age to call forth the vocation of the laity.

The voice of Christ the shepherd is muted by the incessant propaganda which calls souls away from his flock. The sacred dimension of life is not taken seriously. Exaggerated claims, based on psychological surveys or polls on behaviour, are taken as the basis for moral guidelines. The authority of God is replaced by a spurious democracy which settles for the lowest common denominator of agreed morality. At this lowest level, societies have condoned abortion and easy divorce.

Moral vagueness has stifled the voice of conscience to such an extent that for many, sin is no longer a word in their working vocabulary. Foggy thinking, which claims that all religions are more or less the same, has clouded the unique light of Jesus Christ, the word made flesh. Materialistic progress is promoted as the purpose of life. Amplified stimulation of the brain through loud music, flashing lights and accelerated change has shattered that quietness of mind which was conducive to reflection and growth in wisdom. These are the thieving voices which steal and kill and destroy members of the flock.

The threatened flock of Christ needs to hear a loud call to the values of the gospel, which are radically opposed to many of the accepted norms of secular society.

But how can they hear unless there are dedicated disciples who give their flesh and blood to embody the voice of Christ for the world of today? The challenge to the destructive voices must come through fearless proclamation of the Christian message and selfless dedication to the service of others, but especially through the witness of how we live.

Vocations Sunday renews the challenge of Christ to every disciple. Am I following the voice of Christ the shepherd and the values of the gospel? Or is my life a denial of the gospel, or a smug compromise which picks and chooses from any source? A Sunday Christian and a six-day pagan?

Am I concerned for the future of the Church? Am I prepared to serve? To give my life to full-time service of the Church? Or to serve with my time and co-operation in the local community? As a faith-friend to even one person?

Do I support those who give themselves fully to the parish mission? Do I pray for the perseverance of those who have given themselves to the service of the Church? Do I pray for the future of the Church and that many young men and women will answer the call of Christ to lead the Church into the third millenium?

Fifth Sunday of Easter

These words of consolation and encouragement are set in the context of the farewell conversation of Jesus at the last supper.

The apostles were very troubled by all that he had said about being betrayed and going to death. Now Jesus draws up their minds to that higher vision which will enable them to understand how his physical departure will prepare for a more powerful coming to them.

John 14:1-12
I am the way, the truth and the life.

Jesus said to his disciples: "Do not let your hearts be troubled. Trust in God still, and trust in me. There are many rooms in my Father's house, if there were not, I should have told you. I am going now to prepare a place for you, and after I have gone and prepared you a place,I shall return to take you with me; so that where I am you may be too. You know the way to the place where I am going." Thomas said, "Lord, we do not know where you are going, so how can we know the way?" Jesus said: "I am the Way, the Truth and the Life. No one can come to the Father except through me. If you know me, you know my Father too. From this moment you know him and have seen him."

Philip said, "Lord, let us see the Father and then we shall be satisfied." "Have I been with you all this time, Philip," said Jesus to him, "and you still do not know me? To have seen me is to have seen the Father, so how can you say, 'Let us see the Father'? Do you not believe that I am in the Father and the Father is in me? The words I say to you I do not speak as from myself: it is the Father, living in me, who is doing this work. You must believe me when I say that I am in the Father and the Father is in me; believe it on the evidence of this work, if for no other reason. I tell you most solemnly, whoever believes in me will perform the same works as I do myself, he will perform even greater works, because I am going to the Father."

Good News
Jesus Christ is the house where the Father dwells.

It is in Jesus that we meet the Father, for he is the way: in Jesus, we hear his revealing word, for he is the truth: in Jesus, we share in the energy of divine action, for he is the life.

First Reflection
In My Father's House

I have one special wish for my death-bed. I long to have somebody reading these consoling words of the farewell discourse of Jesus.

What seems at first sight to be a departure is now understood in faith as a coming and as a more powerful mode of presence.

In the light of these words, death will not be a departure but a more complete coming of the fulness of life. In the writings of John, eternal life is not postponed until after death: many times he repeats that the believer has eternal life. The resurrection of Jesus Christ means that he is alive here and now in the community of the baptised.

'There are many rooms in my Father's house.'

What is meant by the Father's house?

Jesus Christ is the house of the Father. He is the new temple of divine presence on earth. He is the sacred meeting-place with God. In his own words: 'I am in the Father and the Father is in me.'

Jesus said that there are many rooms in the Father's house. In one sense it suggests that there is no shortage of places for us all. In another sense it expresses room for a great diversity of people, talents and ministries. In today's second reading Christians are exhorted to become 'living stones making a spiritual house.'

The new temple of God's presence on earth is no longer a temple of lifeless stones. Now God lives and works on earth in the living members of the community of the Lord.

The compassion of God comes to people through hearts that are full of tenderness and love. The words of God are heard from mouths that proclaim in his name. The caring acts of God are performed in hands that serve. The eyes of God see through the human eyes of attention and sensitivity.

The presence and action of God on earth is now operative in the community of believers in whom the risen Lord lives. In their diverse talents they are like a house with many rooms.

The wonderful flow of divine energy comes through these living stones which form the sacred house of God's presence.

Yet sometimes we sigh for a more visible or tangible sign of

God's presence. 'Oh, if I could only set my eyes on Jesus for five minutes! If I could only hear the tone of his voice! See the look in his eye! Even touch the hem of his garment!"

But among those who did experience the physical presence of Jesus, there were relatively few who followed him. Some turned their backs on his teaching, some plotted against him and finally crucified him.

Knowing Jesus in the days of his physical presence on earth did not bring faith. The works he performed then were signs that pointed to the greater workings of grace that would follow the days of his new presence in the church. Hence these startling words: 'Whoever believes in me will perform the same works as I do myself, he will perform even greater works, because I am going to the Father.'

The power of God now works through the community of believers. The bread of divine life is shared, sinners are reconciled, souls dead in sin are restored, leprous minds are cleansed of guilt, wounded travellers are bandaged up and healed.

The departure of Jesus brought about a powerful release of the Spirit upon the disciples. We believe that the risen Jesus lives in the Father and the Father lives in him. He is the sacred house of the Father. Through our baptismal union with Jesus, we too dwell in the Father's house. Through the risen Lord Jesus we are adopted into direct relationship with the Father.

In him, we too can pray: 'Our Father'.

Second Reflection
I am the Way, the Truth and the Life

Last Sunday we heard Jesus say, 'I am the gate of the sheepfold.' Today we hear another of the seven great 'I am' claims of Jesus.

'I am the way, the truth and the life.' The words 'I am' echo the divine name as revealed to Moses.

Each of these seven statements should be pondered over and over as each text reveals some aspect of how God, in Jesus Christ, relates to our lives.

I am the way

As life is a constant process of change, as we are ever leaving one day to move on to the next, we find it easy to think of life as a journey. Jesus says that he is the journey, he is the road of life, he is the way.

The gospel does not give us an abstract theory of life: nor a comprehensive code of ethical behaviour. It is the story of God's revelation in the human life of Jesus Christ. We are given a model or example in a way of life that knows solitude and community, joys and pains, loyalty and desertion, serenity and anxiety, good health and the pains of dying. Throughout all the experiences of life, the foundational motive of his life is love. The value which casts light on everything is his love of the Father's will and his outreach of love to every person he meets.

If we wish to know if our decisions are for the right road, all we need to do is ask whether this is the road that Jesus would travel. He is the way.

I am the truth

In Jesus Christ, we believe that the ultimate truth, God's thought, was spoken in the word made flesh. God spoke in a language we can understand, the example of a human life.

We accept that the full concept of God is too vast and mysterious for our limited minds to comprehend. Just as the sunlight is too bright for our eyes to gaze at directly and its unfiltered brightness is a darkness to us.

Yet, within the limits of our minds, we can have a true concept of God. While we cannot take in the entire ocean, yet we can fill our buckets with its true water. We do not claim that our little bucket contains the vastness or mysterious depths or majestic storms of the ocean. But nonetheless the contents are true ocean water. If you wish to fill your bucket with the true knowledge of God, drink deep ly from the gospel of Jesus Christ.

When Francis of Assisi wrote a rule of life for his followers, he summed it up as observing the gospel of Our Lord Jesus Christ.

It was a happy choice of word: for observing expresses the need to pay attention as well as the need to obey. Francis knew that the truth he required would be found in Jesus Christ.

I am the life

If we follow his way we will grow in his likeness. Increasingly the power of Jesus Christ will work through us.

'As I, who am sent by the living Father,
myself draw life from the Father,
so whoever eats me will draw life from me.' (Jn 4:12)

Our world will then mirror the beauty of God's thought in creating.

How do we respond to Jesus Christ as our way, our truth and our life?

We must find the space and time each day to savour the wisdom of the gospel where we meet the truth of God in human flesh and blood. Our plans and directions of life should all be guided by and subject to the way that Jesus travelled.

We must let go of sinful ways in order to invite the life and energy of God to flow into the world through us.

Sixth Sunday of Easter

Our gospel for this Easter day is again taken from the mystical words of Jesus at the last supper. Deep consolation and tremendous encouragement are offered to the apostles. As Ascension Day and Pentecost draw near, the departure of Jesus is transformed from the sadness of departure to the joy of a dynamic presence of God within us. The secret power of this transformation is in the gift of the Holy Spirit.

John 14:15-21
I shall ask the Father and he will give you another Advocate

Jesus said to his disciples: "If you love me you will keep my commandments. I shall ask the Father, and he will give you another Advocate to be with you for ever, that Spirit of truth whom the world can never receive since it neither sees nor knows him; but you know him, because he is with you, he is in you. I will not leave you orphans; I will come back to you. In a short time the world will no longer see me; but you will see me, because I live and you will live. On that day you will understand that I am in my Father and you in me and I in you. Anybody who receives my commandments and keeps them will be one who loves me; and anybody who loves me will be loved by my Father, and I shall love him and show myself to him."

Good News
In the coming of the Holy Spirit, God lives in us and we live in God. The soul's delight is in carrying out the Father's will.

First Reflection
A New Presence

The evangelist John had a liking for pairing things off in opposites. Black or white, life or death, flesh or spirit, light or darkness. But the wonder of Jesus Christ was that in him all conflict was overcome and now the opposites can be held together.

So, when John wrote about Jesus being lifted up from the earth he conveyed both his elevation on the cross to die and his rising to new life. Death no longer contradicts life but leads to a more full life... eternal life. The failure of the mission of Jesus becomes his moment of victory.

The tree of our falling becomes the tree of salvation. And the

104

departure of Jesus from physical presence is changed into his coming in a greater, more dynamic presence.

Jesus speaks of another Advocate, another Helper, who 'will be with you for ever.' The disciples are not left without leader, guide or father: 'I will not leave you orphans.' The most astounding promise of Jesus is about sharing his own relationship with the Father with us.

'On that day you will understand that I am in my Father and you in me and I in you.'

The liturgical readings for Easter continually bring before us the changeover from the old way of thinking to the new: from the old life which is left in the water-tomb to the new life of sharing in the resurrection of Jesus Christ. For the apostles it meant changing from their old contact with Jesus in a physical way to their new contact of faith: the change from outward seeing (as 'the world' sees) to inner believing (in faith). It meant that they had to move from following a man they admired to becoming his living members charged with his spirit and his mission.

The question behind the Easter stories is : 'Where is Jesus to be found?' And the answer: do not look for the outer, physical body of his presence. He is no longer there for your eyes to see, but he is now within the believing community: and in every person who is a member of that community.

The secret of the changeover is the Holy Spirit.

The word 'spirit' means breath. The air that we breathe is unseen but absolutely essential. We would stifle and choke without it. We long for a deep breath of fresh air to renew our vitality.

The breath of God's life is given to us in the Holy Spirit.

We receive a call to be no longer merely human. We are called to let God live in us, know in us, work in us and love through us.

In baptism we acquire a new identity: we are in deep relationship with the three divine persons.

I have been loved into new life by the indwelling Spirit:

I share in the life of Jesus Christ, the beloved Word of the Father:

I am entitled now to pray with Jesus to God as my Father.

In a beautiful phrase of prayer a psalmist sang:

105

'I thank you, Lord, for the wonder of my being.'
Even more wonderful is my being now sharing in divine life.
I thank you, Lord, for the wonder of my new creation:
for the wonder of your presence within me:
for the life and love of God that is shared with me.

Second Reflection
Divine Indwelling

Yuri Gagarian, the first Russian space-traveller, reported that in the great up-there he had seen no evidence of heaven, much less of God. But a priest of the Russian Orthodox Church replied: 'How could anybody see God up there if he had not first met God in here,' pointing to his heart. The eye of faith is in the heart, not in physical sight. The Easter readings greatly emphasise the transition from outer contact (as the world sees) to inner believing.

When Jesus sat at the well with the woman of Samaria, they were talking at first about water and buckets and wells. But Jesus drew the conversation into the thirst of our inner hearts. 'Whoever drinks this water will get thirsty again; but anyone who drinks the water that I shall give will never be thirsty again: the water that I shall give will turn into a spring of water inside him, welling up to eternal life.' *(Jn 3: 13-14)*

One of the key discoveries of prayer-life is in recognising that spring of the Spirit within the heart.

'He is with you, he is in you.'

It is to advance from talking about God out-there to knowing the warm presence of God in-here: to come from a cold, impersonal attitude to God into a personal relationship with Father, Son and Holy Spirit. It means growing from a religion of serving God in the out-houses to living with God in the inner rooms of the soul. Theologians have called it the indwelling of God.

Indwelling means that my soul is at home in God: and God is at home in my soul. 'On that day you will understand that I am in my Father and you in me and I in you.'

Did you know that our word 'enthusiasm' comes from the Greek words for in-God? The word was originally used to express the zeal for God shown by those who felt the powerful presence of God in their hearts.

The surest test that this zeal is genuine will be obedience to the Father's commandments. 'If you love me you will keep my commandments.' When the Spirit is the dynamic source of energy in the soul, then observance of the commandments will not be regarded as a heavy burden. It will be the soul's delight: just as the Father's will was the food that sustained the energy of Jesus.

We have a traditional list of seven gifts which distinguish the ways in which the Holy Spirit is the light and strength of God in the soul.

The Spirit's gift of wisdom elevates the mind's vision to the height and breadth of God's timeless, comprehensive view of all affairs.

Understanding is the gift that enables the mind to grasp and accept the truths of faith. Without this inner light one labours with the mind of the 'world': 'it neither sees nor knows him.'

Knowledge enables the mind to recognise the hand of God in all created things and in the everyday affairs of life. In particular it raises the mind to share in God's view of people and their complexities.

Counsel directs us towards making the proper choices: it enlightens conscience in making moral judgments: and gives discernment in the direction of souls.

God's presence in the soul is a source of great fortitude: in this gift one meets with a courage and serenity beyond human explanation.

Piety is the divine gift which fills the soul with prayerfulness and zeal for the worship due to God.

The seventh gift of the Spirit-within is a proper, reverential fear of God. It is seen in humility of mind before the inscrutable designs of God. And it is heard in language that deeply respects the name and operations of God.

The Spirit of God dwells in the soul and is truly that spring of water which Jesus promised, 'a spring inside, welling up to eternal life.'

'The waters of a river give joy to God's city,
the holy place where the Most High dwells.
God is within, it cannot be shaken.' (Ps 45, Grail Trans.)

The Ascension of the Lord

For forty days, a full period of preparation, we have been growing with the new life of Easter. In the readings of the liturgy our minds have drunk from the fountain of the church's memory of the risen Lord. The day has now arrived to celebrate the full confirmation of two aspects of Easter life: the glorification of Jesus Christ in his return to the Father's side; and the new maturity of the disciples who are sent out to continue his mission of the kingdom.

Matthew 28:16-20
All authority in heaven and on earth has been given to me

The eleven disciples set out for Galilee, to the mountain where Jesus had arranged to meet them. When they saw him they fell down before him, though some hesitated.

Jesus came up and spoke to them. He said, "All authority in heaven and on earth has been given to me. Go, therefore, make disciples of all the nations; baptise them in the name of the Father and of the Son and of the Holy Spirit, and teach them to observe all the commands I gave you. And know that I am with you always; yes, to the end of time."

Good News

Jesus Christ has returned to the glory and authority of heaven. But he remains Emmanuel, God-with-us, who accompanies those who proclaim his message, baptise in his name and teach his way of life.

First Reflection
A Mountain in Galilee

'Great things happen when men and mountains meet.'

I'm not sure who wrote the line but Matthew would like it. Matthew wrote of five mountains: just as his book is composed of five parts in imitation of the five books of the law, the Pentateuch.

The first mountain *(Mt 5:1)* was the elevated scene of the great sermon in which Jesus set out his overview of the kingdom: of what life on earth could be like if the rule of God were taken seriously.

The second mountain was where Jesus went by himself to pray. *(14:23)* Even Jesus needed to withdraw from the pressures of the crowd. The mountain of prayer represents withdrawing to solitude and climbing up above the pressing throng to a place of perspective. Prayer needs the solitude and perspective of the mountain.

The third mountain(15:29) was the scene of many healings. The crowd was astonished and they 'praised the God of Israel.'

The fourth mountain, we are told, was high. (17:1) Up there he took Peter and James and John where they could be alone. The deep religious experiences of Moses on Mount Sinai (Ex 24) and of Elijah on Mount Horeb (1 Kings 19) were relived when the face of Jesus shone like the sun and he was transfigured.

The fifth mountain was in Galilee.The apostles were instructed to go there by the angel who spoke to the women at the empty tomb. Here took place the final meeting of the risen Lord with the disciples. The meeting offered full confirmation of two aspects of the Easter message: the glorification of Jesus Christ; and the continuation of his message through the disciples.

When the disciples saw Jesus they fell down before him. They adored him, as the Magi had adored the Infant King. Yet there was a certain hesitation in their adoration: this expresses the mixture of light and darkness in faith. Throughout Matthew, the mixture of good and bad, of strong and weak in the church, is a recurring theme.

The gap between the God of glory and our limited condition can only be bridged by the initiative and approach of God. That is why Jesus 'came up' to them, just as he had approached the three prostrate apostles on the mount of transfiguration.

He spoke of his glorification in words that recalled a vision of the prophet Daniel: 'All authority in heaven and on earth has been given to me.'

Matthew does not give us Luke's more physical picture of Jesus rising up towards the skies. What Matthew conveys is the universal, cosmic authority of Christ. This is the authority that St Paul expresses in today's second reading: 'He has put all things under his feet, and made him as the ruler of everything, the head of the Church; which is his body, the fulness of him who fills the whole creation.' (Eph 1:22-23)

After this confirmation of the glory and authority of Jesus Christ, the second aspect of Easter life to be confirmed is the continuing presence of the Lord through the mission of the church community.

In the course of his gospel Matthew wrote of how Jesus proclaimed the ideal of the kingdom and worked closely with the selected disciples to make them ministers of the kingdom. The church would be the means of the kingdom throughout the world.

The ministry of Jesus was confined to Jewish territory: but the mission of the church community would be to all nations. That is why the final mountain of meeting is in 'Galilee of the nations'. From there, the disciples are sent out to proclaim his kingdom to all peoples, to baptise in the name of the three Divine Persons, and to teach the way of the commandments.

They would never be alone. He, the risen Lord, would be with them always, to the end of time.

Matthew's first news of Jesus was the annunciation to Joseph of the birth of one who would be Emmanuel, God-with-us.

And his last word is again of God-with-us.

Second Reflection
Head in the Air, Feet on the Ground

There is much to celebrate today: to make us lift our hearts in the air, raise our vision heavenwards and sing for joy.

Jesus Christ is glorified, made the ruler of everything and given all authority in heaven and on earth.

After his humiliating death on the cross he was raised on high and given the name which is above all other names. All beings, on earth and in the underworld should bend the knee at the name of Jesus and every tongue should acclaim Jesus Christ as Lord, to the glory of God the Father. *(cf Phil 2: 9-11)*

The ascension of Jesus Christ is a source of great hope to us. In the words of the preface of the feast:

'Christ is the beginning, the head of the Church;

where he has gone, we hope to follow.'

This Christian hope is expressed by Luke in Acts as Christ coming back to us again: 'Why are you men from Galilee standing here looking into the sky? Jesus who has been taken up from you, this same Jesus will come back in the same way as you have seen him go there.' *(Acts 1:11)*

While we are raised up in hope and hold our heads high in the air, yet we do not spend our days looking at the sky. The eye of the Christian disciple scans humanity's landscape. The feet of the disciple are firmly planted on the ground. Not standing still, but stepping forward on the mission of claiming the world for the authority of the risen Lord.

As we wait for the coming of the Lord to take us to himself in glory, we must not be found in idleness. We are to work in his name to claim the world for justice, peace and joy. For these, according to Paul, are the qualities of the kingdom.

If religion were regarded only as marking time until one is called home to heaven, then it would be a dangerous opium: which is what Karl Marx rightly criticised.

But if love is the essential ingredient of religion, then it is no opium for idleness but a power-packed programme for action. And the source of this power is the divine energy of Emmanuel, God-with-us.

'As long as we love one another God will live in us and his love will be complete in us.' (1 Jn 4:12) The mission of Christ needs to be completed in the mission of Christians.

God's love is seen on earth in the countless Christian works of service... nursing, caring, providing, educating, peace-making and reconciling. A million hearts burn with his love, a million hands perform his works and a million feet travel with his message to the ends of the earth.

But there are people and places that can only be reached when one more apostle is added to the million.

And that new apostle of Christ is you.

Brother/Sister in Christ, this Ascension Day hold your head high in the hope of heaven, but set your feet firmly on the road wherever the call of Christ directs you.

And remember, he will be with you.

Seventh Sunday of Easter

We are in the great novena of the church, the nine days of waiting and praying between Ascension and Pentecost. These were the days when the disciples were gathered in the upper room in continuous prayer. The gospel draws us up into the upper room of Christ's mind. We are privileged to listen in on the intimate conversation of Jesus with the Father. He prays for the glory of the Father. And then he prays for the disciples who continue to represent him in the world.

John 17:1-1
Father, glorify your Son

Jesus raised his eyes to heaven and said: "Father, the hour has come: glorify your Son so that your Son may glorify you; and, through the power over all mankind that you have given him, let him give eternal life to all those you have entrusted to him. And eternal life is this: to know you, the only true God, and Jesus Christ whom you have sent. I have glorified you on earth and finished the work that you gave me to do. Now, Father, it is time for you to glorify me with that glory I had with you before ever the world was. I have made your name known to the men you took from the world to give me. They were yours and you gave them to me, and they have kept your word. Now at last they know that all you have given me comes indeed from you; for I have given them the teaching you gave me, and they have truly accepted this, that I came from you, and have believed that it was you who sent me.

I pray for them; I am not praying for the whole world but for those you have given me, because they belong to you: all I have is yours and all you have is mine, and in them I am glorified. I am not in the world any longer, but they are in the world, and I am coming to you."

Good News

The Father and the Son are one in an intimate communion of knowledge and love. Christian disciples are given the beginnings of this knowledge and are called to share in this love.

First Reflection
Prayer in the Upper Room

Today could be called the Sunday of the upper room. We can consider the upper room as that part of the inner self where we go to when we need to raise our eyes to heaven, as Jesus did when he began to pray. The classical definition of prayer as the raising of the mind and heart of God is symbolised in going to the upper room.

The evangelist John, under divine inspiration, did what was humanly impossible. Have you ever observed anybody rapt in deep prayer? How could you ever attempt to capture in words what is taking place in that deep, intimate giving of God's knowledge to a heart that returns in beats of love? And if the intimate prayer of ordinary mortals is difficult to describe, how much more is it humanly impossible to capture in words the prayer of Jesus?

In divine inspiration the Holy Spirit became the light of the writer's mind, the energy in his hand, the ink on his pen. John, so divinely inspired, enables us to enter into the mind of Jesus at the moment when his life reaches its destined climax. In the upper room, after sharing the meal of the new covenant with the disciples, Jesus raised his eyes to heaven: 'Father, the hour has come.'

Viewed from the human perspective it is the hour when all is falling apart and the entire movement is crashing about him. Judas has walked out from the meal. Night had fallen. The drama leading to his death had just begun. But in prayer, raising his eyes to heaven, Jesus returns to the centre where all is one. There is a serene unity between Father and Son at a level far beneath the storms of life. Unity of purpose, unity of will. Nothing, not even betrayal and death, can break this inner core of unity. It is precisely when all the externals are stripped away and shattered in death that the inner core of divine obedience is most clearly shown to the world. In this unity of wills can be seen the glory of the Father.

Jesus prays that his disciples too will share in this inner centre of divine knowledge and love. The fulness of life is 'to know you (Father), the only true God, and Jesus Christ whom you have sent.' We, the disciples of Christ, remain 'in the world.' And whenever we experience failure, or everything seems to be crashing about us, then it is time to raise our minds to the upper room and return to the centre. It is significant that in these days of pressures, changes and tearing apart, the Holy Spirit has directed many people to what is called centring prayer: that is, the practice of holding the mind on one simple, uncomplicated word or thought of God at the inner centre of our being.

Too easily we let our minds be submerged by the bad news: we neglect the inner heart of stillness. We fret our days in anxiety because life seems to be out of our control. Patterns of social behaviour, fashions of dress and popular tastes change for no logical reason. Nothing is sacred and everything is questioned. Familiar practices are debunked with no better replacements. Technology has outstripped our ability to control it. The mass media of communication are preoccupied with sensational stories and depressing news. If you want to spend your life alternating between anxiety and depression then join the club of those who are compelled to catch the radio news at each hour and view the news each night on at least two TV channels. You will know every gruesome statistic of the latest catastrophe from Chile to China, you will be in touch with industrial unrest, the violence of the gunmen, economic failures and factory closures. You will succumb to the attitude that all is falling apart. And you will spend your life in the lower room, in the dark cellar where all is hopeless.

Like Jesus at the hour of climax we must go to the upper room and raise our minds to heaven. We return to the centre where God in-dwells. There one receives the gift of knowing God, the only true God, through Jesus Christ sent to reveal him.

The message of this Sunday in the upper room comes in three stages: Return to centre. Wait in continuous prayer. The Spirit is not as far away as the world would lead you to think.

Second Reflection
The Lord's Prayer

The prayer of Jesus in the last supper room is known as his priestly prayer, or his consecration prayer, or as the preface to his sacrifice. Its great solemn tones and contemplative theme would certainly suggest some liturgical title.

But this prayer can also be regarded as a more solemn and soaring version of the Our Father.

It was expected of a religious leader to teach his disciples a distinctive prayer which would summarize his teaching for them. Hence the request of one of the disciples to Jesus: 'Lord, teach us to pray, just as John taught his disciples.'

The Our Father expresses in spare and simple words the essence of Jesus' teaching about God and the central thrust of his mission. His relationship with God is expressed in the name Father: who is as distant as heaven but as near as Father to child: whose name is to be revered but whose providence is to be trusted.

The central work of Jesus was to set up on earth the kingdom of the Father. The kingdom means a society where God's will is the rule of life. It means that there is bread each day for all: no more injustice, discrimination or selfishness but the fair sharing of the resources of mother earth.

In the kingdom there is full forgiveness and perfect reconciliation: no more tearing apart within us or fighting between us.

Kingdom people persevere faithfully as temptation is resisted and evil is totally conquered.The prayer of Jesus in the upper room repeats the great themes of the Our Father, though in John's swirling cycles of thought rather than the simple and clear lines of Luke or Matthew. The name which dominates this prayer again is Father. The infinite otherness of God is expressed in the recurring theme of glorification.

Just as the Our Father then becomes a prayer for the kingdom on earth, so too the upper room prayer intercedes for the disciples in the world. Jesus has glorified the Father on earth by doing his will and making his name known. Now that his earthly hour is completed, he hands on his mission to the disciples. 'I am not in the world any longer but they are in the world.'

The instrument of the kingdom is now the earthly church-in-the-world. The glory of Jesus himself is now reflected in the works of the church...'in them I am glorified.'

In many forms of charitable sevice the church brings bread to the hungry, sets up clinics and hospitals for the sick, runs day-centres and night-shelters.

The church experiences God's forgiveness so deeply that there is a special sacrament of reconciliation to celebrate it. Desiring to share the joy of reconciliation, the church preaches peace and encourages an understanding that is greater than hurt, a blessedness that overcomes cursing. And through various ascetical practices the church helps people to counteract temptation and to be delivered from the clutches of the evil one.

The prayer of Jesus in the upper room is John's great spiral of contemplative thought expanding upon the simple words of the Our Father.

Pentecost Sunday

In John's gospel the sending of the Holy Spirit is part of the first day of the new creation. It is the beginning of the new age when the mission of Christ is given to the church. The disciples are sent out in the power of the Holy Spirit. It is the birthday of the church.

John 20:19-23
As the Father sent me, so I send you. Receive the Holy Spirit

In the evening of the first day of the week, the doors were closed in the room where the disciples were, for fear of the Jews. Jesus came and stood among them. He said to them, "Peace be with you," and showed them his hands and his side. The disciples were filled with joy when they saw the Lord, and he said to them again, "Peace be with you. As the Father sent me, so am I sending you."

After saying this he breathed on them and said: "Receive the Holy Spirit. For those whose sins you forgive, they are forgiven; for those whose sins you retain, they are retained."

Good News

The first divine mission was that of Jesus Christ, sent by the Father. Now the disciples are given the power of the Holy Spirit and are sent out to continue the mission of Jesus.

First Reflection
First Day or Fiftieth

John celebrates the coming of the Holy Spirit on the first day of the new age. Luke, however, sets the story of the Holy Spirit on the fiftieth day, that is Pentecost.

John writes of the Holy Spirit in the context of Easter, the first day of the week, the beginning of the new age when the human race is raised to new life. The Spirit is bestowed upon the disciples and they are co-opted into the mission of Jesus Christ. It is the day of their commissioning and the birthday of the church. In the power of the Holy Spirit they are sent out as harvesters into the fields of the world.

Luke however writes out of a different perspective to John. He sets the coming of the Spirit in the context of the Jewish feast of the fiftieth day, Pentecost. Pentecost was a Jewish harvest festival which followed on fifty days after the feast of Unleavened Bread. In the fields the harvest was now completed and Pentecost celebrated the solemn offering of the harvest fruits to God. In the symbolic use of numbers, the fiftieth day marks the beginning of a new age after the completion of seven weeks, a fulness of time.

The ending of one period is always the beginning of another. When the grain is harvested, the work of the reaper is completed but the task of the miller has just begun. As Jesus completed his mission, the task of the church was just beginning. He set the wheels in motion. He breathed on the disciples and said: 'Receive the Holy Spirit.'

On that day the words of the psalmist attained a new meaning: 'You send forth your spirit; they are created;

and you renew the face of the earth.' *(Ps 103, Grail trans.)*

How does this new breathing of the Spirit change and renew? What are the fruits of this new life? Paul tells us that it is not the spirit of slavery and fear. 'The spirit you received is not the spirit of slaves bringing fear into your lives again'; it is the spirit of children who recognise God as the loving Father. *(cf. Rom 8: 14-15)* Nor is it the spirit of timidity and weakness but 'the spirit of power and love, and self-control.' *(2 Tim 1:7)*

When the fiery tongue of the Spirit ignites a soul, the interior fire will be manifested in many ways. Religion will be no half-hearted affair dominated by servile fear but a full, joyful celebration of God who is good and loving. The Spirit of power and divine energy moves even gentle, little people to astonishing initiatives and even more astonishing courage in perseverance.

The presence of the Spirit is always marked with joy, even in the midst of suffering. There is none of the sadness of sin nor lives of 'quiet desperation.' God is praised, goodness is observed and life is celebrated.

In the power of the Spirit there is a clear conviction that goodness is greater than evil. The hurts and malice of life are overcome by the greater power of patience, forgiveness and kindness. The decrepit sadness of sin is cast off. A great breath of divine freshness sweeps through the land. God renews the face of the earth.

John is correct in celebrating the coming of the Spirit as the first day of the new age of renewed humanity. But equally, Luke is correct in celebrating the presence and power of the Spirit on the fiftieth day, the day of blessing God for the harvest fruits.

In the eyes of God a thousand years are as a single day, so it is a futile search trying to pinpoint a precise moment or day for the Spirit's coming. John and Luke both give us valuable insights. Every time the Spirit moves a person it is part of the new age, the first day. But it is also the fiftieth day, for the Spirit's gift is part of the harvest gleaned by Christ.

The day of the Spirit cannot be tied down: for the work of the Spirit is as free as the wind.

'The wind blows wherever it pleases;

you hear its sound,

but you cannot tell where it comes from or where it is going.

That is how it is with all who are born of the Spirit.' *(Jn 3:8)*

Second Reflection
The Spirit of Forgiveness

John and Luke both write that the coming of the Holy Spirit inaugurates a mission unto the forgiveness of sins.

According to John, in the power of the Holy Spirit, 'those whose sins you forgive, they are forgiven.' While Luke records the promise of the risen Lord that, in his name, they would preach repentance for the forgiveness of sins to all nations, when they received power from on high. *(cf Lk 24: 46-49)* This power from on high, or divine energy, can be seen in 'a variety of gifts and all sorts of service, working in all sorts of different ways in different people.' *(1 Cor 12: 4-5)*

The Spirit which hovered over the formless void in the act of creation is even more beautifully manifested when a broken life is re-created: when beauty can grow out of an ugly situation: when life can flourish out of death. The true church, the authentic community of disciples, is found where memory is full of love and compassion, and empty of bitterness and hatred.

People often confess that they cannot forget what has been deeply registered on the brain. Trying to forget can be dangerous: it can lead to the repression of anger: and repressed anger will be a trouble-maker. But remembering with bitterness is not helpful either. One is saddened by the war memorials which are erected and the annual parades which are mounted 'lest we forget.' That sort of remembering is too often used to fan the embers of bitter memory and sustain old rivalries.

The Spirit's way is to remember with a love that refuses to be poisoned by the other's hatred: with a compassion that will not be blinded by the other's malice: with a prayer that will not be blocked by the other's cursing.

The supreme model is Jesus Christ who 'was insulted and did not retaliate with insults: when he was tortured he made no threats but he put his trust in the righteous judge.' (1 Pet 2:3)

On the cross he prayed for the forgiveness of his executors.

How can a woman forget the husband who has deserted her? How can a child forgive the reckless driver who killed a parent? How can a grieving family forgive the one who planted the bomb that removed the loved one from their lives?

Whenever you see a noble forgiveness which is greater than the atrocity perpetrated, then you have seen the Spirit. The Spirit of forgiveness in a true disciple reaches out a healing invitation to the sinner.

If the sinner is melted by the love that is offered he will find forgiveness and, in the power of the Spirit, his life will be re-created.

But if he refuses the offer of the Spirit's healing, then he is 'retained' in his sinfulness.

I am sending you out...
not in your own power,
nor on your feet heavy with fear and anxiety,
but in the power of the Spirit
and on the wings of the divine breath...
so that you might love, understand and have compassion,
in my name,
and bring about repentance for sin,
offering my salvation to the ends of the earth.

Trinity Sunday

After celebrating the great saving events of Easter-Pentecost, before we resume the cycle of the Sundays of the year, we are today invited to reflect on the inner life of God and how we are adopted into that life. The feast of the Blessed Trinity draws attention to the movements of God's love towards us and in us. It is important not to reduce the feast to a discourse in Greek philosophical language about person and nature. The mystery of God is to be savoured and enjoyed rather than probed for an explanation.

John 3:16-18
God sent his Son to save the world through him
Jesus said to Nicodemus:

God loved the world so much that he gave his only Son, so that everyone who believes in him may not be lost but may have eternal life. For God sent his Son into the world not to condemn the world, but so that through him the world might be saved. No one who believes in him will be condemned; but whoever refuses to believe is condemned already, because he has refused to believe in the name of God's only Son.

Good News
God the Father loved his world so much that he gave his Son to save us and prepare us for the Holy Spirit who breathes God's own life into us.

First Reflection
John Three-Sixteen
The words of Jesus to Nicodemus are a summary of the entire gospel of John. Indeed, the opening verse stands on its own as a summary of the entire message of evangelisation. Certain evangelical groups value this verse so much that one often sees at sporting events or public parades the banner proclaiming John 3:16. Through the eyes of TV cameras, the world is invited to look up that text and read the message of good news:

'God loved the world so much
that he gave his only Son,
so that everyone who believes in him may not be lost
but may have eternal life.'

The good news (evangelisation) is a story in three acts: the story of the three divine persons in our lives.

First is the story of God the Creator: not as a clinical, scientific cause or mechanical trigger: but a Father who lovingly wishes to share life. Why did God create? Great minds have offered us their answers to that question.

Love did not permit God to remain alone, suggested Thomas Aquinas. God wished to have co-lovers, according to the Franciscan Dun Scotus. In the Genesis story of creation, when God looked at his handiwork each day, he saw that it was good. And after making man, male and female in his own image, God saw that it was very good. Each of us was first a beautiful thought in the mind of God: just as a building is first a thought in the mind of the architect before it is erected in steel and stone. But when we open our eyes and look about us we see that all is not quite so beautiful. There is much moral ugliness in society and in each one of us. The theological name for this ugliness is sin. Clearly there is a spanner in the workings. The gift of freedom, which is an essential part of love, has been misused. The noble image of God in man has been tarnished. We have wandered away from God down the ways of falsehood and compromise.

Did God desert us because we had strayed away on the path of sin? The second act of the drama of salvation is the story that God loved the world so much that he sent his only Son to be our Saviour. Born in the flesh of Mary, he was called Jesus, meaning God-saves.

It was the Father's love that sent the Son to us, desiring to call back his straying creatures and to heal their brokenness. The mission of Jesus was not to pronounce damnation but to announce salvation. He did not come to trample the fallen into the ground but to lift up all who would take his hand. He came to take away the sins of the world... so that through him the world might be saved.

When we hear the story of Jesus the Saviour, the question comes to our lips: 'What must we do to gain that salvation?' The short answer given to Nicodemus is: 'believe in the name of God's only Son.'

This is the third act in the drama of evangelisation. To believe is to give oneself in heart and mind to Jesus Christ as the only Saviour of the world. But to take this step one requires the grace of the Holy Spirit. No one can say that Jesus is Lord unless moved by the Spirit.

Through the waters of baptism one is born again by the gift of the Holy Spirit. The seed of divine life is planted, destined to grow into the fulness of eternal life. To believe is to accept Jesus Christ as one's way, truth and life.

But if anyone goes the way of sin, settles for the deceptions of darkness and falls for the blandishments of false god, that person refuses to believe and will be automatically condemned.

The subject of the good news is not some remote, mysterious power up-there or out-there. God is called Father, for he is the one whose love planned me, created me and upholds me. God the Son is my Saviour whose love did not desert me in my sinfulness but who came to free me, heal me and lead me. God the Holy Spirit is my Sanctifier who raised me up to share in divine life, breathing in me, living in me and loving in me.

Three relationships of God with me: yet one God.

Three candles glowing in the room of my life: yet one light.

Second Reflection
Movements To and Fro

God so loved the world that he gave his only Son so as to draw us back into sharing in the divine life.

There are two movements of God in our regard: sending out and drawing back. God's life is a dance of love: to and fro: forward and back again: out and in.

The first movement is the Father's expression of himself in one perfect Word, the Son. In the fulness of time the Father sent the Son to us in human flesh. The Son lived among us until the time of his return to the Father. This is also called his glorification. The return of the Son is through the drawing power of the Holy Spirit who is Divine Love. The Son has so united himself with those who believe in him that they too are drawn back to the Father in the power of the Spirit. Already they share in divine life: God dwells in them and they live in God. Through baptism we are caught up in the double movement of God sending to us and drawing us back.

We can use the in-and-out rhythm of breathing as corresponding to God's double movement of to and fro.

As I draw in my breath I am receiving the gift of God, creator of all life.

I hold that breath for a while and make it my own. It becomes part of me. It represents the gift of life which is mine too for a while. I make it my own life in freedom. But life, like breath, is only on loan from God.

I return my breath to the surrounding all-present. And at death I return the gift of life to God.

My intake of breath is a response to the outward movement of God, who utters his Word and gives his Son.

My return of breath represents yielding to the loving magnetism of the Spirit who draws all back to the Father.

As I breathe in I receive the Son who is sent to us.

As I breathe out I return with the Spirit.

My breathing becomes a trinitarian prayer as my intake of breath forms the name, Jesus.

And my return of breath whispers Spirit.

The Body and Blood of Christ

In recent weeks the liturgical readings have brought before our minds the great doctrines about God dwelling in us and how we are raised up to sharing in the very inner life and relationships of the Blessed Trinity. On this feast of the Body and Blood of Christ we celebrate the Eucharist as the sustaining food of divine life within us.

John 6:51-59
My flesh is real food and my blood is real drink

Jesus said to the Jews: "I am the living bread which has come down from heaven. Anyone who eats this bread will live for ever; and the bread that I shall give is my flesh, for the life of the world." Then the Jews started arguing with one another: "How can this man give us his flesh to eat?" they said. Jesus replied: "I tell you most solemnly, if you do not eat the flesh of the Son of Man and drink his blood, you will not have life in you. Anyone who does eat my flesh and drink my blood has eternal life, and I shall raise him up on the last day. For my flesh is real food and my blood is real drink. "He who eats my flesh and drinks my blood lives in me and I live in him. As I, who am sent by the living Father, myself draw life from the Father, so whoever eats me will draw life from me. This is the bread come down from heaven; not like the bread our ancestors ate: they are dead, but anyone who eats this bread will live for ever."

Good News
In the eucharistic meal we are fed on the body and blood of Jesus Christ. We live in him and he lives in us. We draw the energy of divine life from him: energy to be his representatives today and energy to grow into unending life in the great tomorrow.

First Reflection
The Bread of Life

You could say, I suppose, that Adam and Eve ate their way out of paradise. Jesus, who was reversing the fall of Adam, thought up a way of eating our way back into the fulness of life. Ever since Adam's Day people have hungered in body and in spirit. Bread for the support of bodily life is earned in sweat and toil. 'With sweat on your brow shall you eat your bread until you

124

return to the soil as you were taken from it.' *(Gen 3:19)* But even this hard-earned bread was not sufficient to meet the hunger of the spirit.

People have not always been able to identify what they hunger for. Moses explained to the people how God schooled them through forty years of desert experience: 'He humbled you, he made you feel hunger, he fed you with manna which neither you nor your fathers had known, to make you understand that man does not live on bread alone but that man lives on everything that comes from the mouth of God.' *(First Reading, Deut 8:3)*

The deprivations of the desert were used by God to sensitise the people to the hunger of the spirit for divine refreshment. The manna was not the complete answer. The human spirit still hungered for the paradise that had been lost.

Jesus provided the answer that the world had been waiting on: 'I am the living bread which has come down from heaven. Anyone who eats this bread will live for ever.'

The sentence of death which followed Adam would be lifted when Jesus gave his life for the world. The gates of paradise were opened again and humanity's invitation to the fulness of life was restored. The saving merits of Jesus Christ are made available to us in the Eucharist. Words about life are repeated and renewed in the spiralling song of John:

'Anyone who does eat my flesh and drink my blood has eternal life, and I shall raise him up on the last day... He who eats my flesh and drinks my blood lives in me and I live in him... Whoever eats me will draw life from me... Anyone who eats this bread will live for ever.'

When we sit to table and eat our dinner, that food is digested and changed into our energy. But it is the reverse with the food of the eucharist: we are changed into it. We grow in the likeness of Christ and increasingly take on his way, his truth and his life. Our lives are more truly patterned on his way: our minds are more enlightened with his truth: and our lives are empowered with divine energy.

This sacred energy must not be locked away in individualistic piety nor lost through indifference. For God's energy is a love that should send us out with Christ's heart, eyes, feet and hands. The privilege of receiving the Lord brings the responsiblity of representing him. Mother Teresa of Calcutta expresses the need to respond in life to what we receive: 'The Holy Hour before the Eucharist should lead us to the Holy Hour with the poor. Our Eucharist lacks something if it does not lead us to love and serve the poor.'

Jesus is the living bread come down from heaven...
to be eaten by us...
that we might live by his life...
to the glory of the Father.

Second Reflection
Prayer before the Tabernacle
God is present everywhere. Even the vast expanse of sky on a starry night cannot contain God. Yet God has answered the smallness of our minds and set up special meeting-places where we encounter his presence in a personal way.

The supreme encounter with God was in Jesus Christ. On the night before he died, Jesus, in a moment of divine inventiveness, set up a new meeting-place with God: Bread.

Since hunger is an experience of every time and every place, he chose bread to express his continuing presence to us:

I am the living bread which has come down from heaven...
and the bread that I shall give
is my flesh for the life of the world.

The liturgical feast of the Body and Blood of Christ began in the thirteenth century. People at that time received Holy Communion very rarely. For instance, St Francis of Assisi, who was a deacon but not an ordained priest, received Holy Communion often, according to his early biographers. 'He burned with love for the Sacrament of our Lord's Body with all his heart, and was lost in wonder at the thought of such condescending love, such loving condescension. He received Holy Communion often and so devoutly that he roused others to devotion too.' *(Bonaventure, Major Life 1X, 2)*

We get a clue as to what is meant by often from the parallel life of St Clare. In the Rule of St Clare the sisters are exhorted to receive Communion seven times a year, on certain specified feasts. Francis and Clare, who were very devoted to the Eucharist, received no more frequently than once every two months or so.

What about those who were less devoted?

Instead of receiving Holy Communion the practice grew up of looking at the sacred host. After the consecration at Mass the priest held up the host for 'the gaze that saves us.' The popularity of exposing the Blessed Sacrament in a suitable showing-vessel or monstrance grew. Eventually came the custom of a public procession as a form of homage to Christ present in the Eucharist.

Frequent reception of the Eucharist has been restored. But there is the danger now that familiarity has dulled our sense of wonder at God's graciousness. While the liturgical prayer asks us to say we are unworthy, yet our casual approach scarcely expresses a sense of profound humility.

The practice of prayer before the Blessed Sacrament reserved in monstrance or tabernacle is to be highly recommended.

Prayer can happen anywhere, for God, who is present everywhere, can be encountered anywhere. Yet for an ongoing prayer-life we need specially recognised meeting-places with God. The Sacred Bread is such a meeting-place.

The subdued atmosphere of a quiet chapel, the soft flicker of light and scent of flowers all help to create a setting that helps us to control our racing minds. Our attention can more easily focus on Jesus who has become the living bread of heaven for us. God, who is everywhere, is more accessible to our limitations here.

One thinks of the witness of Bishop James Walsh, a Maryknoll missionary, who spent more than twenty years in a communist prison in China. His prayer-life was sustained by a daily hour before the Blessed Sacrament. In a communist prison !

The nearest church he knew of was in Japan, so each day he faced Japan for an hour of eucharistic prayer. What difference did a thousand miles make? In the eyes of faith a thousand miles is no greater than a thousand millimetres.

The Sacred Bread is before me. There is enough seen to focus my attention, my thoughts, my emotional response. But what is seen is only the invitation to pass on to what is hidden and inexpressible. Faith alone can make the step beyond the senses.

Staying here becomes the test of faith: and the school of faith. For the Eucharist is the mystery of faith.

Second Sunday in Ordinary Time

We are still at the stage of preparation for the public ministry of Jesus. John the Baptist, whose task was to prepare the way, points to Jesus as the one who was to come, the one on whom the Spirit of God rests.

John 1:29-34
This is the Lamb of God who takes away the sins of the world

Seeing Jesus coming toward him, John said, "Look, there is the lamb of God that takes away the sins of the world. This is the one I spoke of when I said: A man is coming after me who ranks before me because he existed before me. I did not know him myself, and yet it was to reveal him to Israel that I came baptising with water." John also declared, "I saw the Spirit coming down on him from heaven like a dove and resting on him. I did not know him myself, but he who sent me to baptise with water had said to me, 'The man on whom you see the Spirit come down and rest is the one who is going to baptise with the Holy Spirit.' Yes, I have seen and I am the witness that he is the Chosen One of God."

Good News
The Spirit of God rests on Jesus who is about to commence his mission to take away the sins of the world.

First Reflection
The Lamb of God

Every time the Eucharist is celebrated the words of John the Baptist about Jesus are recalled: 'Look, there is the lamb of God that takes away the sins of the world.'

The biblical writers had no hesitation about mixing their metaphors. Jesus is sometimes the shepherd of the flock and sometimes the lamb!

The image of Jesus as lamb grew out of a rich and complex vein of Jewish thought. The blood of the lamb, sprinkled on doorposts, was the sign to save the Hebrew people from the destroying angel: that was when Moses led them out of their Egyptian slavery. The annual remembrance of that liberation became the Passover Feast, the climax of the Jewish year. Lambs in the great numbers were slaughtered and family groups ate the meat of yearling lamb in the sacred meal which bound them together in very

128

close fellowship with one another and with God. They ate it standing, dressed for a journey.

In the chronology of John's gospel, the death of Jesus took place at the very time when the passover lambs were being slaughtered. And the ritual instruction regarding the sacrificial lambs applied also to Jesus: 'Not one bone of his shall be broken.' *(Jn 19:36)*

The Christian community favoured the symbol of the lamb from the very earliest times. Little more than twenty years after the death of Jesus, a passing reference in a letter of Paul suggests that his readers were already familiar with the symbol: 'Christ, our passover, has been sacrificed.' *(1 Cor 5:7)*

Another important idea behind the symbol of the lamb was the practice of sacrificing animals as a substitute for what people owed to God. Through the sacrifice of an animal thanks were returned to God for the birth of the first-born. And it was through sacrifice that expiation was paid on behalf of a sinner. That idea of payment through subtitution comes through the words of 1 Peter 1: 18-19: 'Remember, the ransom that was paid to free you... was not paid in anything corruptible, neither in silver or gold, but in the precious blood of a lamb without spot or stain, namely Christ.'

The choice of Isaiah 49 for the first reading today invites us to interpret the gospel passage in the light of Isaiah's picture of Chosen Servant of God. Indeed, the scholars tell us that the word translated as lamb of God might equally have been translated as servant of God. In the light of Isaiah's Song of the Servant, Jesus is understood as a gentle, innocent lamb who is led to death on behalf of others. 'Ours were the sufferings he bore, ours the sorrows he carried.' *(Is 53:4)*

As the sacred host is raised before our eyes at Mass, the words of John the Baptist are heard again to express our faith: 'Look, this is the lamb of God who takes away the sins of the world.'

Truly blessed and happy are those who are called to this banquet. In the Eucharist Jesus is the passover lamb whose flesh is eaten by those who are ready for the journey out of slavery:

Jesus is the lamb who substituted for us and in whose blood our baptismal robes are washed clean again:

Jesus is the innocent, gentle lamb, on whom the Spirit of power and dove of peace comes to rest.

Second Reflection
He Carried Our Sorrow

The heaviest burden that the world knows is guilt. What a blessed day it was when John the Baptist could point towards Jesus as the one who would take away the sins of the world. He is God who became our brother so as to carry our burden. 'Surely he has borne our grief and carried our sorrow.' *(Is 53:4)*

What we call redemption is the third act in the great story of the world. The first act is about God... one and true, good and totally desirable. The second act is the story of sin which is the antithesis of God... with divisions and deceptions, bad will and hatred.

The third act of the drama is the connection between the God of goodness and the world of sin. God so loved the world that he did not forsake the unhappy sinner but sent his only Son to lead back the stray and to carry the wounded on his shoulder. It was a dramatic moment then when the Baptist pointed towards Jesus as the one who would carry off the guilt of the world.

On the road of life we can be laden with many heavy burdens, such as illness or handicap, loneliness or desertion, poverty or injustice. But the burden that is heaviest to bear and most difficult to off-load is guilt, because it is carried within the person.

Spiritual writers of a bygone age depicted the sinner as downcast in demeanour and dark in countenance. The weight of guilt drags one down to a pit of self-hatred, blaming and constant self-criticism. There are people who are so imprisoned in their past failures that they have totally lost the light of idealism. And people who are so worn out and jaded by fault-finding and anxious fretting that it is years since they could relax or let go in a hearty laugh.

Guilt is a very serious blockage to religious growth. People will shy away from any close contact with God when they are burdened with a deep sense of being too unworthy to face him. Let me sort myself out first and then I can face God. But the truth is that God wants me to come even as a sinner. And without him I cannot sort myself out.

When guilt eats away at one's inner contentment, it is usually projected outwards in poisoned energy. Sometimes the self-hatred comes out in a cloak of self-pity which generates impure compulsions or the excuse for over-indulgence in drink: all of which only increases the inner guilt.

Negativity comes out in those who are incapable of offering an affirmative word to another, but are animated and alive when the conversation turns to the faults of some third party. The reason is that all they have ever heard within themselves are voices of guilt and blame. And then there are those who are totally threatened by goodness. How else can one explain the insane hatred which crucified Jesus Christ. His truth and goodness were a threat to the unadmitted guilt of others. If they crucified Jesus Christ, they will also crucify his church as long as its goodness is a light to hurt sore eyes. Watch the zeal of some people to pick up some criticism of any new movement in the church. And when you hear an unbalanced, vitriolic attack on the church, the chances are that you are hearing the voice of repressed self-hatred.

Who can rescue us from what St Paul called 'this body doomed to death?' With a deep sigh of relief he could answer: 'Thanks be to God through Jesus Christ our Lord.' *(Rom 7:24)*

A psychiatrist can help one sift through the rubble of memories for the root cause of guilt. A counsellor can help one come to terms with the situation. But the only power that can remove sin is God's love which is greater than sin.

John the Baptist had wrestled with the burdens of people.

Preaching the coming of judgment, he could frighten people into making a positive effort. He gave them a programme of penance which acted as a therapy to cleanse the system of guilt. But there was, as yet, no joy in his tone of voice until he saw the Spirit of God come down upon Jesus of Nazareth and rest on him.

John brought water of cleansing. But Jesus brought the Holy Spirit of God and new life. Truly it was a blessed day when John pointed towards Jesus as the new lamb of sacrifice... no ordinary lamb, but the lamb of God... whose divine love would be greater than sin and hatred.

If we lay claim to what Jesus offers us the burden will be lifted. There will be lightness in our steps, joy on our faces and purpose in our bearing. For, in Jesus, we see how God became our brother to bear our griefs and to carry our sorrows.

Third Sunday

*The voice of John the Baptist is now silenced behind prison walls.
It is time for Jesus to begin. In four swift strokes of the pen Matthew
describes the beginning of Jesus' mission:*
- He sets it in a geographical location rich in memory of the prophets.
- Jesus begins to preach: Repent for the kingdom of heaven is at hand.
- He calls the first followers.
- The first mission of Jesus brings good news and deeds of healing.

Matthew 4:12-23
He went to Capernaum, that the prophecy of Isaiah be fulfilled

Hearing that John had been arrested Jesus went back to Galilee, and leaving Nazareth he went and settled in Capernaum, a lakeside town on the borders of Zebulun and Naphtali. In this way the prophecy of Isaiah was to be fulfilled:

Land of Zebulun! Land of Naphtali! Way of the sea on the far side of Jordan, Galilee of the nations! The people that lived in darkness has seen a great light; on those who dwell in the land and shadow of death a light has dawned.

From that moment Jesus began his preaching with the message, "Repent, for the Kingdom of heaven is close at hand."

As he was walking by the Sea of Galilee he saw two brothers, Simon, who was called Peter, and his brother Andrew; they were making a cast in the lake with their net, for they were fishermen. And he said to them, 'Follow me and I will make you fishers of men.' And they left their nets at once and followed him.

Going on from there he saw another pair of brothers, James son of Zebedee and his brother John; they were in their boat with their father Zebedee, mending their nets, and he called them. At once, leaving the boat and their father, they followed him.

He went round the whole of Galilee teaching in their synagogues, proclaiming the Good News of the kingdom and curing all kinds of diseases and sickness among the people.

Good News
The kingdom of heaven is among us. The power of God is released upon the world. For a world in darkness there is light: for people haunted by death there is life: for those laid low by sickness there is uplifting and hope.

First Reflection
The Kingdom ... Another Way

Jesus had a dream for our world: he called it the kingdom of heaven. He dreamt of life on earth being a mirror of heaven. Towards the realisation of this dream he began to tell people that there is another way.

Instead of the nightmare of war, he spoke of brothers and sisters in the one family of God.

Instead of bitterness and retaliation, he spoke of love that refuses to be poisoned and makes one pray for the oppressor. In place of the spectre of famine which will always haunt a greedy, grasping world, he set up the practical criterion of how we feed the hungry and clothe the naked.

In place of the murky world of deeds of darkness, Jesus wanted all of life to be a clear reflection of the light of heaven. He prayed that the will of the Father be done on earth as it is in heaven. Where God's will holds sway, there is where God is king. And that is the kingdom of heaven on earth.

In Matthew's understanding (and he is our evangelist for the rest of this year), the work of Jesus was to set up the kingdom of heaven upon earth. Matthew describes it as a work progressing in five stages.

First he announced that the kingdom was close at hand. Then he travelled with the words of good news and deeds of mercy. He lit a beacon on the height of a mountain where he preached the charter of life in the kingdom. In the second stage he worked closely with selected disciples, the nucleus of the church, who would give legs to the message for the spread of the kingdom. In the next stage he spoke mainly in parables to prepare them for the pains and struggles of slow growth, disappointments and opposition. After that he worked again with the disciples, organised them under Peter and instructed them at greater depth about the way. Finally, he spoke of the glorious future of the kingdom when he would come again in glory.

So, when Jesus began to tell the people that there is another way, his first words were about letting go of the old, sinful way of life. Repent ... let the old hatreds go ... put on a new mind ... enter a new system of values ... be born again of water and the Holy Spirit.

The message of the kingdom was a call to revolution. Minds would have to turn the full circle. Accepted values and standards were turned upside down. The greatest in the kingdom would not be the one who receives most but the one who gives most. The richest in the kingdom would not be those who possessed most but those who had the greatest emptiness for God. The voice that would be greatest would not be the loudest or most commanding but the whisper of those who go to the inner room and pray to God in the secret recesses of the heart.

In the kingdom the first shall be last and the last shall be first.

Jesus began to preach his dream. There is another way. The world is meant to be a mirror of God's love ... the kingdom of heaven on earth.

To realise the dream we must let worldly values be turned upside down. We must repent.

Second Reflection
The Kingdom and the Church

The kingdom is the ideal. The church is the means towards the ideal: as human as you or I: but capable of heroic greatness by the grace of God.

Immediately upon announcing that the kingdom of heaven was close at hand, Jesus set about recruiting his task-force.

He called Peter and Andrew, James and John.

Two were casting their nets. "Follow me and I will make you into fishers of men," he promised.

Two were mending their nets. "Follow me and I will make you into menders of a broken world."

Ordinary people called to an extaordinary task: the first hint of the church in service of the kingdom.

Casting nets and mending torn bits: some to venture on the high sea of mission; and some to stay on the home shore, mending and supplying.

All this happened in Capernaum.

Visiting the Holy Land, I was surprised at how small the town must have been. Archeologists and historians tell us that it was once a very busy, bustling place. But it was so small by our standards.

Yet I should have known better.

For has it not always been God's way to choose the weak to confront the strong, and the simple to confound the worldly wise? Isn't it a pity when the church tends to forget its humble origins.

When it begins to congratulate itself ... as if we had done what only grace can achieve. And when it rewards itself by aping the conceits of the world in wealthy embellishments and the titles and trappings of self-important authority.

And yet the church has been the mother of the greatest workers for the kingdom, caring and educating, peace-making and developing, beautifying and uplifting, nursing and protecting, striving for justice and challenging tyranny.

The church of Francis and Clare, Mother Teresa and Jean Vanier, Maximilian Kolbe and Oscar Romero, Matt Talbot and Edel Quinn ... this is the church splendidly serving the kingdom.

Ordinary people called to extraordinary greatness by God's grace. Casting nets for the cause of Jesus Christ: mending brokenness. Peter and Andrew, James and John, called in every age, and leaving everything to follow Jesus.

An ever-young church in service of the eternal kingdom.

Fourth Sunday

Matthew's gospel is built around five great sermons of Jesus on the kingdom of heaven, now begun on earth. For six Sundays we will take our gospel reading from the first of these sermons, usually called the Sermon on the Mount.

Today we begin with the beatitudes which capture the essence of the Master's vision of an alternative life which radically challenges the accepted values of worldly wisdom.

Matthew 5:1-12
Happy are the poor in spirit

Seeing the crowds, Jesus went up the hill. There he sat down and was joined by his disciples. Then he began to speak. This is what he taught them: "How happy are the poor in spirit; theirs is the kingdom of heaven! Happy the gentle: they shall have the earth for their heritage. Happy those who mourn: they shall be comforted. Happy those who hunger and thirst for what is right: they shall be satisfied. Happy the merciful: they shall have mercy shown them. Happy the pure in heart: they shall see God. Happy the peacemakers: they shall be called sons of God. Happy those who are persecuted in the cause of right: theirs is the kingdom of heaven. Happy are you when people abuse you and persecute you and speak all kinds of calumny against you on my account. Rejoice and be glad, for your reward will be great in heaven."

Good News

Jesus did not change the social or political conditions of life, but he brought a vision which can see the presence and blessedness of God even in difficult circumstances.

First Reflection
Kingdom-Attitudes and Kingdom-Actions

Jesus had proclaimed that the kingdom of heaven is at hand. It was a plea that the life of heaven would be mirrored on earth. It was time now for him to teach in more detail what he meant by 'kingdom'.

In the days of old, Moses had received the covenant with God on the mountain in Sinai. The atmosphere was awesome and terrifying. Now had come the time for the new covenant. Again the mountain was the rightful place to light the beacon. But here the atmosphere is gentle and intimate as Jesus sits down with his disciples and begins to teach them. This is the age of Emmanuel, God-with-us. The kingdom is among us.

The beatitudes capture the essence of all that Jesus would teach about life in his ideal society. Matthew likes to use the device of inclusion, which is a way of wrapping up a section by having the last sentence repeat the opening. So we find that the first and last beatitudes are in the present tense: "theirs is the kingdom of heaven." In between, there are six promises of future reward and justification.

The kingdom is both future and present: its fulness of realisation is of the future; but it is of the present since the seed has been planted and the process of growth towards perfection has already begun.

Jesus did not change the outer structures of social conditions or political organisation. But he gave the new light of faith to the inner eye which can now see with a different set of values. Perfect justice may belong to the future, but growth towards it has begun. However, the words of Jesus imply that it will be a painful process.

The new vision of life inspires four attitudes and four forms of action. The key attitude is being poor in spirit. In the light of today's first reading, we can understand this as an attitude of humility before God and obedience to his command. (cf. Zeph 2:3) It is about having a sense of our own inadequacy and our creaturely dependence upon God. Only those who come empty before God can receive of his giving: 'theirs is the kingdom of heaven.'

It follows that whoever has this sense of utter poverty before God will deeply respect all of God's creation. This is the second attitude, gentleness. Gentle people delight in letting all creatures be themselves, and feel no need to dominate or manipulate anything. It is no idle coincidence that Francis of Assisi, who jealously wed his soul to poverty, was also the gentle saint who deeply respected all creatures of the earth as his brothers and sisters. 'They shall have the earth for their heritage.'

The third attitude is mourning, or the sadness which means repentance for one's own sins and reparation for the evils of society. It is the attitude of heartfelt sorrow for any offence against the

137

love of God. Those who are sad for God's sake will be comforted.

The fourth attitude of the kingdom-member is hunger for justice in society and thirst for an end to the disorders caused by sin.

These kingdom-attitudes inspire kingdom-actions.

Kingdom gentleness is shown most beautifully in the work of mercy and forgiveness. Even the ugliness of another's behaviour becomes an occasion for showing the power of love.

The attitude of sadness for sin inspires repentance: it makes a person pure in heart. That means being single-minded or undivided in seeing things from God's point of view. If it is true that everything looks yellow to the jaundiced eye, it is equally true that all things can be seen in their goodness by the God-filled eye. 'They shall see God,' is the promise.

The kingdom's hunger for justice will inspire action for peace. Peacemakers shall be called children of God.

As the eighth beatitude echoes the first, the fourth action is inspired by the first attitude, namely poverty of spirit. The poor have nothing to lose so they will witness fearlessly in the cause of right, even in the face of persecution and death. Theirs, already, is the kingdom of heaven.

This vision of life radically challenges the value system and power which dominate society. History shows that the challenge of the kingdom is no lightweight voice which can be disregarded or reduced to ridicule. It deeply threatens the rulers of this world, because it works on their repressed conscience. And repressed conscience is most uncomfortable.

And so ... Jesus was crucified by those whose darkness he threatened. The disciples at Matthew's time of writing were being abused and persecuted in the cause of right. Ten thousand catholic priests and religious died in Nazi concentration camps. And in recent times kingdom-visionaries like Ghandi (whose favourite text was the sermon on the mount), Martin Luther King ('I have a dream') and Archbishop Oscar Romero have been assassinated. The prophet of the kingdom exposes the darkness of the worldly mind. Prophets have always been persecuted.

When the church is no longer the target of secular critics, it will indicate the absence from its policies of the radical, threatening mind of the kingdom. The voice of the church is of service to the kingdom only when it presents Christ's alternative way to the materialistic, sensual, and domineering attitudes which the worldly mind accepts.

Second Reflection
Blessed and Happy

There were many people who were disappointed with the teaching of Jesus. After all he did not advocate a political uprising nor did he outline a social utopia. There would still be poverty, oppression, injustices and reasons to lament. What he did offer was a new way of seeing how God can be present and operative in these situations. And if God is there, it is blessed.

How do we translate the beatitudes? Do we say 'happy' or 'blessed'?

'Happy' suggests a feeling of well-being, satisfaction and contentment: one is the recipient of favourable chance happenings. 'Blessed' is a word that reaches deeper than feelings or chance happening. It expresses the belief that God is at work in this particular circumstance. On the level of feeling there may be very little experience of well-being or contentment. But if God is involved in the happening, then the believer has an eye for goodness, even though the superficial experience may be of darkness and emptiness, mourning and misunderstanding. To the outer eye things may appear to be all suffering and pain, defeat and mistakes. But the inner eye sees that God is here ... and all shall be well, and all is well.

Deep trust in God is the most profound basis for peace of soul. And there can be happiness at a profound depth in the soul of a believer even while storms of adversity are raging on the surface of life. St Paul liked to open his letters with a greeting, first of grace and then of peace. Peace and happiness would follow as a result of knowing that one was the recipient of God's grace. Blessed first, then happy.

People may have been disappointed that Jesus did not set up a system of ending poverty and pain. People would still have to live in imperfect conditions.

What he did present was that interior disposition of mind and heart which could discern the working of God even in those imperfect conditions.

And where God is at work, it is a blessed situation.

And those who know that God is here are happy.

Fifth Sunday

The sermon on the mount continues. After the master vision of the beatitudes, Jesus tells his disciples that they are the salt of the earth and the light of the world. Salt and light are two elements which achieve their usefulness only when in contact with other things.

Matthew 5:13-16
You are the light of the world
Jesus said to his disciples:
"You are the salt of the earth. But if salt becomes tasteless, what can make it salty again? It is good for nothing, and can only be thrown out to be trampled underfoot by men. You are the light of the world. A city built on a hill-top cannot be hidden. No one lights a lamp to put it under a tub; they put it on the lamp-stand where it shines for everyone in the house. In the same way your light must shine in the sight of men, so that, seeing your good works, they may give the praise to your Father in heaven."

Good News
Kingdom-people are so charged with the Spirit and power of God that they are called to bring to the earth all the qualities we associate with salt and light.

First Reflection
Salt of the Earth, Light of the World
People are easily mesmerised by evil. I suppose it goes back to the fascination of the forbidden fruit. It is sad to see how many people feel compelled to buy the latest blockbuster novel, seething with crime and unbridled passion... but they never take up the good news of scripture.

It is amazing that so many people are compulsive listeners to the rasping, aggressive voices on radio, stirring up every possible pot of controversy for the sake of controversy: they forget their option to switch off and enjoy the silence. It is sad too that so many minds must feed off the amoral husks of the soap opera menu of corruption and violence, adultery and infidelity.

Are we to passively suffer the persistent erosion of tradition and morality? And all the while people wonder why they have no peace of soul.

They are too fretful to relax, too disillusioned to hope and too mixed up to hold a clear meaning of life. In the name of being liberal or progressive, we succumb to the fascination of evil. Our world is mesmerised.

A great pope of an early century, St Leo, issued this clear call to all Christians: 'Christians, know your dignity as Christians.' The dignity of Christians is that in them the kingdom of heaven is present in the world. And the kingdom is a life of love and hope, beauty and fidelity, in direct opposition to the world of hatred and disillusionment, ugliness and infidelity. It is the power of uplifting beauty set against the weight of downgrading ugliness.

Jesus said to his kingdom-people: 'You are the salt of the earth.' As salt preserves the goodness of things, you have the power and responsibility to preserve moral goodness and conserve the valuable truths of revelation for the world.

As salt brings out the taste of things, you are to show forth and celebrate the presence of God's face in the affairs of life and in the good things of creation. As salt heals the septic wound, you are to heal the putrid areas of society. And salt stings as it heals, so you are not to be afraid of hurting in order to heal, by confronting, challenging and correcting. It is the salt that makes the ocean water stimulating beyond all other water, and likewise your lives are to be vibrant and fresh and stimulating.

Jesus then said to his kingdom-people: 'You are the light of the world.' You are the light of revealed truth to stimulate the searching mind. You are the light of moral guidance to teach the way of living. You are the beacon-light to warn of dangers and guide the ships safely home.

Jesus did not say: 'You are to become the salt ... the light.' He said : 'You are.' It is not in our own talents or by our own doing that we are the salt and light. It is a dignity and responsibility given by God and implanted in us.

The kingdom of heaven is here. Its work is taking place. Its power is operative because Christ's Spirit is living in us and working through us. You are the salt of the earth and the light of world.

Your call is to let Christ-in-you be seen through your attitudes and actions ... seen like that city on the hill-top which cannot be hidden.

Second Reflection
Light in the Darkness

The secularistic society, in which God or religion are not in any way relevant to what happens between Monday and Saturday, will be enlightened only by beacons of good example. So the injunction of Jesus: 'Let your light shine in the sight of men, so that, seeing your good works, they may give the praise to your Father in heaven.'

Today's responsorial psalm lists many of the qualities of life and good works which express the kingdom of light in a world of darkness. Kingdom-people, fired with the Spirit of Christ, are generous in attitude, merciful in heart and just in action.

Their generosity is in contrast to the jungle society where self is always number one and what I have is mine to use in any way I wish.

Their mercy is a softness of heart in contrast to the hard heart which stores bitterness and seeks revenge and punishment.

Their concern for justice shines out in the midst of corruption, untruthfulness, chicanery and sharp practices.

Kingdom-people never waver. They are conscious that God is ever faithful and unchanging in love. So, their promise is fully meant and their commitment is faithful.

Infidelity is a mark of the Godless world. The sands are always shifting so there is no solid foundation to build on. Even the ethics of the secularistic conscience are situational, for it seems that there are no absolute values. Relationships are transient, marriages are until further notice, and everything changes with the conditions.

But the love of God is everlasting and unconditional. Kingdom people are inspired by this: they never waver.

Kingdom-people have no fear of evil news, such is the firmness of their trust in God. God is in control of the world and all shall be well. Without trust in God what is there to keep one from succumbing to the bad news? Many people today are so disillusioned that they can no longer trust anybody, even themselves. They are settling for the philosophical view that life is meaningless and absurd.

The sadness of this atmosphere has dragged far too many people down into the pits of depression where they could no longer find sufficient reason to continue living.

The question used to be: is there life after death? The question for many minds today is: is there life after birth, a life worth living?

Kingdom-people are the salt of the earth and the light of the world. It is not of their own doing but by the power of the Holy Spirit in them.

The Spirit inspires:

a steadfast heart that will not fear;

an open-handed nature that gives to the poor;

and a justice that stands firm for ever.

When Moses came down from the mountain after his encounter with God, his face was too bright for the people, so they asked him to wear a veil over it.

Christians, who have listened to Christ on the mountain, are fired with his light. As St Paul wrote: 'It is the same God that said, "Let there be light shining out of darkness", who has shone in our minds to radiate the light of the knowledge of God's glory, the glory on the face of Christ.' *(2 Cor 4:6)*

In baptism we have received the light of Christ. And so, the words of Christ on the mountain to his disciples were: 'Your light must shine in the sight of men, so that, seeing your good works, they may give the praise to your Father in heaven.'

Sixth Sunday

For the third consecutive Sunday the gospel is from the mountain sermon where Jesus sets out his programme for the kingdom. Today's extract gives us some of the rules of the road. But there is a huge contrast between the understanding of laws as presented by the scribes and Pharisees and the deeper meaning of religious conversion as preached by Jesus.

This passage specifically highlights the laws forbidding murder, adultery, divorce and swearing. Jesus does not stop at the letter of the law but reaches into the virtue which gives meaning to the law.

Matthew 5:20-22, 27-28, 33-34, 37

Such was said to your ancestors; but I am speaking to you

Jesus said to his disciples: "I tell you, if your virtue goes no deeper than that of the scribes and Pharisees, you will never get into the kingdom of heaven.

"You have learned how it was said to our ancestors: You must not kill; and if anyone does kill he must answer for it before the court. But I say this to you: anyone who is angry with his brother will answer for it before the court;

"You have learned how it was said: You must not commit adultery. But I say this to you: if a man looks at a woman lustfully, he has already committed adultery with her in his heart.

"Again, you have learned how it was said to our ancestors: You must not break your oath, but must fulfill your oaths to the Lord. But I say to you: do not swear at all. All you need say is 'Yes' if you mean yes, 'No' if you mean no; anything more than this comes from the evil one."

Good News

Jesus teaches us that religious laws are pointers to inner integrity and the fulness of life. Greatness in the kingdom consists in growing in the virtues or strengths of soul which are signposted by the commandments.

First Reflection

A Kingdom of Passion and Energy

There is a growing body of Catholics who should sign the initials of their denomination not as R.C. but as C.B.: 'I am a Catholic But ...' But I don't agree with all the rules of the church. But I don't see why we have to wait until we're married. But this is a just war and they are the occupying forces. But it's none of the Pope's business.

This is an age when law and order is challenged on every level, when discipline is throttled by permissiveness, and when laws are regarded as restricting the inflated goal of self-fulfilment.

The teaching of Jesus strongly affirms the need for rules; but rules are to be understood as the means to the end, which is a life of spiritual strength and commitment.

The Greek philosopher, Plato, four hundred years before Christ, wrote of the two horses in the human heart, Passion and Reason. Passion is the wild, untamed horse with boundless strength and energy, but very hard to control and direct. Reason is the tamed horse, accustomed to the reins, disciplined in stride and responding to directions. A chariot hitched to a pair of Passions might go anywhere but would surely crash or overturn before long. However, a charioteer who selects a pair of Reasons will be too cautious and fearful to go anywhere worthwhile. But if Passion and Reason can be paired, then the powerful energy is harnessed and the journey of life can be enjoyed.

Jesus found that the religious leaders of his time concentrated too much on the controlling reins. The scribes were the legal experts who knew their way through the unbelievably complicated maze of rules which had come in from various sources. The Pharisees, meaning the separated ones, reacted against the influence of foreign culture which threatened the nation and religion of Israel. Increasingly as the scribes and Pharisees gained control over the minds of the people, the very purpose of religion seemed to be protection of oneself from the risk of defilement, whether moral or ceremonial.

The scribes were lecturing people on the signposts and complicated directions: the Pharisees were lecturing on all the potholes and muddy pools to be avoided. The rules of the road had become more important than the journey.

With this pair of horses hitched to the chariot, people simply could not find the passion and energy needed for the journey of the soul to God.

And as for the sinner ... there was no hope at all.

Accordingly, when Jesus outlined the kingdom which

would mirror heaven on earth, his voice rang out on the mountain: 'You have learnt how it was said ... but I say this to you.'

His challenge was to bring passion and energy back into religion. One by one he took examples of religious commandments to restore the ideal of full life towards which they pointed.

The wild energy of anger must be tamed and become the disciplined energy of thirsting for justice and working towards reconciliation. The passion of attraction must be pruned of all lustful self-seeking so as to flower in unselfish love. The difficulties of a marriage must be worked at creatively so as to reflect the fidelity and unconditional nature of God's love. Zeal for truth must be so apparent on one's face that 'yes' means 'yes' and 'no' means 'no', without the need to bolster up statements by swearing.

Jesus brought back the true meaning to the religious journey. He confirmed the need for rules, not for their own sake, but as giving direction and discipline to our passions and energies.

The scribes and Pharisees hitched two horses of Reason to their chariot ... so they debated endlessly and moved nowhere.

Modern permissiveness hitches two horses of Passion and the chariot rushes headlong to catastrophe.

Jesus matched the discipline of rules to the energy of the heart ... and he set us on our journey.

Second Reflection
Redeeming Our Energies (1)

Newspaper editors and Radio/ TV producers have no problem today in packing their pages and panels with the embittered minds and sour faces who can be counted upon to rant and rave about the restrictive mind of Catholicism. And yet, if one were to go by the criterion that by their fruits you shall know them, these very critics are scarcely in a position to lead the morality of the nation.

It cannot be denied that it is an occupational hazard for any church that it might take on that negative, restricting influence once held by the scribes and Pharisees. But the ideal is that religious rules represent a discipline which favours the growth of virtue and strength of character. The habit of virtuous action is strengthened through repeated practice of the virtue. The good habit is called acquired virtue. And acquired virtue is the most fertile ground for receiving the seed of God's grace (called infused virtue). Religious rules create the favourable disposition for the development of our inner potential and for redeeming the energies which will enslave a person if they are left unchecked.

Spiritual masters have identified seven basic energies which are the sources of sin if they remain unchecked. These are the seven capital (or source) sins: pride, greed, lust, envy, anger, gluttony and sloth. Each of these comes from a powerhouse of energy which can lead either to sin or to goodness. Today's gospel invites us to reflect on two of them, anger and lust.

Anger is an energy that is released when one experiences a hurt or wrongdoing, be it real or imaginary. A physical reaction is set in motion as adrenalin is released, blood rushes to the face and muscles are tensed up for action. Uncontrolled anger leads to an explosion which usually wreaks further destruction. But sometimes the anger is not released. And when it is not admitted then either of two things can happen. We try to repress it, but it is like pressing in the bulge in a balloon. Press it in here and out it pops there. Repressed anger eats away at health of mind and body. It causes tension and anxiety. It leaves one fatigued because one is drained from living in the state of constant alert. Or else the anger comes out sideways, rather like a crab walking. Sideways anger comes out in resentment or uncharitable remarks about a third party (but never spoken to the object of the remarks).

When anger is redeemed then the energy is directed positively and creatively towards the correction of the fault and the pursuit of justice. A character incapable of anger would be a very weak person, incapable of determination.

Lust is the disturbing energy that is released by sexual stimulation of mind or body. Jesus repeated the warning of certain rabbis against adultery of the heart, the eye or the hand. One extreme position tries to repress or deny sexual energy: the other extreme goes for unrestrained sexual activity. In between the extremes is the possibility of developing this energy into the powerhouse of unselfish love.

The futile effort to repress sexual life usually results from trying to deny its existence and importance. But as Blaise Pascal warned, those who pretend to be angels usually end up as beasts.

This denial of reality may result in compulsive auto-eroticism, or the guilt-ridden mind unable to concentrate on any pursuit, or a dreadful fear of close contact with anybody. Sometimes the energy is projected outwards in inflamed condemnation of others. Obviously in a church ruled by celibates, this negative, condemnatory attitude is an occupational hazard. Just listen to the energy behind many sermons on the 'fightin' sixth and ninth'!

The opposite extreme, that is unrestrained sexual licence, develops an unhealthy self-centredness which damages one's potential for unselfish, faithful and unconditional love. If one does not recognise control and restraint in oneself, then one will not know how to trust any other. The virtue of chastity is a power-house of unselfish love, whereas selfish lust is a barrier to love.

A three-step plan helps to tap the potential in these wayward energies:

First admit the existence of anger or lust or whatever energy is causing the trouble. It is dangerous to pretend that the energy does not exist.

Then, secondly, try to see the positive potential in this energy, for after all, it is part of God's creation. Anger can be the beginning of great determination and initiative. Lust indicates a desire for relationships. Channel this desire properly and it leads to warm-hearted sharing with others. If we are incapable of lust then we are incapable of loving. The only day you should worry about impure thoughts is the day you have none, for then you are on the way out.

It's like the weeds in the garden. See them in the forest and you call them wild flowers and admire them. There are no such things as weeds: only flowers in the wrong place. All our energies are basically good: they sometimes happen to get into the wrong garden.

The third step is to pray about it and work with God's grace to use the energy for growth. Thank God for this power, even if it is presently causing trouble. God is the source of all our energy, so it must be good. We must learn how to praise God in the storm.

Religious rules, when exaggerated, depress growth and inner development of character. But when prudently applied they point the direction towards the fulness of life and love and the redeeming of our wayward energies.

Seventh Sunday

Again we are on the mountain listening to Jesus share his vision of how our life on earth might reflect the kingdom of heaven.

The ideal is that we would share in the Father's huge, generous and unconditional love. Here the gospel probes with the incisiveness of the surgeon's steel. At the core of our being we are challenged about the extent of our generosity and whether we allow the evil of others become a source of poison in our hearts too.

Matthew 5:38-48

Love your enemies

Jesus said to his disciples: "You have learned how it was said: Eye for eye and tooth for tooth. But I say this to you: offer the wicked man no resistance. On the contrary, if anyone hits you on the right cheek, offer him the other as well; if a man takes you to law and would have your tunic, let him have your cloak as well. And if anyone orders you to go one mile, go two miles with him. Give to anyone who asks, and if anyone wants to borrow, do not turn away.

"You have learned how it was said: You must love your neighbour and hate your enemy. But I say this to you: love your enemies and pray for those who persecute you; in this way you will be sons of your Father in heaven, for he causes his sun to rise on bad men as well as good, and his rain to fall on honest and dishonest men alike.

"For if you love those who love you, what right have you to claim any credit? Even the tax collectors do as much, do they not? And if you save your greetings for your brothers, are you doing anything exceptional? Even the pagans do as much, do they not?

"You must therefore be perfect just as your heavenly Father is perfect."

Good News

God is our Father in heaven whose love goes further than strict justice and is not blocked by enmity or rejection.

Kingdom-people, children of God, share in the same passion of love which refuses to be blocked or diverted.

First Reflection
Perfect Love

Jesus called his kingdom-people to perfect love. 'You must therefore be perfect just as your heavenly Father is perfect.'

Perfect here means a love that is universal and complete.

It is not based on natural attraction which makes us like some people more than others.

The ideal is that we would share in the huge, generous and undiscriminating love that the Father has for all the children of his creation. Sunrise and raindrops come the same for all. But we are tempted in two ways:

- to restrict the energy of love to the minimum demanded in strict justice:

- to allow our rivers of love become infected and poisoned by the evil attitudes of others.

Jesus addressed the accepted morality of the time: 'You have learnt how it was said: Eye for eye and tooth for tooth.'

In fact, that law of equal vengeance represented a huge advance on the primitive lust for unmitigated revenge. But in Jesus' mind any form of retaliation was a contradiction of love.

He spoke out of a nobler vision of life. And the strength he admired was inner strength of character.

He invites us to imagine the petty tyrant who insults you by slapping you with the back of his hand on your right cheek. If you can preserve your dignity and calmly turn the other cheek, then you will have shown an inner strength much greater than the imagined superiority of the bully.

Or think of the greedy moneymaker who would claim his rights even by taking your undergarment. Let him have his greedy way. And give him your cloak as well (which the law would not permit him retain overnight because it had to serve as the night's blanket). Be prepared to stand there naked, knowing that you are clad in a dignity which the greedy man, for all his wealth, will never attain. One remembers Francis of Assisi letting his earthly father have the last stitch of clothing off his back, for he would henceforth be seen as a child of the heavenly Father.

Then Jesus invites us to think of the soldier who had the right to commandeer someone, as happened to Simon of Cyrene, to carry his baggage for a thousand paces, one mile. Carry it for two miles instead and let him see that your spirit of helpfulness is mightier than his strong-arm policy.

Do we let the brutish bullyboys, the greedy moneymakers or the advocates of military superiority continue to rule society with their small minds? Or do we try to open up their vision by challenging the standards which the world too easily accepts?

The sick society of today will only be cured if it is challenged by the counter-culture of gospel living. The gospel's view is that God is the Father of us all and we are the one family of brothers and sisters. Our dignity comes from knowing this and trying to live up to it.

Kingdom-love is a deliberate commitment to generosity as an alternative to the tyranny and coercion exercised by the self-appointed little gods. It thinks more of my responsibilities to others than my rights from them. It is a powerful river that will not be blocked or diverted by any obstacle. It is a pure stream that will not be infected by the poison of any enemy.

Kingdom-love is unlimited and complete. It is perfect, as the love of the Father is perfect.

Second Reflection
Redeeming Our Energies (2)
In God's kingdom upon earth, love is a powerful decision to push forward the cause of goodness and beauty without letting oneself be infected with the poison of whatever evil or hatred may be encountered. This decision draws its strength from the prayerful remembrance of God, who always loves the sinner even while despising the sin.

Oh, but what a waste of much-needed resources and technology when they are put into the manufacture of weapons of destruction to maintain the balance of hatred between the so-called great powers!

And what a waste of God-given energy there is in the individual life which is soured by hurt, hatred and areas of unforgiving! When hatred is allowed to boil over in open confrontation it disrupts the harmony of relationships.

But hidden and repressed hatred may be more dangerous, for it burrows into one's reserve of energy and leaves the victim listless and fatigued. Or else it comes out in cynicism and that negative, knocking attitude which is a sure sign that inner hatred is being projected outwards onto the screen of some other person or cause. Negativity usually says more of the subject who shows it than of the object of his attack!

All this wasted energy is to be redeemed and healed. The challenge of the kingdom is to let go of all hatred and to be converted unto love. The greatest source of healing is that prayer which draws us more unto the mind of God. As Jesus said: 'Love your enemies and pray for those who persecute you.' Kindgom-love is a reflection in our lives of the love of the Father who cares for all his children, even the sinners.

Obviously this sort of love goes far beyond the scope of natural attraction. And it keeps on giving even when one is spurned, despised or injured. To keep on giving is to be forgiving. Kingdom-love is determined not to be infected by the poison of the other's evil. Like the man who wished 'Good morning' every day to his unresponsive newspaper-seller. He defended his action by saying that he was not going to allow the surly reaction of one individual put a halt to his desire to wish well to all.

A typical scenario in daily life might go like this:

Somebody hurts me, hates me or wrongs me: then he has a problem in his soul. But if I am infected by his poison and respond in hatred or thoughts of revenge, then I too have a problem. My anger or hatred belongs to nobody else but me.

I have allowed my streams of energy to be polluted by the situation. I think up horrible names, breathe fiery language and let imagination stir up a great justification of hatred. If I reflect on the situation, I see that the problem now has two aspects:

- the wrong done by the other (which is his problem);
- and the amount of unredeemed energy within me (which is my problem).

I may come around to seeing that my enemy does me a service by opening up my inner heart and revealing to me my need of healing and reconciliation.

We are not asked here by the Lord to convert our enemy but to be healed of our own hatred. And when we cope with our own problem our Christian dignity may inspire him to deal with his. As Abraham Lincoln remarked in the context of dealing with the defeated side in war, the best way to destroy the enmity of another is by mak ing him your friend.

This sort of love goes beyond the scope of natural inclinations. It is a supernatural love which is attained only by a gift of God. That is why Jesus spoke of prayer as the solution to enmity. When we feel that we have reached the limits of our own ability to love and forgive, then we must hand it over to God and invite his love to invade our hearts.

We pray that we might see and understand the pain and complexity of our enemy, with the understanding that the Father has. If my enemy treats me in this way, I can be sure that he treats others badly too. He does not need me as another enemy: what he needs is pity and understanding.

In prayer we are opened up to the growth of God's mind in us. We come to see how the Father always loves his creature here; how the Son loved him unto the cross: and how the gentle breeze of the Holy Spirit would fan his tiniest spark of love back into flame.

Our Father in heaven ... may your kingdom come ... within our hearts.

Forgive us our trespasses ... and heal the poisoned memories which warp and block us.

May we so deeply experience your healing and forgiveness that we will passionately want to pass on forgiveness to others.

May our love be perfect as your love is perfect.

Eighth Sunday

In the sermon on the mount Jesus shares his vision of what life would be like if we truly belonged to the kingdom. The principles of the kingdom clash head on with the philosophy of today's consumeristic society. If our faith and trust were strong we would let go of our search for security in material surroundings and be rid of our anxiety about tomorrow.

Matthew 6:24-34

Do not worry about your life and what you are to eat or to wear

Jesus said to his disciples: "No one can be the slave of two masters: he will either hate the first and love the second, or treat the first with respect and the second with scorn. You cannot be the slave both of God and of money.

"That is why I am telling you not to worry about your life and what you are to eat, nor about your body and how you are to clothe it. Surely life means more than food, and the body more than clothing! Look at the birds in the sky. They do not sow or reap or gather into barns; yet your heavenly Father feeds them. Are you not worth much more than they are?

"Can any of you, for all his worrying, add one single cubit to his span of life? And why worry about clothing? Think of the flowers growing in the fields; they never have to work or spin; yet I assure you that not even Solomon in all his regalia was robed like one of these.

"Now if that is how God clothes the grass in the field which is there today and thrown into the furnace tomorrow, will he not much more look after you, you men of little faith? So do not worry; do not say, 'What are we to eat? What are we to drink? How are we to be clothed?' It is the pagans who set their hearts on all these things. Your heavenly Father knows you need them all.

"Set your hearts on his kingdom first, and on his righteousness, and all these other things will be given you as well. So do not worry about tomorrow: tomorrow will take care of itself. Each day has enough trouble of its own."

Good News

God, whose power and beauty can be seen in the adornment of the fields, will surely provide for us, his children.

First Reflection
Anxiety or Trust

The materialistic culture of today represents a thinking that is diametrically opposed to the understanding of life outlined in Christ's kingdom.

By their fruits you shall know them. Where life is based on materialistic values, people are insecure, fretful and anxious. Whereas kingdom-life shows serenity, confidence and joy in all things, for its foundation is the sure love of God, from whose eye nothing is hid den, and in whose memory nobody is forgotten.

In today's first reading Isaiah reassures us that God has the loving memory of a mother. 'Does a woman forget her baby at the breast, or fail to cherish the son of her womb? Yet even if these forget, I will never forget you.' *(Is 49:15)*

We are familiar with the words but we still let God's love be blocked off from our lives. We let a defensive screen obscure God's light like clouds blocking the sunlight. The golden light of sunshine travels 93 million miles to beautify our day. But very often, in the last half-mile of its journey, a grey cloud of vapour blocks off its golden rays. That is how God's love is beaming down on us, but we let our inner, unredeemed areas project out clouds which obscure God's light and lessen his warmth in our lives.

There are three clouds in particular which we tend to produce. Out of our past comes up the cloud of guilt which makes us want to hide from God for we think we would be uncomfortable in his closeness. Out of our present non-acceptance of others comes the cloud of anger. And anger is scared of being thawed out and melted by the warmth of love. Out of our thoughts about the future comes up the cloud of anxiety. We worry and fret and show no signs of a foundational trust in God.

Jesus tells us not to worry about the parts that make up the jigsaw of life ... food, drink and clothing. The totality of life, which is God's dear creation, is so much greater than the parts. He invited his audience on the mountainside to open their eyes and their hearts to the creatures of field and sky all about them.

We might be inclined to regard this as poetic naivete. But Jesus did not say that food and clothing are unimportant. Nor did he advocate that we should not plan ahead or work hard. Remember the birds have to work very hard for their food. And growing plants use their every root and leaf and stem in the process of growth. What Jesus did say is that the beauty and adornment of creation is the language of God's overall, providential plan. And surely the children of God are most important in this care. 'Are you not worth more than they are?'

The maternal heart of God already knows our needs. Can we not trust in our Divine Mother's care? If our heart sincerely prays 'Thy kingdom come,' can we not be totally confident in asking for our daily bread?

Each passing day leads us into situations where we respond in anxiety or trust.

The breakdown of community behaviour, the increase in violence and vandalism can shake our basic peace of mind. Do we respond in increased anxiety and pessimism? Or do we have the calm trust of knowing that this is still God's world?

Someone we deeply care about strays into troubled ways. Do we fret ourselves into ill-health? Or are we moved to pray with full confidence that the Good Shepherd is searching for the stray? Our pattern of life is unexpectedly shattered, say by illness or accident or bereavement. When one responds in anxiety then everything falls apart for the centre no longer holds. But to respond in faith is to see God at work in this breaking. It may be beyond our understanding now, but faith accepts that God has a loving purpose in this. It may be to test us; or deepen us; or to move us from our familiar life to a new level which as yet we do not understand. Sometimes, with hindsight we can see how our most painful experiences proved to be very enriching.

The frantic, loud, fretful and distressed society of today is hurtling down the hill towards despair and self-destruction.

It will be saved through the witness of kingdom-people whose deep trust, undisturbed peace, and quiet joy proclaim that this is God's world, that he has not forgotten us, and that he cares for us dearly.

'Set your hearts on his kingdom first, and on his righteousness, and all these other things will be given you as well.'

If the centre of your prayer is 'Thy kingdom come,' then there will be no anxious fretting as you confidently ask, 'Give us this day our daily bread.'

Second Reflection

Thirsting for God

According to the Master, it is a pagan heart that is set upon material things: but the kingdom-heart is set first upon God and his righteousness. And you cannot have a heart that is set equally in both directions. 'You cannot be the slave both of God and of money.'

To set your heart first upon God is to thirst for God beyond all lesser striving, contentment or satisfaction. It is God or nothing. There is no room for compromising or for half-hearted faith.

From the days of Egyptian monasticism comes the story of the young initiate asking the Spiritual Father to teach him how to pray. The Father led the young man to a river bank and asked him to plunge his head under water. He pressed his hand on the head to keep it under a while. Then he let the young man surface for air. The process was repeated, the head being held under for a longer time. Then the third time, the Master held the pupil's head under longer still. Then he let him surface and asked him how he felt.

'Bursting for air,' he gasped.

'When you begin to thirst for God the way you were bursting for air, you will be ready to learn about prayer.'

Whatever we set our hearts on, whatever we value most, will receive our attention, our time and our energy. If our values are of a low order, if we settle for inconsequential things like passing fashions, the chances are that we will never recognise the eternal thirst of our hearts.

When our values are low, our attempts at prayer will resemble the pagans who sought to twist the arm of the deity to their own favour and advantage. The prayer that comes out of half-hearted faith is invariably an attempt to use God for self. It tries to make God's will come around to what we want.

The psalms are the greatest school of faith-filled prayer to instruct us. We need go no further than three examples. These are verses to learn and repeat until we not only know them off by heart but we know them in our hearts.

In God alone is my soul at rest;
my help comes from him.
He alone is my rock, my stronghold,
my fortress: I stand firm." *(Ps 61, today's Responsorial Psalm)*

157

O God, you are my God, for you I long;
for you my soul is thirsting.
My body pines for you
like a dry, weary land without water. *(Ps 62)*

Like the deer that yearns for running streams,
so my soul is yearning for you, my God.
My soul is thirsting for God,
the God of my life. *(Ps 41) (Grail Translation)*

Ninth Sunday

In this closing section of the sermon on the mount we are given the images of sand and rock. We can build our lives on the solid rock of Christ's words or on the sands of changing fashion. Moses, in the first reading today, calls obedience a blessing and disobedience a curse.

Matthew 7:21-27
The house built on rock and the house built on sand

Jesus said to his disciples: 'It is not those who say to me, "Lord, Lord," who will enter the kingdom of heaven, but the person who does the will of my Father in heaven. When the day comes, many will say to me, "Lord, Lord, did we not prophesy in your name, cast out demons in your name, work many miracles in your name?" Then I shall tell them to their faces: I have never known you; away from me, you evil men!

'Therefore, everyone who listens to these words of mine and acts on them will be like a sensible man who built his house on rock. Rain came down, floods rose, gales blew and hurled themselves against that house, and it did not fall: it was founded on rock. But everyone who listens to these words of mine and does not act on them will be like a stupid man who built his house on sand. Rain came down, floods rose, gales blew and struck that house, and it fell; and what a fall it had!'

Good News

There is good news here for our age which has suffered deeply from the floodtide of change and the collapse of changing structures: the teaching of Jesus is a solid rock on which the house of life can be built, to withstand all seasons, climates and changes.

First Reflection
From Dream to Reality

In the sermon on the mount Jesus outlined his dream for the world. He pictured a blessed society in which the Father's love is mirrored on earth by our attitudes and actions. Such a world would be the kingdom of heaven among us.

To make the dream a reality he had to reverse many of the accepted values of the world. He recalled our wayward energies to fuel the passion of faithful and selfless love. He brought back the true meaning to religious rules.

159

But his followers had to learn that there would be no discipleship without discipline. The road from dreaming about the kingdom to its realisation is lifelong and costly. Its doctrine is drawn from the words of the Lord: its morality is acting on them.

Matthew gives prominence to Jesus' warning about self-appointed prophets and religious charlatans who use nice-sounding religious words but lack the discipline of obedience. The scholars tell us that Matthew, at his time of writing, had to address the undisciplined teachers who ignored certain moral obligations, and the unrestrained healers who were upsetting community peace. Obviously these words are of the utmost relevance today when so much harm is being done from within the ranks of the church by dissent and disobedience.

Not every statement addressed to the Lord is genuine prayer. Nor is any song or reading suitable for liturgy just because it mentions words like peace, justice, love or heaven. Not every healing or extraordinary phenomenon is an authentic sign from God: there are far too many unexplored areas of subconscious energy for us to be sure of the origin of the phenomenon.

The one sure sign of authentic discipleship is obedience to the full teaching of Jesus Christ. The true kingdom-member 'does the will of my Father in heaven.'

Sometimes the ways of disobedience receive the false blessing of misguided priests ... shepherds in the mist.

There are spineless leaders who rate high in popularity because they know how to please but not how to confront. One type will have the young liberals on his side because, while he denounces social injustice and selected areas of church practice, he totally ignores the Lord's teaching on lust and adultery (which are far more relevant to the lives of his audience).

His counterpart will please the wellheeled conservative because he attacks the decadence and vandalism of the others while exercising a polite deafness to the radical church teaching on social justice (which might upset his audience).

Then there is the darling of the media who can be guaranteed to tell us about the compassion of Jesus Christ in order to paint a black picture of a hard-line church. Notice what a soft ride he will get on the popular chat-show.

If we have learnt anything from the sermon on the mount it

is that the kingdom is a beautiful dream but very demanding.

The grace of God comes as an unmerited, free gift: but responding to grace, that is discipleship, is very demanding. In the oft-quoted words of Chesterton: 'Christianity has not been tried and found wanting: it has been found hard and left untried.'

Over fifty years ago, Dietrich Bonhoeffer, wrote that the deadly enemy of the church is cheap grace. 'Cheap grace is the preaching of forgiveness without requiring repentance, baptism without church discipline, Communion without confession, absolution without personal confession.' It wants to bypass discipleship and dispense with the cross. The true disciple knows it is costly to follow the one who said, 'Take up your cross and follow me.'

There is today a fog of vagueness regarding doctrine and a grey mist of unclarity about morality. Many follow the trend towards selective Christianity, a menu a la carte, where you choose what you like and comfortably ignore what is unpleasant. Under the umbrella of pluralism there is a reprehensible tolerance of disobedience to the commandments.

The Lord's sermon on the mount concludes with a black or white choice: full obedience to his teaching or else disobedience. There is no room allowed for grey mists, half-baked theology, a la carte morality or lukewarm spirituality.

'You are neither hot nor cold. I wish you were one or the other, but since you are neither, but only lukewarm, I will spit you out of my mouth." (Rev 3: 15-16)

Second Reflection
The Rock and the Sand

I am singularly blessed these years to be living in very close proximity to the mystery of the sea. Near our retreat centre is a perfect horseshoe bay which we call Lucky Shell. It is protected from the North Atlantic by a long promontory of weathered rock.

Water is soft, the rock is hard, but the sea is relentless. It searches every weakness and probes every fault. At one place there is a gully where long ago the sea found a fault. Rolling storm-waves act like frightened monsters when they are trapped in this narrowing gully. The water howls terrifyingly as it crashes forward before it is forced to spout dramatically in the air as a geyser.

How long before the sea forces its way through and the

promontory is cut off to form a rocky island? A day, two days perhaps. For in the life of rocks a day is a million years. It helps us to understand God with whom a thousand years is like a single day. For today, at least, the sheltered bay is safe. Sunlit, it reposes like a sunbather showing off its golden skin to the skies.

Yet it is a different beach from last week. The high tides have changed its contour. The sands keep shifting. The sand-dunes are receding noticeably each year.

Not far from here the marram grass, which roots the sand, was cut too low and the mouth of a sea inlet was gradually silted by blown sand until it was eventually blocked. And what was once a salt-water swamp is today a freshwater lake. Some of the old people can remember the fine farm and house buried under the wind-borne sand. They tell of the auctioneer standing on the roof of the house selling off the contents.

The old and not so old can also remember when life was more simple and contentment more common. Boredom was unheard of and depression had not yet been invented. There was no confusion of doctrine. And everybody had a clear sense of right and wrong. You never had to lock a door and your bike was safe.

The whirlwind of change has whipped up a sandstorm. It stings your face; you have to cover up your ears and screen your eyes. It is hard to hear and impossible to see.

The new culture has lost contact with time and eternity. It is all about now, the present moment. Its totem is the digital watch which shows the instant now with no relation to past or future. Stability is gone, mobility is here.

The rocks have the wisdom of the ages in their story but the sands have only the shifty foolishness of the shallow instant. Is there any solid foundation for life and wisdom? Today's psalm prays to God:

'Be a rock of refuge for me
a mighty stronghold to save me,
for you are my rock, my stronghold.
For your name's sake, lead me and guide me.'

Jesus promised to build his church upon the rock of Peter and he said: 'Everyone who listens to these words of mine and acts on them will be like a sensible man who built his house on rock.' Yes, there is a solid rock to build on: the words and the way of Jesus Christ.

Tenth Sunday

The closed minds of the Pharisees were incapable of taking in the beauty of God's love which was reflected in the care and mercy of Jesus towards sinners. Love and mercy please God far more than sacrifice and self-righteousness.

Matthew 9:9-13
I did not come to call the virtuous, but sinners

As Jesus was walking on he saw a man named Matthew sitting by the customs house, and he said to him, 'Follow me.' And he got up and followed him.

While he was at dinner in the house it happened that a number of tax collectors and sinners came to sit at table with Jesus and his disciples. When the Pharisees saw this, they said to his disciples, 'Why does your master eat with tax collectors and sinners?' When he heard this he replied, 'It is not the healthy who need the doctor, but the sick. Go and learn the meaning of the words: What I want is mercy, not sacrifice. And indeed I did not come to call the virtuous, but sinners.'

Good News
The merciful, faithful love of God is the heart of true religion. Jesus came as the saviour of sinners, as the physician for the sick.

First Reflection
The Separate Ones

How very important it is not to make a religion out of religion! What I refer to is that brand of religion which is no longer responding to the call and love of God, but is more concerned with the preservation of the religious group.

That is what happened to the Pharisees, whose very name means the Separate Ones. They came into existence as a group out of the determination of many Jews not to be contaminated ... in doctrine, in food, in touching, in anything.

It has always been a useful tactic of the tempter to so fascinate the eye with evil that it no longer sees any beauty and goodness.

This attitude continues to produce the self-appointed defender of pure religion who can write essays of learned criticism but is incapable of a word of encouragement: who can tell you what is wrong with any plan but cannot see its potential for good: whose energy rises in condemning the decadence of society but who cannot raise a whimper of breath to talk of the beauty and love of God.

Even the good Lord himself was not acceptable to the Separate Ones. As sunlight hurts the sore eye so is beauty a threat to the ugly soul. When Jesus in mercy sat to table with sinners, it severely discomforted the Pharisees.

The pure Pharisee and the sinful tax collector together represent the saint and the sinner in each one of us. As sure as summer and winter, as sure as day and night, there is light and darkness in each one of us, saint and sinner. Trouble arises when the two do not meet and sit down to table together. The sinner is left to stew in his sinfulness without hope while the self-canonised saint stands aloof in a religion of cold correctness.

How beautiful that day when Jesus saw a sinner to whom he said, 'Follow me.' Then he went in to sit at table with a rare assortment of sinners. But the Separate Ones would not go in ... nor would they go in to face the darkness of their own lives.

How beautiful today is the church of Jesus Christ that is sufficiently catholic to inspire the heroic sanctity of the saints while offering a harbour of refuge to the storm-tossed sinners. It is not the church of saints: nor the church of sinners: but the church of saints who are sinners and sinners who could yet be saints.

'There is so much good in the worst of us
And so much bad in the best of us,
That it ill-behoves any of us
To speak ill of the rest of us.'

In Jesus, we see how 'Mercy and faithfulness have met, justice and peace have embraced.' *(Ps 84, Grail)*

Second Reflection
The Call of Matthew

Matthew had a lovely name: it means the gift of God. But his name had an echo of irony to those who suffered from the shady practices of a tax collector.

The Jews had an ingrained prejudice against paying taxes, more than any other nation. Fundamentally they maintained that God alone was king and everything belonged to him. No earthly ruler, then, had the right to levy tax on what really belonged to God. To rub salt into the wound, the taxes were now being collected for the occupying, colonial power. So, anybody who collected for the Romans was a collaborator with the national enemy.

Furthermore, the system of taxation was so loose that the local collector had ample scope to line his own pockets to a considerable extent. To become a tax collector was tantamount to admitting that one had neither religious principles nor national pride: only the poli cy of looking after number one.

One can understand the decision to debar all tax collectors from the synagogue.

Matthew, the gift of God, was the very contradiction of his name.

Then, the moment of grace.

Jesus walked by and looked at Matthew. He saw a man involved in sinful ways but called by name to be a gift of God. And to this sinner he said, 'Follow me.'

The Pharisees stood outside because all they saw was the scandal, the contamination with sinners, the accusation.

What did Matthew himself see?

In that glance of Jesus he saw enough to leave his customs booth, his counting table and weighing scales. He saw enough to become a disciple. Later he heard his name called to become one of the twelve apostles. And as his road lengthened with the years he became one of the great sources of the Good News of Jesus for all time.

Matthew, by the grace of God, followed Jesus and became his name, a gift of God to others. And we who are happy to study the gospel that bears his name rejoice that Matthew becomes a gift of God to us.

Lord, as we spend our time with Matthew, your gift to us, let your face again shine on your servants, and save us in your love.

Eleventh Sunday

The appointment of the apostles serves as a lead-in to the second of the five great sermons on the kingdom which form the backbone of Matthew's gospel. The sermon on the mount was the grand picture of the ideal of life in the kingdom. This sermon is about the involvement of apostles in spreading the kingdom as labourers in a great harvest. The next two Sundays also will give us extracts from this apostolic sermon.

Matthew 9:36 – 10:8
He summoned his twelve disciples, and sent them out

When Jesus saw the crowds he felt sorry for them because they were harassed and dejected, like sheep without a shepherd. Then he said to his disciples, 'The harvest is rich but the labourers are few, so ask the Lord of the harvest to send labourers to his harvest.' He summoned his twelve disciples, and gave them authority over unclean spirits with power to cast them out and to cure all kinds of diseases and sickness.

These are the names of the twelve apostles: first, Simon who is called Peter, and his brother Andrew; James the son of Zebedee, and his brother John; Philip and Bartholomew; Thomas, and Matthew the tax collector; James the son of Alphaeus, and Thaddaeus; Simon the Zealot and Judas Iscariot, the one who was to betray him. These twelve Jesus sent out, instructing them as follows: 'Do not turn your steps to pagan territory, and do not enter any Samaritan town; go rather to the lost sheep of the House of Israel. And as you go, proclaim that the kingdom of heaven is close at hand. Cure the sick, raise the dead, cleanse the lepers, cast out devils. You received without charge, give without charge.'

Good News
Jesus felt sorry for the plight of the straying souls. In his compassion he commissioned apostles who would extend his own mission to wider horizons.

First Reflection
From Disciple to Apostle

Today's gospel extract is the lead-in to the second of the five great sermons on the kingdom. Preaching on the mountain height, Jesus had outlined his programme for living as members of God's kingdom upon earth. Those who received his word and acted

166

upon it would build on solid rock. They would be his disciples.
Now the time had come for the development from disciple
to apostle. A disciple is one who listens and learns and follows: an
apostle is one who is sent. Jesus called twelve of the disciples to be
apostles and he began to work at greater depth with them. The
pupils were being trained to become teachers. Those who had
received God's gift were asked now to share what they had received. In this way Jesus was gradually unfolding his plan of using
chosen disciples, the future church, as the means towards realis-
ing his ideal of the kingdom of heaven on earth.

Among the twelve chosen to be apostles was Matthew, the
tax collector. We met him in last Sunday's gospel. His calling is
the model of all apostles. It verifies the old saying that what God
wants to achieve in many people he first accomplishes in one.

Matthew, as a tax collector, had been numbered among the
sinners and religious outcasts. He was called to follow, to be a disciple. Now he is chosen to be an apostle, to be sent out to give to
others. He who used to take from people, now receives from God
and gives to people. He is true to his name, which means the gift
of God. Every apostle of the kingdom is a Matthew: a sinner who
receives a call from God to become a gift of God to others. 'As you
go, proclaim that the kingdom of heaven is close at hand. Cure the
sick, raise the dead, cleanse the lepers, cast out devils. You received without charge, give without charge.' By the grace of God,
every apostle brings to people the same gifts of instruction, healing and fulness of life that Jesus brought.

The motivating power behind the call of the apostles is the
compassion of Jesus for the lost sheep, who were harassed and
dejected, for they were left as sheep without a shepherd.

'He felt sorry for them.' This is a key sentence in the passage.
Matthew's gospel rarely mentions emotion, so now when he does,
it must be regarded as important.

The motivating power within the apostolate is care and concern for all whose way of life is far from the kingdom. The sinner
is not despised and kept away. Compassion sits to table with sinners and offers them every chance of entering the kingdom.

The strategy of Jesus was to work deeply with a small number even though he recognised that the harvest is vast and the
labourers few. He went for quality in depth rather than quantity in

167

numbers. And when he sent out the first apostles, their territory was confined to the lost sheep of Israel: not even to the neighbouring Samaritans. It was a strategy of immense pastoral patience.

One is reminded of the man who summed up his life's journey like this: When I was twenty I thought that all the world was wrong and needed conversion. When I was forty I thought that all the people around me had problems and should be converted. Now that I am seventy I understand that what God was really asking was that I would be converted.

Christian apostolate begins at home. Jesus began with a small number with whom he worked at greater depth. An apostle must first be a disciple: one who listens and learns: and who is then called by God to go out to the sinner in compassion of heart. 'You received without charge, give without charge.'

Second Reflection
The Apostles

Where could the Lord have found more unlikely candidates to front his new organisation? Their obvious limitations are the surest proof of the power of the Holy Spirit in the founding of the church. Such limited men could never have got any organisation off the ground by their own steam. Although little enough is said about the individual apostles, we can at least put together a small dossier on some of them. Simon, whose name was changed to Peter is the best known. His new name indicated that he was to be the rock as foundation of the structure.

Some rock! More like fickle sand with his quick temper and changing moods. So eager to be near the Lord that he would walk on water ... but conspicuously absent from Calvary. One moment the spokesman of great faith in Jesus and moments later the spokesman of Satan. Boastful of his loyalty to Jesus, but that same night swearing on oath that he never knew him.

The sons of Zebedee, James and John, were extreme characters. In Mark's list of the apostles we read that Jesus gave them the name Sons of Thunder, Boanerges. Something of that extreme streak emerged one day when they wanted to call down fire from heaven to burn up a town in Samaria which had been inhospitable. They must have inherited something of their mother's ambitious nature, for she approached Jesus about getting the two best jobs in the kingdom for her boys. Away from Jesus they would have been proud, ambitious, extreme characters. But in his healing presence their characters matured and their excesses became their virtues. James developed the extremes of courage needed to sustain him as the first of the apostles to face martyrdom. *(Acts 12:2)* John's extreme striving grew into the depth of contemplation on the mystery of the incarnation which was the source of the fourth gospel, which bears his name.

We have a soft spot for Thomas, doubting and pessimistic. When Jesus announced that he would face the opposition and travel to Bethany when Lazarus was ill, all Thomas could see was the inevitable death. Yet bravely he said, 'Let us go too, and die with him.' *(Jn 11:16)* What he is best remembered for is his difficulty in accepting the resurrection. 'Unless I see the holes that the nails made in his hands and can put my finger into the holes they made, and unless I can put my hand into his side, I refuse to believe.' *(Jn 20:25)* He is so important in the story, for if a Thomas could believe, then anybody could!

Then there was Simon known as a Zealot. Zealots were extreme nationalists who did not hesitate to resort to violence. As a young lad he would have daubed the walls with slogans such as 'Romans Out! Peace In!' The paint-brush of youth has prepared many hands for the sword or gun of later years. But in the vision of the new society outlined by Jesus, Simon the Zealot can live and work with Matthew, a tax collector who had collaborated with the Romans. In different circumstances Simon would have thought it his duty to eliminate Matthew.

Some of the apostles are virtually unknown to us apart from their names. But one of them, Judas, went out into the night and betrayed Jesus.

Actions speak louder than words. And certainly the action of Jesus in appointing these particular men as the front men of his kingdom speaks volumes of how he came as saviour and healer of the sinner. It is very reassuring that the foundation stones of the church were of such unlikely material. Surely it is the greatest proof of the presence and power of the Holy Spirit in the church. And after such a start, how can anybody ever be shocked if the human frailty and sinfulness of church leaders is apparent? Personally, I find it encouraging that at such a table of sinners there is room for me.

Twelfth Sunday

This is the second extract from the great apostolic sermon in Matthew. Jesus makes a threefold plea to the apostles not to be afraid in the face of opposition.

Today's first reading gives a clear instance of severe opposition experienced by the prophet Jeremiah.

Matthew 10:26-33
Do not be afraid of those who kill the body

Jesus instructed the Twelve as follows: 'Do not be afraid. For everything that is now covered will be uncovered, and everything now hidden will be made clear. What I say to you in the dark, tell in the daylight; what you hear in whispers, proclaim from the house-tops. Do not be afraid of those who kill the body but cannot kill the soul; fear him rather who can destroy both body and soul in hell. Can you not buy two sparrows for a penny? And yet not one falls to the ground without your Father knowing. Why, every hair on your head has been counted. So there is no need to be afraid; you are worth more than hundreds of sparrows.

'So if anyone declares himself for me in the presence of men, I will declare myself for him in the presence of my Father in heaven. But the one who disowns me in the presence of men, I will disown in the presence of my Father in heaven.'

Good News
Those who suffer rejection and persecution because of their witness to the gospel are very precious in the eyes of God. Jesus will testify in the heavenly court on behalf of those who witness to him on earth.

First Reflection
The Courage of an Apostle

I write in an Ireland that is rapidly changing. Not long ago it took courage of a sort not to take part in church practices here: to swim against the social tide which equated church-going with respectability. Increasingly, situations are arising where it now takes courage to witness to Christian beliefs and principles of behaviour. It takes moral courage to say the words which confront, correct and challenge. It is all too easy at times to disown one's moral responsibility by staying silent. But for evil to triumph all that is required is that the good people would say nothing.

It takes courage to express one's religious beliefs in the face of sophisticated agnosticism, yuppie materialism or the taunts that one is out of date. It is easy enough to witness or share a religious experience in the welcoming warmth of a prayer meeting, but to speak in the daylight or from the housetop is a very daunting challenge.

The words of St Paul to Timothy are even more relevant today than when he first wrote them: 'Proclaim the message and, welcome or unwelcome, insist on it. Refute falsehood, correct error, call to obedience – but do all with patience and the intention of teaching. The time is sure to come when, far from being content with solid teaching, people will be avid for the latest novelty and collect for themselves a whole series teachers according to their own tastes; and then instead of listening to the truth, they will turn to myths.' (2 Tim 4:1-4)

The witness of Christian action will raise a thousand situations calling for courage – to stand apart from wrong behaviour: to commit oneself to some cause or organisation or ministry, knowing that this will cost time and comfort: to visit a difficult relation or neighbour who will probably abuse you more than thank you: to work for peace and the preservation of the environment: to oppose political policies that are unjust or harm family stability or place monetaristic considerations above the welfare of people.

A time of change is a time of challenge. And a challenge will always make or break people. While many are falling away, others are discovering a new level of commitment because of the challenge. There is nothing like a challenge to draw out the potential of people. A priest from Poland gave this as the reason for the strength of the church in his country: 'We have the advantage of a visible enemy,' he said, 'while you have the disadvantage of an invisible one.'

In these days of challenge and criticism it is good to hear again how the Lord prepared the first apostles to face opposition. Three times in this short passage alone he encouraged them not to be afraid. 'Do not be afraid.' The phrase is repeated throughout the bible so often that it virtually corresponds to the number of days in the year.

Let us recap at this point the growth stages of the kingdom:

Those who listen to the teaching of Jesus and act on it are his disciples. Disciples then are sent out to share the message with others: they are called apostles. Now, as apostles, they are encouraged not to be afraid of the opposition which is inevitable. The pattern of growth remains true for us today ... to be disciples of Jesus ... to be apostles for Jesus ... to be courageous with Jesus.

Second Reflection
The Backlash

Opposition to the gospel is inevitable. So much so, that whenever the church experiences no opposition it is time to undertake a serious examination of conscience. Lack of opposition almost certainly indicates a church which has lost its nerve in proclaiming the gospel's radical reversal of worldly attitudes and actions.

Contradiction and opposition were certainly the lot of Jesus. Even in his earliest days he was announced to the nations by the old man Simeon as a sign of contradiction: destined for the rising and the fall of many: a sign to be rejected. As Jesus began to share his mission, he forewarned the first apostles that they too would have to face opposition, rejection and persecution. 'You will be hated by all men on account of my name.' *(Mt 10:22)* 'If they persecute me they will persecute you too.' *(Jn 15:10)* And in today's extract from the Lord's apostolic exhortation, three times he tells them not to be afraid. Three times, corresponding perhaps to the three sources of opposition – from within oneself, from the resistance of others and from the backlash of the evil spirit.

Opposition to the gospel challenge will come from our own darkness as we fear the discomfort, and dread the cost of commitment. We know what it is to lack the fundamental trust to let go of lesser securities and put all our hope in God.

But the Lord tells us not to be afraid. We are called to grow. To be pruned so as to bear fruit. And what is but a prayer whispered now in private will become a brave public proclamation, and what is shared only with friends will become a courageous witness from the housetops for all to hear and see.

Opposition will come, secondly, from outside oneself: from all whose sick eyes are hurt by the light of goodness. Those who do wrong hate the light and avoid it for fear their actions should be exposed. The light of Christ's teaching will uncover what is covered up, and will make clear what is hidden.

Goodness is a terrifying threat to those whose consciences are compromised with evil. They will reply in cynicism, scoffing, argumentation and eventually blind violence. Jesus himself was done to death by the conspiracy of fears and jealousies of those who had compromised themselves for religious power, political advancement or money. Once again, the exhortation of the Lord is not to be afraid. Those who torture the body, could they but realise it, are only making the determination of the spirit more firm. And those who kill the body have never learnt of the immortality of the spirit. For history shows that the blood of martyrs is the seed of Christians. And the courage of every witness who dies is a candle that will light a thou sand more.

The ultimate source of opposition to the gospel is the evil spirit. The advance of the kingdom of God will inevitably provoke a backlash from the deposed evil spirit whose lordship of lives has been usurped. 'For it is not against human enemies that we have to struggle, but against the Sovereignties and the Powers who originate the darkness in this world, the spiritual army of evil in the heavens.' *(Eph 6:12)*

One sees a satanic hatred on the faces of those who have totally sold their souls and principles. When people are trying to break out of addicition to alcohol or drugs, or seriously trying to deepen prayer life or follow a religious calling, they can expect severe opposition and temptation. The lives of certain saints appear to have been the battleground for souls snatched from the evil spirit. Heroic confessors like St John Mary Vianney, St Leopold Mandic and Padre Pio had to suffer severe physical assaults from the enraged despot of darkness. The Lord told the apostles to respect this enemy: 'Fear him rather who can destroy both body and soul in hell.' But however terrifying the backlash of evil may appear, we can trust in the greater power of the loving Father. Not a hair falls out, not a sparrow hops about, but the eye of the Father sees. And his heart cares.

Very precious in the eyes of the Father are those who suffer rejection and opposition because of their witness to the good news. 'Blessed are those who are persecuted in the cause of right: theirs is the kingdom of heaven.' *(Mt 5:10)*

Thirteenth Sunday

The apostolic sermon closes with a double message: Christian apostolate comes at a great cost to selfishness: but it will bring a great reward, not only to the messenger of good news, but to all who welcome the messenger.

In today's first reading, an episode from the career of Elisha illustrates the reward of fertility that comes to those who welcome the bearer of God's word.

Matthew 10:37-42

Anyone who does not accept his cross is not worthy of me. Anyone who welcomes you, welcomes me

Jesus instructed the Twelve as follows: "Anyone who prefers father or mother to me is not worthy of me. Anyone who prefers son or daughter to me is not worthy of me. Anyone who does not take his cross and follow in my footsteps is not worthy of me. Anyone who finds his life will lose it; anyone who loses his life for my sake will find it. Anyone who welcomes you welcomes me; and those who welcome me welcome the one who sent me. Anyone who welcomes a prophet because he is a prophet will have a prophet's reward; and anyone who welcomes a holy man because he is a holy man will have a holy man's reward.

"If anyone gives so much as a cup of cold water to one of these little ones because he is a disciple, then I tell you solemnly, he will most certainly not lose his reward."

Good News

Following Jesus Christ is a costly investment, but it brings the reward of finding the fulness of life.

First Reflection

A Costly Following

Beware of cheap religion! Beware of any version of religion that comes across as soft and easy, where the burning cost of receiving God's light is never mentioned, and where conscience is never challenged and disturbed. Cheap religion will wrap you around in the comforting warmth of God's love, but it will never tell you that the same fire of love must burn out and purge all the impure vestiges of selfishness. Purgatory, here and hereafter, has gone out of fashion.

We are strong today on comfortable religion. Go to the funeral of the greatest scoundrel in the parish and you are likely to hear a comforting panygeric in tones of pious waffle. We are so reluctant to cast judgment on anybody that the terrorist, who dies while attempting to kill people, will be accompanied to the grave with full ecclesiastical platitudes.

We will happily use the God-factor to our own advantage. But are we ready to be used by God? We will set the terms of religion to God. But will we come on his terms? A God who gives will be approached. But a God who demands is not wanted.

Again, it is the modern a la carte approach to religion. Self-denial, sacrifice and asceticism are not fashionable words on the modern menu. It takes some extraordinary phenomenon, like the experience at Medjugorje, to shock people back into the meaning of fasting or the need to make a deliberate option for the life of the spirit over the constant gratification of the body. Yet the gospel tells us clearly that anybody who is not prepared to make a painful option, or practise self-denial, or take up one's cross, is not worthy of the Christian name. The burning fire of God's love is also the Spirit of truth whose coming unmasks the amount of selfishness that can reside under cov er of our virtues.

Jesus took the example of something very precious ... family relationships. It is highly desirable that we should enjoy strong family ties. Yet if this becomes an obstacle to a higher calling one must be prepared to cut the tie. Too much mothering becomes smothering. Too much family togetherness becomes a suffocating atmosphere which will stifle freedom. What is good may be shown up as an obstacle to what is better.

Our contemporary cult of self-fulfilment makes this gospel message sound very strange. But the way to grow in life is in willingness to die constantly, just as the way to travel is by departing from wherever we are now. It is in losing one's life for Christ's sake that one finds it in greater fulfilment. We must let go in order to follow.

From the earliest days of the church, the cost of the Christian calling has been 'carrying the cross after Christ'. 'Anyone who does not take up his cross and follow in my footsteps is not worthy of me.' Any version of Christianity which overlooks the cost of the cross is bogus. It is not worthy of Christ.

Nobody has surpassed St Paul's expression of how the pattern of Christian life is the recurring rhythm of dying and rising with Christ: 'Always, wherever we may be, we carry with us in our body the death of Jesus, so that the life of Jesus too, may always be seen in our body.' *(2 Cor 4:10)* He had come to the realisation that the difficulties and buffetings of life are all part of the dying to self which to tal love of God demanded.

The call to follow Jesus Christ is a wonderful free gift of grace. But receiving this gift will be very costly to our self-centredness. Cheap Christianity is suspect.

Second Reflection
Welcoming the Word

The Lord's sermon to the apostles comes to a surprising conclusion. He has called them, motivated them, encouraged them in the face of opposition and told them clearly the cost of being an apostle. But now his final words are about the people who would welcome disciples because they were disciples. It's as if the Lord were saying, 'that's enough for the moment about you, apostles. Here's something for those who must listen to you.'

The passage affords us an opportunity to reflect on how we should welcome the word of God as it comes to us from reading or hearing the scriptures or through sermons which are drawn from the sacred words.

The first quality of welcoming the word is humility. We must humbly admit our ignorance and darkness. We recall that the risen Lord told the two dejected disciples on the Emmaus road that they were foolish. And then he explained the scriptures to them. Our minds hunger for the food of God's revelation which is found in the word. Our spirits thirst for the solace and comfort which made those Emmaus disciples feel their hearts burning within them as the Lord opened up the scriptures to them. Without the light and warmth of the sacred word our world is left in darkness and foolishness.

The second quality of welcoming is faith in the word. The words of sacred scripture are not to be approached as one might take up a newspaper or novel. This word is a precious gift of God to us. The Spirit, who helped the author of the text, will help us to read and hear it as a word that is alive and active, penetrating our lives, judging and challenging us on how we think and act. It is the living word of God for my life each day. Faith in the word as God's gift is expressed by our prayerful approach to it.

Always begin with a prayer to the Holy Spirit before reading the sacred word. It is a very good practice to pray for the preacher before we listen. The energy that we spend in criticising preachers might be better spent in praying for them! Pray that God's word for your life will come from his lips.

Reverence towards the word is shown in little gestures like kissing the page with love, having a respectable cover on the sacred book, and keeping it in a becoming place when not in use.

A third quality of welcome is being prepared to spend time with the text. If we receive a visitor to our home we know that we should sit down, relax and spend time ... like Mary at Bethany who chose the better part. We must sit with the word, listen to God through the text and respond to him, as in good conversation. It is better to take a short portion each day and spend time with it than to take a long reading in careless fashion. Read the text a second time or third until your heart is touched by a living word. Those who are called to the ministry of the word through preaching, teaching or reading, have received a noble calling. It is a ministry that should not be treated lightly.

The most basic preparation of a reader is to have the correct pronunciation of the words and a clear sense of the meaning of the passage. But any reader who believes in the sacredness of the text would never presume to read the word of God to others without first having prayed with it. The more time we spend in prayerfully welcoming the sacred word of God, the more we will be at home in the word. And if we are at home in it, a day without God's word would be a day in exile.

Here are two verses taken from hymns in the breviary, expressing a welcome to the word.

O God of truth, prepare our minds
To hear and heed your holy word;
Fill every heart that longs for you
With your mysterious presence, Lord.

In the Scriptures, by the Spirit,
May we see the Saviour's face,
Hear his word and heed his calling,
Know his will and grow in grace.

Fourteenth Sunday

*First we were given the great vision of the kingdom, then the apostles
were chosen and prepared, and now the third section of Matthew's gospel
is about the mounting opposition and hostility to his preaching.*

*Today's extract draws us into the inner heart of Jesus in the emerg-
ing situation. His heart rises up to bless the Father and reaches out in a
loving invitation to all to come to him and accept his way.*

Matthew 11:25-30
I am gentle and humble of heart

Jesus exclaimed: "I bless you, Father, Lord of heaven and of
earth, for hiding these things from the learned and the clever and
revealing them to mere children.

"Yes, Father, for that is what it pleased you to do. Everything has been entrusted to me by my Father, and no one knows
the Son except the Father, just as no one knows the Father except
the Son and those to whom the Son chooses to reveal him.

"Come to me, all you who labour and are overburdened,
and I will give you rest. Shoulder my yoke and learn from me, for
I am gentle and humble in heart, and you will find rest for your
souls. Yes, my yoke is easy and my burden light."

Good News
God is to be praised in all situations, hard as well as pleasant. When the cross is accepted as part of God's loving will it is no
longer a laborious burden too heavy to bear.

First Reflection
A Heart of Praise

The most precious moments in scripture are when we are
allowed to enter into the prayer of Jesus. It is like peeping through
a window into where he is at home with the Father.

'Master, where do you live?' they asked him once.

'Come and see.'

In this moment of prayer we see where his heart is at home
as his words rise up to bless the Father. Jesus, the Word made
flesh, continues to return everything to the Father.

'I bless you, Father, Lord of heaven and earth.'

Blessing is a twofold movement. First it is the movement of

178

God, source of all goodness, to us. The recipient then appreciates the gift and returns to God in thanks and praise: thanksgiving centres on the thought of gift but praise goes straight to the giver.

As the ministry of Jesus progressed he experienced rejection and opposition. He has just reproached the towns by the lake for their failure to repent. He must have felt disappointed, somewhat deflated and not a little angry. Yet, before his Father his prayer is still a blessing: he accepts the painful situation and praises the Father.

The psalms invite us to praise God at all times, to have his praise ever on our lips. Not only when things are going along pleasantly and favourably, but in the hard times too.

The example comes to mind of the saintly Capuchin from Detroit, Solanus Casey. He was deeply revered by the people and many have attributed great favours to his intercession. The policy of Father Solanus was to encourage people to thank God right in the middle of their trying situation. He so trusted in the goodness of God at all times that he would tell people to start praising God now, and not to wait until after a favour. His motto was, 'Thank God ahead of time.'

Psychologically our problems are often a heavier burden than they need be, because we do not fully and consciously accept the unpleasant situation. Healing therapy depends to a great extent on the person's ability to accept the situation through telling its full story.

Telling the story, confessing one's guilt, is of course an integral part of the sacrament of Reconciliation. Perhaps at times we have overemphasised this part of the sacrament to the neglect of other parts: too much emphasis on guilt tended to overshadow the grace of God. And then the sacrament becomes a terrible burden that is reluctantly faced. The wider sense of reconciliation sees the story of our sins in the context of the greater power of God's love and mercy. And real healing unto joy takes place when one discovers that God can still be praised even from the pits of guilt.

However great our guilt is, the love of God is still greater. So, blessed be God, for his love endures for ever.

What happens then is that one finds that the enslaving chains of sin fall off. We are amazed to see that there were no locks on these chains, only our own rigid hold, wrapping ourselves around with guilt and self-hatred for years. And when the chains fall off, the courage is found to be free from alcoholism or thieving, impure compulsions or irresponsibility. Martin Carothers wrote of his experience of discovering praise, in a book appropriately entitled, 'From Prison to Praise'.

Bless the Lord at all times.

As his ministry ran up against rejection and hostility, as the deflating experience of failure hit him, Jesus prayed: 'I bless you, Father, Lord of heaven and earth'.

His example invites us to praise God in defeat and darkness, in sin and sorrow, in fretting and fear.

Second Reflection
A Heart of Compassion

After rising up to the Father in praise, the heart of Jesus reaches out to all who are heavily burdened.

When Matthew related these words he intended a special appeal to the Jews who were burdened under the heavy yoke of the Jewish Law. As St Paul found in his own life, the law gave the sense of guilt but offered no way of relieving that burden. Only the Spirit of Jesus Christ gave him release. Matthew, in this most Jewish of the gospels, appealed to his fellow Jews to consider belief in Jesus Christ very seriously.

But the Law was not the only burden that comes into the scope of the invitation of Jesus to come to him. The gentle and humble heart of Jesus reaches out to people with any sort of burden.

He is gentle and will not crush the fragile reed.

He is humble and will not push away the little people.

Although Jesus did say that his followers must carry the cross after him (as in last Sunday's gospel), here he promises that his burden will be tolerable and not beyond our strength.

'Light and easy', he said.

While the body still has to carry the burden, yet the soul is at rest when one takes up the cross as a sharing in his cross.

This text on the gentle and humble heart of Jesus is at the centre of the traditional devotion to the love of Jesus Christ known as the Sacred Heart devotion. The words of the Lord open with an invitation: 'Come to me'. We can hear a threefold invitation in the Sacred Heart devotion.

The first invitation is to reflect more on the great love and compassion which Jesus showed all through the gospel: his love of the Father and his absolute obedience to the Father's will; and his love for us which brought him through the pains of the passion for us.

The second invitation is to make reparation for our failures to appreciate his love. This failure is expressed so poignantly in the words heard by St Margaret Mary: 'Behold this heart which has so loved people and is so little loved in return.'

We can make reparation by spending more time meditating on his love, by acts of sacrifice and self-denial, by repeated prayers and ejaculations.

The third invitation is to contemplate the final piercing of this heart from which poured out blood and water: blood of life and water of cleansing.

When our hearts are shattered with sorrow or pierced through by disappointment, then we are to look upon the one who is pierced. And we learn that even in our sorrow and loneliness we are not alone.

His pierced heart forever tells us that he is suffering with us.

His is a heart full of compassion.

He is gentle and humble of heart.

And it is in the contemplation of his heart that 'you shall find rest for your souls'.

Fifteenth Sunday

This is the first of three Sundays when we read from the third great sermon in Matthew. This sermon is a collection of parables about the kingdom. Three dominant themes recur throughout the sermon: the kingdom is growing; it involves a mixture of good and bad; and it is worth any cost.

For the weekly homilist this block of parables offers the opportunity to reflect on the mystery of the church at a time of opposition and hostility.

Matthew 13:1-9

A sower went out to sow

Jesus left the house and sat by the lakeside, but such crowds gathered round him that he got into a boat and sat there. The people all stood on the beach, and he told them many things in parables.

He said, "Imagine a sower going out to sow. As he sowed, some seeds fell on the edge of the path, and the birds came and ate them up. Others fell on patches of rock where they found little soil and sprang up straight away, because there was no depth of earth; but as soon as the sun came up they were scorched and, not having any roots, they withered away. Others fell among thorns, and the thorns grew up and choked them. Others fell on rich soil and produced their crop, some a hundredfold, some sixty, some thirty. Listen, anyone who has ears!"

Good News

Our experience shows that faith encounters many obstacles, but the word we have received is a divine seed which is destined to grow unto a great harvest.

First Reflection

Stories for a Hostile Climate (1)

A parable is a story for all times. It gives you just enough of its original setting to make you do your own thinking for your own time and situation. The gospel context here is the mounting opposition to the mission of Jesus. Opposition raises a barrage of questions. Jesus tells a story from everyday experience which offers space to get behind the questions. As we today reflect on the parable of the sower, we can distinguish three levels of time, each with its own set of ques tions.

182

a) On the level of what Jesus experienced, questions arise about why was he rejected. How did a mission of such obvious goodness run up against so much hostility? In spite of the signs and wonders he worked, why was his preaching campaign so unsuccessful? And the biggest question of all – how did the crucifixion come about?

b) On the level of the time when Matthew was writing, the questions which occupied his mind were, why have Christians been so despised and persecuted? How could some believers have fallen away from such a precious faith? Why was it that so few of the Jewish scribes recognised Jesus as the fulfilment of Old Testament texts? Many scholars think that the author of this gospel was himself a former scribe who converted to Christ. Indeed, this sermon of parables closes with a final appeal to the scribes: 'Well then, every scribe who becomes a disciple of the kingdom of heaven is like a householder who brings out from his storeroom things both new and old.' *(Mt 13:52)*

c) In our own day too there are questions which constantly recur. Why is there such a falling off in Church attendance? And in so far as one can discern, in faith? The ideals of the kingdom are very noble and attractive, but why have they so little influence in an increasingly secular, materialistic and promiscuous culture?

We believe that we have the supreme revelation of God in Jesus Christ, meant for the whole world. But two thousand years on, in spite of easy travel and the media of communication to reach people everywhere, how come that the message has not penetrated every part of the globe?

What is it that sparks off the raging cries of criticism on press, radio and television after the public statements of church leaders? How is it that some people become incoherent with rage at the very mention of church or religion?

Jesus offered the parable of the sower as an illustration of the differing reactions which are set off in the meeting of God's grace with human freedom.

Matthew takes up the story in the church of his experience. He reaches out to the Jewish scribes by quoting from Isaiah on the difference between believers and unbelievers. The believer, or disciple, is one who sees, hears and understands: and the more faith one has, the more one grows. 'Grace in return for grace', as St John phrased it. *(Jn 1:16)*

The unbeliever belongs to a nation whose heart 'has grown coarse'. Coarse living renders the spiritual ear less sensitive and leaves the eye blind. And while the believer increases in faith, the person who falls away from faith becomes extremely hostile.

'They have shut their eyes, for fear they should see with their eyes, hear with their ears, understand with their heart, and be converted and be healed by me.'

Matthew's experience of virulent opposition from the scribes throws light on the vehement outbursts of today's post-Christian scribes and radio/television pundits. 'There is nothing new under the sun,' remarked old Qoheleth. The damburst of negative energy that we see today is what Matthew witnessed, and it is exactly what Jesus experienced. The culpable rejection of grace sparks off the most illogical hatred ... witness the crucifixion.

But the good news is that, in spite of obstacles and hostility, the kingdom grows and the harvest is as sure as God's grace. The promise is clearly written in today's First Reading: 'The word that goes from my mouth does not return to me empty, without carrying out my will and succeeding in what it was sent to do.' There may be hostile soil in hard hearts, shallow minds and a culture that chokes spirituality, but the disciple of Jesus Christ hears the good news, sees the exciting, good things that are happening, and understands.

'Listen, anyone who has ears!'

Second Reflection
The Soil of my Soul

Parable comes from a Greek word which expressed the picture of parallel movements. Lay this storyline along the story of your own life and see if you are losing your direction. A parable is a story that makes you do your own thinking.

The parable of the sower and the different kinds of soil invites one into a self-examination about 'what kind of soil do I present to the seeds of the Kingdom?'

Guides to the Holy Land point out a little horseshoe bay as the place where Jesus got into the boat and taught the people on the shore. One can easily picture him pointing to the farmer on the upland field scattering the seed with generous abandon.

A first batch of seed fell on a pathway. After the previous

year's harvesting, people would walk through the field and some well-trodden paths would be quite hard. Remember that in the Palestinian agriculture of that period, the seed was scattered before the ground was ploughed. By the time the plough arrived to open up the soil, birds had stolen the seeds from the well-trodden paths.

The picture of the well-trodden path suggests the life which is hardened now under well-trodden routine. All freshness and vitality have been snatched away. A dreadful fog of mediocrity has descended. Nominally we may be dedicated to some religious body and we may be surrounded by proven practices of religion, but mediocrity will squeeze out the life-blood and sap from our lives. We might dutifully recite ten psalms each day and never experience a word of prayer there.

We can 'say Mass' (what a horrible expression!) or attend Mass every day but never celebrate the Eucharist.

We might confess our sins in number and detail without ever celebrating the work of reconciliation.

We read and hear the gospel until we virtually know it by heart, but has it the power of the living word of God in our lives – incisive, challenging, consoling or uplifting our lives each day? When mediocrity leads us down the well-trodden path, then we are numbered among those who believe with their lips but their hearts are far away.

The comfortable lifestyle of our age breeds mediocrity. T.S.Eliot made this observation some fifty years ago in 'Choruses from The Rock':

'Our age is an age of moderate virtue
And of moderate vice
When men will not lay down the Cross
Because they will never assume it.'

What the mediocre life needs is a thorough ploughing up to make it receptive to the seeds of the kingdom.

Some of the soil, which received the seed, looked good on the surface, but there were stones immediately underneath. It promised well but proved shallow. We make resolutions and begin well, but once the cost of commitment is called for, our enthusiasm begins to wane. It is the price of saying 'yes', of making a weekly commitment, of giving time to a person or a project, of digging deeper into our resources of generosity or stamina.

In some people the stone that blocks the root is a hard lump of unforgiveness in the heart. It is not easy nor pleasant to recognise the grudges and grievances that we have held on to under years of self-justification.

What happens when the roots hit such a rock? Perhaps we do nothing, just opt out and let the momentum die. Or we dig up these hard rocks so that the next sowing will be in fertile ground.

In between doing nothing and the removal of the rock is a compromise policy: we apply a little water regularly, enough to help the plant to survive. But will it be strong enough to bear fruit? It is the policy of personal survival and you meet it in all sorts of minimum versions of Christianity. Duty is done, but where is the growing, blossoming, fruitful life?

You will find the world's most comfortable bachelors ensconced in some presbyteries: and the most self-sufficient survivors in some convents. Lives that promised well but proved shallow.

And then there are the thorns that choke the growth: the worries of this world and the lure of riches. The Lord comes knocking on our door and we cannot let him in. The sign says 'House Full'. There is no space left because we are preoccupied. The fascination of material things, the temptations of the flesh, or the curiosities of meaningless pursuits divert the energies of the mind from God. We allow ourselves be diverted from the kingdom of heaven on earth. It is not the central pursuit of our lives. We are being choked.

Lay your life along the line of the story. There is no limit to what might emerge in our thinking. A parable is a spring that never dries up, a story that never dies.

Sixteenth Sunday

We continue today with the parable sermon in which Matthew reflects on the opposition which grew against Jesus and which mounted up against the church of his own time. We are invited to draw light from the wisdom of scripture for our own experience of opposition today.

Matthew 13:24-43
Let them both grow together until the harvest

Jesus put a parable before the crowds, "The kingdom of heaven may be compared to a man who sowed good seed in his field. While everybody was asleep his enemy came, sowed darnel all among the wheat, and made off.

"When the new wheat sprouted and ripened, the darnel appeared as well. The owner's servants went to him and said, 'Sir, was it not good seed that you sowed in your field? If so, where does the darnel come from?' 'Some enemy has done this,' he answered. And the servants said, 'Do you want us to go and weed it out?' But he said, 'No, because when you weed out the darnel you might pull up the wheat with it. Let them both grow till the harvest, and at harvest time I shall say to the reapers: First collect the darnel and tie it in bundles to be burned, then gather the wheat into my barn.'"

He put another parable before them, "The kingdom of heaven is like a mustard seed which a man took and sowed in his field. It is the smallest of all the seeds, but when it has grown it is the biggest shrub of all and becomes a tree so that the birds of the air come and shelter in its branches."

He told them another parable, "The kingdom of heaven is like the yeast a woman took and mixed in with three measures of flour till it was leavened all through."

In all this Jesus spoke to the crowds in parables. This was to fulfill the prophecy: I will speak to you in parables and expound things hidden since the foundation of the world.

Then, leaving the crowds, he went to the house; and his disciples came to him and said, "Explain the parable about the darnel in the field to us." He said in reply, "The sower of the good seed is the Son of Man. The field is the world; the good seed is the subjects of the kingdom; the darnel, the subjects of the evil one; the enemy who sowed them, the devil; the harvest is the end of the world; the reapers are the angels. Well then, just as the darnel is gathered up and burnt in the fire, so it will be at the end of time. The Son of Man will send his angels and they will gather out of his kingdom all things that provoke offences and all who do evil, and throw them into the blazing furnace, where there will be weeping and grinding of teeth. Then the virtuous will shine like the sun in the kingdom of their Father. Listen, anyone who has ears!"'

Good News
There may be darnel in the wheat-field; the mustard seed may look very small; and the yeast may be hidden; but the good news is that the kingdom is among us and is growing and advancing. Would that our faith had the eyes to see and the ears to hear the power of God working among us.

First Reflection
Stories for a Hostile Climate (2)
We ought to welcome opposition and criticism.

Any fool will listen to the flattery of his friends, but the wise will heed the criticism of their enemies. As Benjamin Franklin put it: 'Love your enemies for they tell you your faults.' In the history of the church, the times of changing culture and intense opposition produced the greatest of the saints.

Many of the critics of the church today are sincere, idealistic and sensitive people. One may consider the intensity of an outburst to be illogical, or a criticism to be unbalanced and blind to that 90% of the church's work which is admirable in its outreach of caring, educating, healing and uplifting. But we need the critics to continue saying that the other 10% is not satisfactory. There is darnel in the wheat-field and it is important to know it.

The church is a mysterious mixture of divine and human, of grace and free will, of divine seed and human soil. Nobody has the right to expect a field of perfect wheat, a church of total perfection.

Every member of the church on earth harbours the roots of seven varieties of darnel – pride, greed, lust, envy, anger, gluttony and sloth. Unfortunately, there may be more weeds than wheat to be seen in a particular field of the church. We have suffered more than our share of idiotic ecclesiastical pomposity, excessive concentration on money, negative anger in preachers who condemn but do not proclaim, downright laziness and minds that refuse to grow up.

In the parable of the darnel the qualities of God which emerge are patience and wonderful tolerance. Today's beautiful lesson from Wisdom makes the point that God's great lenience and mildness of judgment only prove his strength and sovereignty. However, the patience and tolerance of God must not be taken as a permission to disregard the darnel or turn a blind eye to our faults.

One great lover of the church who always tried to see the wheat rather than the weeds, the potential for growth rather than the possible hazards, was Pope John XXIII. Before his election to the papacy, in his days as Patriarch of Venice, one of his priests was the subject of rumours and complaints. The poor man arrived home one evening to find his bishop waiting in the presbytery. But Cardinal Roncalli did not question the man about the rumours, much less did he launch into an attack. He humbly knelt at the feet of the priest saying, 'Father, would you please hear my confession.'

It was like St Paul reminding his disciple Timothy: 'Fan into flame the gift that God gave you when I laid my hands on you.'

The power and love of God are in the church ... even if there are situations where it is as tiny as the mustard seed and as hidden as the yeast. In these changing times our inherited values, family rules, social practices, fashions of dress and modes of behaviour are under question. It causes great distress to parents when their children reject the familiar practices of religion and regular church attendance. Yet it is important to remember that many of these practices belong to a style of catholicism which is less than a hundred years old.

I have often looked at my garden beds under a green patina of weeds and wondered if the seeds I planted would ever emerge.

As we look for the signs of wheat among the darnel, two practical strategies are emerging.

The first policy is to pick up the traces of the Spirit within the prevalent criticism. Rather than condemn the critics out of hand, be humble enough to consider whether the Spirit is speaking through them ... just as David spared the man called Shimei, who was cursing him and throwing stones at him, because it was Yahweh, perhaps, who was using him.

Might not the Spirit be speaking through:

- the angry voice of social conscience which is critical of the church energy that supports privatised spirituality:

- the repeated word 'boredom' which criticises the absence of religious experience from liturgy:

- the angry attacks on a legalistic system which makes sympathy and understanding very difficult:

- the sadness of intelligent people spoken to like infants?

The second pastoral strategy is to work at a more intense level with small groups. Today's gospel has a verse which the scholars regard as the pivotal moment in Matthew's story: Jesus left the crowds and worked with the small group of disciples. His strategy was to work with the small group for the sake of the wider audience.

Put it this way. If there were ten dedicated communists or ten dedicated terrorists in a town, wouldn't you be alarmed? How would you feel if there were ten dedicated christians, fully committed to the three legs of Christian life, study, action and prayer?

The mustard seed is tiny; the yeast is hidden in the flour.

Just wait and see what happens.

Second Reflection
That Darned Darnel

The Greek word for darnel which Matthew used has a suggestive ring to it: *zizania*. I picture a weed with a zig-zag, binding root system. Pull it up and you will do more harm than good to your young seedlings. And those binding weeds have an amazing resillience. One tiny inch of root system left in the earth, and off it grows again. Would that the plants you want to grow had such resilience!

The perfectionist in us is driven crazy at the sight of a weed. The utter perfectionist had better avoid all gardens ... just settle for some plastic flowers in the corner.

In a sense, there is no such thing as a weed. Many of the weeds we attack with zest in the garden are the wild flowers we admire in the forest, thumbing our way through our nature-guide to find its fancy name. There are no weeds in the garden, only flowers in the wrong place.

I remember my precious vegetable garden in Carlow. Precious at least to me, for the hour I spent there most days helped my sanity (though some might disagree). One spring I planted some French Golden Marigold seeds. We had a splendid border of golden light all summer. When other flowers died, the marigolds stayed faithfully at their posts. Even into the depths of winter. I hadn't the heart to dig them up or cut them back. They popped out seeds which sprouted new marigolds. No, they catapulted seeds to the far corners of the garden.

Like Patrick Kavanagh on Raglan Road, my undoing was that 'I loved too much.' It broke my heart to lift any seedlings. And after four years, no matter what I planted – cabbage, lettuce, turnips – there would be the smiling golden faces among them. All in the wrong places, but I still could not hate them. A garden can be a fertile nursery of wisdom. I have noticed that most of our problems in life are to do with energies which are in the wrong place or are coming up negatively. If we are burdened with an exaggerated expectation of perfection, then we are in trouble.

How many of us really hate part of ourselves!

We are plagued with 'bad' thoughts, forgetting that when God fashioned the human body, he stood back that evening, rubbed his hands in satisfaction and said, 'It is very good.'

Our prayer is destroyed by distractions. Yet these flying thoughts may well be the cries of our suppressed selves which God wants us to listen to that we might nurture a more balanced growth.

Many people hate themselves because they are so far from perfection and they give up the struggle out of sheer desperation. Life is then a matter of quiet hopelessness. The soul never knows the joy of believing and never feels the need to leap beyond self to praise God or to join with others to celebrate God.

There are no weeds, only wild flowers in the wrong place.

Treat your wild energies, not with hatred, but with love and respect. I am not saying to love them too much ... like my marigolds. But with God's grace they can be admired in their rightful place and controlled in the inappropriate situation.

Blessed be God, the master who lets the darnel with the wheat until harvest time.

Blessed be God who loves the crazy shapes that make an interesting landscape and brightens the world in a patchwork of colours.

Blessed be God who enriches us in a complex mixture of light and shadow, energy and rest, aloneness and sociability, matter and spirit, mind and body, laughter and tears, growing and dying.

"Glory be to God for dappled things," wrote Hopkins ...
"All things counter, original, spare, strange;
Whatever is fickle, freckled (who knows how?)
With swift, slow; sweet, sour; adazzle, dim;
He fathers-forth whose beauty is past change:
Praise him." (*Hopkins: Pied Beauty*)

Seventeenth Sunday

Today we conclude the parable sermon of Jesus. The treasure in the field and the pearl of great price illustrate the value of the kingdom, which is worth every penny of sweat and sacrifice. The dragnet is a picture of the mixture of talents and faults, virtues and vices, within each individual, as well as in the community of the church and the whole world.

Finally there is a piece about the scribe who becomes a disciple of the kingdom. He has access to the wisdom of old and new. Some scholars suggest that Matthew the evangelist may have been a Jewish scribe who entered the new way of Christianity.

Matthew 13:44-52
He sells everything he owns, and buys the field

Jesus said to the crowds: "The kingdom of heaven is like treasure hidden in a field which someone has found; he hides it again, goes off happy, sells everything he owns and buys the field.

"Again, the kingdom of heaven is like a merchant looking for fine pearls; when he finds one of great value he goes and sells everything he owns and buys it.

"Again, the kingdom of heaven is like a dragnet cast into the sea that brings in a haul of all kinds. When it is full, the fishermen haul it ashore; then, sitting down, they collect the good ones in a basket and throw away those that are no use. This is how it will be at the end of time: the angels will appear and separate the wicked from the just to throw them into the blazing furnace where there will be weeping and grinding of teeth.

"Have you understood all this?" They said, "Yes." And he said to them, "Well then, every scribe who becomes a disciple of the kingdom of heaven is like a householder who brings out from his storeroom things both new and old."

Good News

God alone is the treasure to satisfy the heart's deepest yearning. Happy are those who discover this treasure and are willing to pay the full price demanded.

First Reflection
Stories for a Hostile Climate (3)

Matthew constructed this sermon of the seven parables to throw light on the mystery of the opposition to Jesus which was growing by the day. In this chapter he had a powerful message for the church of his time. By inviting his readers to reflect on the hostility which Jesus had experienced, they might understand the hostility and mixture of good and bad which was their own daily experience.

We have attempted to understand today's hostile climate and the prevalent criticism of the church in the light of these parables. The parables of the treasure and the pearl ought to raise up our hearts in joy as we think of all that has been given to us in faith: the support of the sacraments, the good example of others and the many reminders of God's love and care for us. It is exhilarating to be raised up but our feet are immediately planted on solid ground as the parable of the dragnet reminds us of the mixum-gatherum people who serve God's kingdom here on earth.

The word to describe a net which brings in a haul of all kinds is 'catholic'.

The time of separation of good from bad is not yet, for the boat is still at sea. While storms of criticism are blowing and our boat is full of all kinds, what is most needed now is balance. Balance is exactly what Solomon prayed for (today's First Reading) ... wisdom of heart ... knowing how to discern between good and evil. Wisdom has been described by the Franciscan preacher, Richard Rohr, as the ability to hold opposites together in balance.

What I love about the church which calls itself catholic is the great wisdom which has maintained the balance between port and starboard, left wing and right wing, progressive and conservative, first world, second world and third world.

In one sense the church is not of this world and great souls have been inspired to withdraw from the bustle of the city into desert, monastery or convent. Yet this same church is the salt of society and the light of minds, educating, advancing the sciences, mothering the arts, pioneering hospitals and every sort of caring service. (Even the unworldly sons of St Francis have invented reading spectacles, set up the first credit unions to counteract usury and manned the first civic fire brigade!)

This unworldly church is full of understanding and compassion to the sinner. A letter on the sacredness of human life condemns all that is contra-the-inception of life: yet it pleads for a compassionate understanding of the pressures and fears and difficulties which couples must face. The ideal of monogamy and faithful love is upheld: yet the church will be deeply involved in support for deserted spouses and in care for the victims of AIDS. Even those who suffer because they did not follow the church's code will find that same church now supporting them in their need. Like a mother who warns the child of danger and is the first to pick up the child who did not heed the warning. The church preaches perfection but makes an industry out of imperfection.

It deals with the realms of faith beyond reason, yet it asks its priests to be trained in the laws of logic and the principles of reasoning. It fears the body and its appetites, yet it regards the body as the sacred temple of the Holy Spirit.

The church does not have the option of being conservative or progressive. It conserves its vitality only by responding progressively to the new needs of the changing situations. Yet it makes progress only when it conserves what is true and good and beautiful in its tradition. The disciple of the kingdom 'brings out from his storeroom things both new and old.'

In a catholic church I find there is room for all my own contradictions and contrary tensions. I can be at home here with my elements of body and spirit, virtue and vice, laughter and tears, rest and activity, growing and dying. It is a pearl beyond price: yet it is a dragnet with a vastly varied assortment of members.

Second Reflection
The Treasure in the Heart

God devised a secret treasure for people and he gave it to the angels to bring it to earth, instructing them to hide it, so that people would have to search for it and might have the joy of finding it. 'Shall we hide it on the highest mountains', asked the angels. 'No,' answered God, 'because only the fittest and healthiest could climb that mountain and the weak would have no chance.' 'Shall we put it on the furthest shores of the ocean?' 'No,' answered God, 'because only the rich people could afford to travel so far and the poor would have no chance.' 'Where shall we put it then?' 'Put it within reach of everybody, rich or poor, healthy or weak. Plant it in the centre of their beings. Hide it in their hearts.'

Let us return to Solomon in today's First Reading *(1 Kgs 3: 5-12):* 'Solomon, as your greatest wish, do you want health and wealth for yourself?' 'No, Lord.' 'Solomon, as your greatest wish, do you want power over your enemies?' 'No, Lord.' again. 'Solomon, as your greatest wish, what do you ask for?' 'Give me, Lord, a discerning heart.'

The strength of a good king is within the heart ... for the kingdom is within us. But if the heart's centre no longer holds, then all falls apart. Our lives at certain times of crisis threaten to fall apart. Then our successes appear empty, our achievements are hollow and the very meaning of life that we once served wholeheartedly is now severely questioned. When the outer walls are crumbling it is a sure sign that it is time to start searching for the cause within. If the church should listen to the cries of its critics, so too must each individual befriend the disturbing voices that come from the well of the heart ... through dreams, feelings of dissatisfaction, blanket anxiety, blind compulsions and fundamental self-questioning.

It is tempting to run from the questions by moving into the faster lane of life and plunge into more diversionary behaviour. Or do we stay with the painful cry and pay the price for the field?

For many people this is their annual holiday time. The kind of holiday one prefers will indicate a quest for more diversion or the opportunity for reflection. Diversion will paper the cracks; the work of reflection seeks the causes which may be deeply buried within.

The two parables of the treasure and the pearl differ in one circumstance. The treasure is something that is uncovered quite by accident: whereas the pearl is found after deliberate pursuit and searching. Whichever way it comes to light, one must sell out everything to lay hands on it as one's own. We have several times learnt from Matthew that there is no cheap grace ... even when it comes free!

Psychologists use terms like the journey to integration or the task of individuation. Mystical writers used the imagery of climbing mountains or moving from the outer courts into the centre of the castle. We are called to grow and asked to pay the price.

But the treasure is worth any price.

And the pearl at the centre of the heart is beautiful beyond words. For its beauty is nothing less than the reflection of God within me. That is the secret treasure hidden by the angels.

And if we discover that divine beauty within ourselves, the price will not be noticed.

Eighteenth Sunday

From today until the twenty-fourth Sunday, seven weeks, our readings will be from the fourth section of Matthew. Jesus has left the crowds and his attention is focussed on the smaller group of disciples. The more intensive formation which the disciples receive prepares them to be the foundations of the church. And it is the church which will be the powerhouse of the kingdom in the world.

The kingdom is the ideal: the church is the means towards that ideal.

A homilist who seeks a thematic plan of sermons might use these seven Sundays to reflect on qualities of being a disciple of Jesus Christ, or aspects of faith for today's Christian.

Matthew 14:13-21
They all ate and were satisfied

When Jesus received the news of John the Baptist's death he withdrew by boat to a lonely place where they could be by themselves. But the people heard of this and, leaving the towns, went after him on foot. So as he stepped ashore he saw a large crowd, and he took pity on them and healed their sick.

When evening came, the disciples went to him and said, "This is a lonely place, and the time has slipped by; so send the people away, and they can go to the villages to buy themselves some food." Jesus replied, "There is no need for them to go: give them something to eat yourselves." But they answered, "All we have with us is five loaves and two fish." "Bring them here to me," he said.

He gave orders that the people were to sit down on the grass; then he took the five loaves and the two fish, raised his eyes to heaven and said the blessing. And breaking the loaves he handed them to his disciples who gave them to the crowds.

They all ate as much as they wanted, and they collected the scraps remaining, twelve baskets full. Those who ate numbered about five thousand men, to say nothing of women and children.

Good News

Even in the empty places and hungry experiences of life God sees us and has compassion on us. He feeds us with bread from heaven and asks us to share it with others.

First Reflection
A Miracle of Compassion

What exactly happened that day when so many thousand were fed with five loaves and two fish?

Trying to visualise it is puzzling. Was there, one moment, this little basket of bread and fish and then, suddenly, a veritable mountain of food for the disciples to draw from? Or was it one by one, as each loaf was lifted another took its place in the basket?

It takes a long time to feed five thousand men ... and women ... and children.

Some commentators suggest that the miracle was not so much on the loaves and fishes but on the hearts of the people. While there is no proper basis for this interpretation, at least it lets our imagina tion build up a story about the miracle.

'Give them something to eat yourselves,' said Jesus to the disciples.

'But,' they said (forgetting that Jesus never liked 'but', for it is an excuse word) ... 'But all we have is our own little basket with five loaves and two fish.'

'Haven't I told you to sell out everything to buy the treasure in your heart? And don't you remember the proverb, "He who gave us teeth will also give us bread." So now, give them something to eat yourselves.'

So the disciples bravely broke up the loaves and cut the fish into little sections and gave a little tit-bit to ... well, some say that as many as forty people got a bit. Not much, but tasty. And then the miracle happened. People were ashamed at their own selfishness when they saw the disciples give away all that they had. And before you knew it, there were packets of sandwiches and boxes and baskets appearing from deep pockets and hoods (like Capuchins') and goodness-knows-where. And satchels of water and fruit-juice, goat's milk and wine.

Everybody was fed and the twelve, who gave away all they had, got back a full basket each. And all who saw what happened that day knew that the smile of God is kind and full of compassion.

'Listen, listen to me and you will have good things to eat and rich food to enjoy.' *(First Reading, Is 55:2)*

At the beginning of the story Matthew tells us that Jesus

took pity on the people. He had compassion on them. Matthew, unlike Luke, rarely mentions emotional life, the language of the heart. There are only three other places where he mentions compassion. When he does mention an emotion it must be significant.

Compassion means that he stood alongside each person, he felt in their feeling, he hungered in their hungering. He could share the pain of others because he had been schooled in suffering. He was just then feeling the pain of John the Baptist's callous death.

Compassion has an identical twin called concern. At least they look the same when you first meet them, but as you get to know them they are different in character. Concern is the cold voice of the logical brain whereas compassion is the warm language of heart and gut. Concern says, 'Send the people away.' Compassion says, 'There is no need for them to go.' Concern takes up causes whereas compassion picks up people. Concern speaks at a safe distance through a microphone or letters to the editor and advocates the need for population control, contraception and abortion. Compassion is at work in the midst of the pain, nursing, feeding, supporting the broken-hearted, befriending the lonely.

Jesus had compassion on the crowd and he healed their sick. And then, when he challenged his disciples to share the hunger of the people, a miracle of compassion took place.

People ask how can God allow such hunger in the world and such inhumane conditions of life.

It will take a huge miracle to feed everybody. The name of the miracle is compassion ... the miracle which changes words of concern into deeds of compassion. Then the monies spent on destructive weapons will be spent on constructive projects. The technology which can reach the moon and beyond it, will stay at home to work for the families who have no food or shelter. What is spent daily on patrolling borders will go towards eliminating barriers.

There is wisdom in the story of the man who prayed in anger to God. 'Why do you allow all this hunger, Lord, if you are kind and full of compassion? When are you going to do something about it?' And because his anger in prayer was sincere and full of concern, God answered him: 'But I am doing something. Didn't I send you?'

Do not send them away... give them something to eat yourselves. And if even twelve people have compassion, a huge miracle can take place.

Second Reflection
The Christian Disciple (1)

A Christian disciple is one who has been deeply nourished in mind and heart by the Lord, and who is charged with the responsibility of sharing this light and compassion with others.

The first group of disciples were deeply involved at every stage of the miraculous feeding of the multitude. Initially, it was their concern for the plight of the people that raised the problem. Then Jesus challenged them to share ... to move from concern to compassion. They were involved in distributing the food and in gathering up the scraps remaining.

The miracle of the loaves and fishes is told in the style of the eucharistic liturgy. The great actions of the Eucharist are seen as Jesus took the elements of food, raised his eyes to heaven in the return movement of blessing, broke the loaves and gave them to the disciples to distribute. The Eucharist is the central source of discipleship. Out of God's compassion and generosity the disciple is nourished in mind and in heart.

The liturgy features two tables: the table of the word to nourish the Christian mind; and the table of the bread to nourish the Christian heart. With the light of Christ in their minds and the love of Christ in their hearts, disciples are sent from the altar to love and serve the Lord everywhere. The celebration in church would be empty if the love of God which is experienced there is not carried out into the streets beyond the chapel door.

The word communion is not about union with God in a cosy devotion. The root of the word is 'munus', the Latin word for the load of responsibility. The disciple who enjoys intimacy with the Lord in the bread of life is charged with the responsibility of sharing and distributing God's love and compassion to others.

'Give them something to eat yourselves.'

The words of the Lord ring down through the ages. St John Chrysostom, a great preacher in the fourth century, challenged his audience on their eucharistic responsibility.

'Would you venerate the Body of Christ? Then do not start by despising it when it is naked. Do not honour it in the church in vestments of silk, only to ignore it outside where it is suffering, naked in the cold. For the one who said 'This is my Body' is also the one who said 'You saw me hungry and did not feed me.' What is the use of loading Christ's table with golden vessels while he is dying of hun ger? Satisfy the starving first; then enrich his table.

'Would you offer him a cup of gold while refusing him a cup of water? Take care lest, in adorning his table, you despise your afflicted brother; for the latter temple is more precious than the former ... Your altar is made up of the members of Christ's Body ... You can contemplate this altar everywhere, in the streets and in the squares, and all day long you can celebrate your liturgy.'

Liturgy is the great act of remembering Jesus Christ. But if we remember Jesus in the mind, we must also re-member him with our hearts, our hands, our mission of compassion to others.

Lord Jesus, I give you my hands to do your work,
I give you my feet to go your way
I give you my eyes to see as you do.
I give you my ears to hear you,
I give you my tongue to speak your words.
I give you my mind that you may pray in me
And above all I give you my heart that through me
You may love your Father and all mankind.

Nineteenth Sunday

Today's gospel is our second story from that section where Matthew concentrates on the preparation of the disciples to be the foundation of the church.

The disciples on the lake, like Elijah on the mountain (1st Reading), encountered the Lord after a terrifying storm and they experienced an awesome sense of adoration.

Matthew 14:22-33
Command me to come to you over the water

Jesus made the disciples get into the boat and go on ahead to the other side while he would send the crowds away. After sending the crowds away he went up into the hills by himself to pray.

When evening came, he was there alone, while the boat, by now far out on the lake, was battling with a heavy sea, for there was a headwind. In the fourth watch of the night he went towards them, walking on the lake, and when the disciples saw him walking on the lake they were terrified. "It is a ghost," they said, and cried out in fear. But at once Jesus called out to them saying, "Courage! It is I! Do not be afraid." It was Peter who answered. "Lord," he said, "if it is you, tell me to come to you across the water." "Come," said Jesus. Then Peter got out of the boat and started walking toward Jesus across the water, but as soon as he felt the force of the wind, he took fright and began to sink. "Lord! Save me!" he cried. Jesus put out his hand at once and held him. "Man of little faith," he said, "why did you doubt?"

And as they got into the boat the wind dropped. The men in the boat bowed down before him and said, "Truly, you are the Son of God."

Good News
The Lord, ascended on high, keeps watch over the church's boat throughout the storms. His message is always one of courage. And our experience of terror can open us up to a greater sense of God.

First Reflection
Developing Faith

This story of the boat in the storm leads to an awesome sense of the nearness of God. Peter calls Jesus 'Lord' and the men in the boat bowed down before him and said, 'Truly, you are the Son of God.' It is a story of faith that develops unto adoration. If you have ever experienced the need to cast yourself down in adoration of God, you have been blessed with a very precious divine encounter.

The gospels are based on the experiences of people in their encounters with God in Jesus Christ, the Word made flesh. These experiences were treasured in memory and retold. The growing Christian community remembered and recalled these experiences for their own edification and strengthening. Matthew has brilliantly reconstructed the memory of the boat in the storm as an instruction for his contemporaries on how faith can develop through the storms of life.

Where is Jesus now? According to the story he is gone up the hills to pray. This is the second of five mountains in Matthew. It is the mountain of prayer and sets the context for a deep experience of God's greatness and nearness. The mountain of prayer anticipates the ascension of the glorified Lord. He is no longer here to be physically seen, or heard, or touched, but his care for the flock is unceasing, for in heaven he is 'living for ever to intercede for all who come to God through him.' *(Heb 7:25)*

The boat of the disciples is surely the church caught in the teeth of a particularly violent storm. It is night-time: for the journey of the church is by the dim light of faith. No longer have they the physical, tangible nearness of Jesus. They are just learning that his care extends through the night. They are to trust that the glorified Lord will come again, though not until the final watch of the night. Until then we chart our course by faith.

Faith is a mysterious balance of light and darkness, the mixture of the absence of God and his presence. The believer steps out into the darkness beyond the light of reasoning and scientific proof. God is not known in the same way that we know one another through contact by the outer senses. We are peering through the night.

St Paul compared it to the imperfect reflection shown in the dull, plate-metal mirror of his day: 'Now we are seeing a dim reflection in a mirror; but then we shall be seeing face to face. The knowledge that I have now is imperfect.' *(1 Cor 13:12)*

The disciples did have faith, but it was still only little faith, baby faith which would have to grow. Peter emerges as their

203

spokesman. He has faith enough to venture beyond what is sensible. He walked on water. But he did not have faith enough to persevere in the face of wind and mounting waves. 'Man of little faith, why did you doubt?' Grown-up faith faces the problems and still does not doubt. It may be very unclear (for it peers through the darkness), but it does not doubt. Its strength comes from hearing the Word: 'Courage! It is I! Do not be afraid.'

The mature believer has this immovable foundation that God is, and God cares for us, and God is watching us through the night and through the storm. The storm can be good for deepening our faith.

In the story of Elijah on the mountain 'the Lord himself went by.' God was there all the time but Elijah did not experience him in the great storm, nor in the earthquake, nor the fire. It was only after these times of terror that Elijah experienced the presence of God in the gentle breeze. He stood in awe at the entrance to his cave and covered his face.

Similarly, with the disciples in the boat, it was when the storm subsided that they bowed down and said: 'Truly, you are the Son of God.' It took the storm which showed up their own helplessness to reveal the greatness of Jesus to them. Their humiliation prepared them for adoration. The story is about the little faith which can grow and become adoration.

Second Reflection
The Christian Disciple (2)

The disciple of Jesus Christ is someone who has heard the words: 'Courage! It is I! Do not be afraid.' Disciples know from experience that on their own they cannot withstand the storms, fears and sinking experiences of life. But they have learnt to reach out in prayer to God: and they know that his hand sustains them, his words give them courage and his presence brings them peace.

Fear is one of the great blockages in life, one of the clouds which can block off the sunlight of God's love from a person. When we no longer feel his light and warmth, our strength is frozen, our ability to deal with life paralysed. It is not surprising that the phrase most frequently repeated in the bible is, 'Do not be afraid.' Somebody has counted more than 360 instances of that message, as if God wishes us to hear it every day of the year.

On the worldwide scale, psychologists discern a sort of blanket depression lying over people. There is an ominous sense of threat. It is as if we have invented a monster threatening to destroy the world. The factors of change appear to be beyond our control and the very foundations of civilisation are creaking. People feel menaced and helpless. Families are under stress as the values and codes which traditionally guided life are questioned or disregarded. Parents are racked with fears about how their children will turn out. And young people have to cope with the anxiety about employment and emigration. Further pressures are put on them by the sexual prowess and materialistic standards they feel expected to reach. All of these factors weigh together in a depressing burden which many are finding too heavy to bear any longer. Through the darkness of night comes the voice of the Lord: 'Courage! It is I! Do not be afraid.'

One of the disciples, Peter, emerges as our model: not because of any greatness on his own part; but because of what he became by the power of God. He had once made the magnificent, blind gesture of leaving everything to follow Jesus. But he still had much to learn about himself and the longterm cost of being a disciple. When Jesus came to them in the storm, again Peter ventured overboard in blind abandon. But in the face of the wind he quickly reverted to relying on his own powers ... and immediately began to sink. At least he had faith enough to cry out, 'Lord! Save me!' And it was here in the moment of weakness he found a strong hand: in the moment of sinking he found a power to sustain him: in the moment of paralysing fear he found a source of courage.

The great gestures of abandonment which Peter made were admirable in their own way. But for his own development it was much more important that he came face to face with his weakness and fear. Peter was the sort of character who would not too easily have admitted to any weakness. But he is now a much greater model because of admitting his weakness than if he had attained the power to walk on every sea. Weakness made a greater man of him than the moment of the daring miracle.

God allows us to experience failures, frustrations and sinkings. These are valuable moments if they make us reach out in trust to the hand of God. Even a little faith, like Peter's, is enough to make one call out to God. And then, what marvels can happen!

By the wondrous power of God the man who was sinking in the lake was called to be the rock of support to others.

And the disciples who were brought to their knees in terror suddenly found that this was the proper posture for adoration.

It is in our weakness that we will find the saving hand of God.

In our abasement we learn his greatness to be adored.

And in our fears we discover the new courage that he gives.

'Our help is in the name of the Lord.'

Twentieth Sunday

This is our third Sunday with that section of Matthew which deals with life in the community of disciples. The Canaanite woman is an outsider who loudly bursts in on the group. She represents the nations of the world who will be welcomed into the people of God.

Today is a rare Sunday when the one theme is common to all three readings. Isaiah opens up the invitation to the holy mountain to all people who act out of justice and integrity. Then St Paul reflects on how the rejection of the Christian message by many of the Jews meant a more determined mission towards other nations.

Matthew 15:21-28
Woman, you have great faith

Jesus left Gennesaret and withdrew to the region of Tyre and Sidon. Then out came a Canaanite woman from that district and started shouting, "Sir, Son of David, take pity on me. My daughter is tormented by a devil." But he answered her not a word. And his disciples went and pleaded with him. "Give her what she wants," they said, "because she is shouting after us." He said in reply, "I was sent only to the lost sheep of the House of Israel." But the woman had come up and was kneeling at his feet. "Lord," she said, "help me." He replied, "It is not fair to take the children's food and throw it to the housedogs." She retorted, "Ah yes, sir, but even housedogs can eat the scraps that fall from their master's table." Then Jesus answered her, "Woman, you have great faith. Let your wish be granted." And from that moment her daughter was well again.

Good News

The good news is that God hears the humble, persistent cry of the outsider.

First Reflection
Working Within Limits

Jesus had withdrawn with the small core-group of disciples to the sea-coast region of Tyre. It was probably intended as a restful retreat but their tranquility was severely shattered. Matthew captures the mood of the moment. Out came this Canaanite, shouting at them and following them. She is an outsider, representing the gentile nations, who loudly bursts in on the introverted Jewish circle. Matthew uses her story to illustrate the history of the first fifty years of the church as it turned increasingly towards the gentile nations. It was a transition that brought its own share of pain.

The mission of Jesus had been limited to a short period of time and confined to the Jews. We hear that restriction first in the observation that he answered her not a word: and then in his statement that he was sent to the lost sheep of the House of Israel.

But the woman's deep need penetrates all boundaries. Her daughter is demented: her people are in a bad way. Her persistent cries upset the disciples and make them bring her cause to Jesus.

She is the first representative of the gentile nations whose plight so touched the conscience of the early church that they turned their mission more towards them. St Paul was proud to be regarded as the apostle of the pagans. *(2nd Reading)*

The short and limited mission of Jesus was the first circle of ripples made by a pebble cast on the lake. It was the task of the disciples to expand the circles. Working within defined limitations always causes tension and conflict. The earliest preaching of Jesus on the ideals of the kingdom was worldwide: ideals on their own are unlimited. But once Jesus began his work with the disciples he accepted the human limitations on his mission. He was confined to a small territory and restricted to the pace that the disciples could match.

The clash between the unlimited vision and the restrictions of reality invariably causes a tension. There are sore feelings and insulting words in this story, indicating the tension.

The early church experienced this same mental agony as they sought to clarify the policy regarding their mission beyond the Jews. Eventually it was resolved in the first council of the church, as recounted in the Acts of the Apostles.

The situation is relevant to the church today. The rapid collapse of traditional culture, freedom of travel, the interchange of ideas from many sources and the prevailing atmosphere of permissiveness have all contributed to a situation which raises new pastoral questions. The answers of yesterday may not be responding to the questions of today.

Big bodies move slowly. The church is a worldwide society

which finds that the very tradition which is the storehouse of wisdom may also be a weight which slows down the speed of response and adaptation to new situations. Some inherited structures, such as the link between parochial authority and length of service in a diocese, are blocking pastoral initiative. Sometimes the laws which are made for the good of the society impinge cruelly on the lives of individuals: and it is a very sad pastoral situation when good kingdom-people have to be refused the sacraments. These are instances where the wider vision does not fit comfortably within the human limitations. Anger is the appropriate response to hurt or the blocking of zeal. However there is a difference between rage, which is a futile waste of energy and the constructive channelling of one's energy towards rectifying the situation.

Jesus might have rushed around in a frenzy of activity to reach as many countries as possible. But that was not his way. He accepted the boundaries on his mileage, the limitations on his time, the restrictions on his pace. He was confined to the lost sheep of the House of Israel and to working in depth with a small core-group of disciples. He threw his pebble into the lake to make the first circle of ripples.

The day when the Canaanite woman loudly burst into this little circle anticipated the widening outreach of the mission of the church. But for the moment his policy was to work in depth with the small group.

In the face of new questions, pastoral patience is needed: the patience to work with the small group even though one is aware of the limited potential of this group. But if the little group helps people to pray, or to study their religion, or to engage in Christian action, then the ripples will expand in God's own time.

Second Reflection
The Christian Disciple (3)

A Christian disciple is someone with faith like that of the Canaanite woman. Jesus called her faith great, whereas he described Peter as a man of little faith. Peter, in his little faith, began to sink, but the Canaanite woman was unsinkable.

Three qualities shine forth in the greatness of her faith: persistence, humility and humour.

Her persistence was remarkable. She reminds one of the

woman of the parable who wears down a reluctant judge with the one weapon she had, persistence. Is this a womanly strength? Or is it something forced on woman as the only way to break through the hard-headed logic of a world organised by men? She must tell them that life is larger than logic. She has to break through the barriers of racial prejudice and cut through the red-tape of ecclesiastical laws. Her daughter at home is sorely demented, and her love for this one sick person charges her heart with an energy that will not be halted or diverted. Official bureaucrats tell her 'it's not done this way'. Doctors in solemn tones tell her 'it can't be done'. Cynics watch and say 'she's act ing strange under the strain'.

But her eyes are set only on the power of God that she has glimpsed in Jesus. And nothing is going to stop her from reaching him. She has no time to waste on theological niceties or racial distinctions. Her heart has only one thing to say: 'Lord, help me.'

The second admirable quality is her humility. She kneels before Jesus. And her prayer is simplicity itself for her hope does not reside in fine words or in her own merits.

Jesus at first did not answer her a word. We have all experienced that feeling in prayer ... that God hasn't heard us. But delay seems to be a tactic that God uses to deepen our sense of dependence. If we got our answers too readily, we might imagine they are due to our own merits or because our prayer is so good. We have to go through the limitations of 'failed prayer'. And God puts us to the test.

Was Jesus testing this woman by throwing back at her the racial insult by which Jews referred to other nations as dogs?

If she reacted in anger then her touchiness about racial identity would be seen to be stronger than her approach to God's power. She, however, lets no insult distract her from her purpose.

Her great faith has the third quality, humour. She can turn a potentially insulting situation into an occasion for quick-witted repartee. If you meet somebody with a great reputation for sanctity but who has no sense of humour, then know that you are not dealing with genuine holiness. Wait around awhile and you will surely see some ungodly anger or prejudice or inhibition of love appear. Lack of humour is always a sign of suppressed energy and a lack of self-honesty.

One must have a sense of humour with God. Otherwise you

cannot let yourself go totally into God's care. If you are too caught up in the dreadfully serious business of self, you will never be able to relax with God. We need a holy humour especially when we are dealing with God about our faults. I am not suggesting that we can laugh our sins away. But if we get angry and deeply upset because we are not perfect, then we are lacking in that humble humour which sees the wonderful mixture of light and dark, of strength and weakness in all visible creation.

The story of the Canaanite woman comes to a fascinating conclusion. Jesus does not simply cure the demented daughter but he draws attention to the great faith of the mother. 'Woman, you have great faith. Let your wish be granted.' It is as if the power of God which she was seeking was to be found in her own heart. The healing God is not remote in a far distant sky. Her great faith discovers the presence and power of God in her heart.

Her persistence, her humiliations and her humour with Jesus had knocked off all corners of selfishness and made her totally receptive to God.

A woman of great faith, she is a model to all disciples of the Lord – persistent, humble, humorous and unsinkable.

Twenty-First Sunday

We are dealing with that section of the gospel where Matthew shifts the scope from the universal ideals of the kingdom to the human limitations of the church. By the power of God this church will be the means of making the dream of the kingdom become a reality.

A moment of climax is reached in today's reading. Simon Peter emerges with a new clarity of faith and, in turn, he receives a divinely appointed role and responsibility.

Matthew 16:13-20
You are Peter, to you I will give the keys of the kingdom of heaven

When Jesus came to the region of Caesarea Philippi he put this question to his disciples, "Who do people say the Son of Man is?" And they said, "Some say he is John the Baptist, some Elijah, and others Jeremiah or one of the prophets." "But you," he said, "who do you say I am?" Then Simon Peter spoke up, "You are the Christ," he said, "the Son of the living God."

Jesus replied, "Simon son of Jonah, you are a happy man! Because it was not flesh and blood that revealed this to you but my Father in heaven. So I now say to you: You are Peter and on this rock I will build my Church. And the gates of the underworld can never hold out against it. I will give you the keys of the kingdom of heaven: whatever you bind on earth shall be considered bound in heaven; whatever you loose on earth shall be considered loosed in heaven." Then he gave the disciples strict orders not to tell anyone that he was the Christ.

Good News
The news of God here is contained in the act of faith that Jesus is the Anointed One, the Son of God.

First Reflection
Moving from Kingdom to Church

Caesarea Philippi is a beautiful spot at the foothills of snow-capped Mount Hermon where fresh, clear water from the melting snow forms inviting pools and charming cascades. At the time of Jesus it boasted of a new temple in gleaming white marble, built by Philip to the honour of Caesar, the Roman Emporer. Philip changed its name from Banias, the place where Pan, the Greek god of flocks and herds was worshipped with wild orgies. The beauty and freshness of the place invited reflection, while its history was associated with changing names and new rulers.

In the freshness of this retreat Jesus asks the question:

'Who are they saying I am?'

It is safe to quote others and in the anonymity of the group several answers are heard. What they tell Jesus is that people are saying that the great days of the past are alive again ... all the great teachers and prophets, all the leaders and miracles are now rolled up into the one person ... 'You, Master.' 'Ah!' said Jesus, 'but you, who do you say that I am?' There is no hiding now, no place for anonymity.

Every group must have a Simon: someone who cannot abide the embarrassing silence: someone who will stick out his neck. 'You are the Christ. You are the Son of God, Lord of all creation!' Christ! The Christ! What a rich name, known only by divine inspiration! (And what a reflection on the shallow faith of any Christian who would use that name as a curse-word.)

Christ means the one anointed with the oil of chrism. People were anointed unto three great roles of religious leadership. A prophet was anointed as one to reveal God and God's message to people. A priest was anointed to mediate with God for the people: to bring people to God and bring God to peoples' lives. A king was anointed to represent God's responsibility and care in leading the people. But now, for the first time ever, the three religious tasks are found in the one person. 'You are no mere human son of man,' says Peter, 'you are the Son of God.'

This moment of recognition is a climax in revelation. The teacher now knows that the pupils have caught his message. In time he can move on, knowing that his message and work will continue.

The message of the kingdom will be maintained. But who is this Simon who has told Jesus who he is? Jesus now, in turn, tells Simon who he is. 'Simon, son of Jonah, everybody knows who you are. You are so up-front that people think there is nothing they do not know of your flesh and blood.' Nobody would disagree.

'But you are more. You are especially blessed by my Father in heaven. You are a new person and you must be given a new name. I call you Peter, my rock. On you, my new rock, I will build my house for all people. A house to stand through life and beyond death itself.'

All could remember the first rock that Jesus had spoken of. At the end of the great sermon on his way of life he gave the option of building on sand or of building on rock. Now the rock was identified. And it was typical of God's ways that he chose the weak to confound the strong and the simple to show up the folly of worldly wisdom, so that it might be clearly seen that what was done is God's doing.

Then he promised to give Peter the keys of the kingdom. Up to this moment the kingdom was the mission of Jesus alone. But now the responsibility would be given to others. The work of the kingdom would be done by the church. Only in time to come would the disciples fully understand what Jesus was saying:

'The nations will turn to your keys to open up my teaching and to close off error. You will open the doors of my house to welcome believers in and you will close the door on unbelievers. What you do with these keys will be ratified in heaven. For your power will be in the keys of the kingdom of heaven upon earth.'

That was the day when Jesus, Son of Man, was recognised as the anointed leader of God's people, the very Son of God. The day when Simon, son of Jonah, is recognised as one blessed by the Father, newly anointed to be the rock that Jesus would build on. It was a decisive day in the transition from the dream of the kingdom to the reality of the church.

The first stone had been set in place.

Second Reflection
The Christian Disciple (4)

In recent weeks we have seen how a Christian disciple is someone:

- nourished by the bread of God's compassion:
- saved from sinking by the hand of God:
- persevering in faith like the Canaanite woman.

Now we see that a true disciple is like Peter, blessed with the divine gift of faith.

There is an old principle in theology that what God wills to accomplish in many he first manifests in one person. That is a way of saying that God writes a headline in one person's life for all the people to copy. Simon Peter is a headline or model of faith. A good model too, because he was moulded from no extraordinary clay. We do not stand back at a fearful distance from Simon as someone of unattainable perfection. We have seen his flesh and blood mixture, being weak and strong, cold and hot, fearful and courageous. And now, into this vessel of ordinary clay God pours an extraordinary gift ... faith.

'It is not your flesh and blood mixture that gave you this light, but my Father in heaven. Simon, son of Jonah, you are the recipient of a great blessing." Faith is a gift.

In the gospel pages it is noticeable that Jesus was amazed when he met with someone who believed: and he was moved to bless the Father in thanksgiving for the faith of the little ones. Yet we today have ceased to be amazed at faith: rather we are surprised and dismayed when we come across someone who does not believe.

If you believe that Jesus Christ is the Son of God and the saviour of the world, then you are truly blessed. You are more than a creature of flesh and blood. Like Simon, you deserve a new name.

Like Simon, you too are a new Peter, a new rock in the temple of God's presence upon earth. Your faith will be a rock of foundation to give you strong roots to withstand the most severe storms and floods of life. Your faith will bring you the keys to open and close the doors of life's mysterious castle. You have the key to open up God's forgiveness and to lock away the terrors of guilt. Your key will open up the light of wisdom, understanding and knowledge: and lock out the powers of darkness.

You have the key of faith to throw open the chains of fear and anxiety which restrict our growth: and to bind in chains the phantoms of terror which come up from the mind's cellar.

You have the key to hope which will sustain you. And the key to love, for if you believe in God's love, then you have the motive for overcoming every denial of love in your life: your love will be greater than the hurts it receives.

In faith you have the key to salvation.

If you have the gift of faith you are truly blessed. You have a gift to be treasured with wonder and amazement: to be carefully protected and daily nurtured by prayer and study.

You have a gift which should move you to thank God and to praise him without ceasing.

Twenty-Second Sunday

How sudden the transition from blessedness to brokeness!

Last Sunday Jesus was identified as the Anointed One, the Son of God: and Simon Peter was identified as a blessed man, the rock-foundation of the new temple, the man with the keys.

Today all is changed. Jesus is destined for suffering and death: and Peter is warned that in his narrow, humanistic mentality he is more of an obstacle than a foundation-stone.

Matthew 16:21-27
If any man wishes to come after me, let him deny himself

Jesus began to make it clear to his disciples that he was destined to go to Jerusalem and suffer grievously at the hands of the elders and chief priests and scribes, to be put to death and to be raised up on the third day.

Then, taking him aside, Peter started to remonstrate with him. "Heaven preserve you, Lord," he said, "this must not happen to you." But he turned and said to Peter, "Get behind me, Satan! You are an obstacle in my path, because the way you think is not God's way but man's."

Then Jesus said to his disciples, "If anyone wants to be a follower of mine, let him renounce himself and take up his cross and follow me. For anyone who wants to save his life will lose it; but anyone who loses his life for my sake will find it. What, then, will a man gain if he wins the whole world and ruins his life? Or what has a man to offer in exchange for his life?

"For the Son of Man is going to come in the glory of his Father with his angels, and, when he does, he will reward each one according to his behaviour."

Good News
The cross is a frightening prospect but the good news is that it is God's way, the way to resurrection and new life, the way to sharing in the glory of the Father.

First Reflection
The Way of the Cross
There are depths in the human heart which are not normally reached except through suffering. One of the key messages of the

new testament is that the way to salvation is the way of the cross. One must die to self in order to live unto God. The wheat grain must die before it fructifies. The bread must be broken before it can be shared. No cross, no crown.

Matthew notes that Jesus 'began to make it clear' what was destined for him. It was such a challenge to the accepted ways of thinking that it would take patient repetition before the idea sank in fully.

We can appreciate the reaction of Peter to the news. He represents our own natural reaction ... which illustrates why Peter is such an appropriate model for us. 'This must not happen to you. How could a kind and loving God demand this?'

We notice that Peter took Jesus aside privately. Is there a hint here that Peter now considered himself somewhat apart from the other disciples, as one on a private line with Jesus. If his new status as the rock gave him notions of grandeur then he must quickly be warned not to let the foundation-stone become a stumbling-block.

Peter was making two mistakes. First of all he did not listen to the full destiny of Jesus. The mention of being raised up on the third day passed over his head unheard.

His second mistake, a more serious but very common one, was to dictate what God's will should be. Genesis says that we are made in the image and likeness of God: our common mistake is to make God to the image of our liking. And this way of thinking is 'not God's way but man's.' This mistake could have such serious consequences that poor Peter is here given yet another new name, the name of the great tempter, Satan. He may have been called the rock, he may have been given the keys, but he is not to use his position to dictate the way. His calling is to follow. 'Get behind me!'

'Heaven preserve you, Lord.' The words of Peter are half a prayer to God and half a challenge to Jesus. His sentiments are echoed every time the question is raised, 'Why the cross?' Why did the Father ask Jesus to travel this hard road?

When we stay in prayer with the question, the love of God that is hidden in the cross begins to emerge.

One great word that grows in the mind is compassion. St Paul offered that word to Titus: 'When the kindness and love of

God our saviour for mankind were revealed ... it was for no reason except his own compassion that he saved us.' *(Titus 3: 4-5)*

The passion of Jesus was not a suffering in isolation. Compassion means that he suffered with the hardships and pains of every person who has been the innocent victim of violence, envy, power-struggles, political policies or greed.

His way of saving was not at a safe distance, removed from the messy, dirty side of life: he did not save us through talk or theory, through debates or white papers. In compassion, his cross on Calvary stands in solidarity alongside all human pain and distress.

Another idea that grows in the mind is from his parables about the mixture of weeds and wheat in the field, and the mixture of good fish and useless ones in the dragnet. These are pictures of life and people, and the same mixture of bad and good is found in the cross.

The cross is the expression of insane hatred and raw bitterness, the backlash of envy and scorn, an invention of savage cruelty. It was the utmost curse.

But in Jesus the cross is healed so that now it expresses love unto death, fidelity unto the end and arms that are open in a world-wide embrace. What was once a curse is now the symbol we use in blessing.

Why the cross?

Because God wished to manifest his love in the mad whirlpool of injustice and violence. And because all cursed trees had to be restored as trees of life and fruitfulness.

How could a loving, gracious Father permit the cross? But think of how much the poorer would be our knowledge of God's love if Jesus had saved us in an easy manner. There are depths in the human heart which are not brought to light until one shares in the cross of Jesus Christ. The way of the cross is the way to salvation and fulness of life. 'Anyone who loses his life for my sake will find it.'

Second Reflection
The Christian Disciple (5)

A Christian disciple is someone who dies unto sin and self-centredness in order to live unto God: who will let go of worldly ambitions in order to concentrate on the eternal: who is willing to be broken on the cross in order to be refashioned however God wishes.

The disciple, who has been blessed with God's gift of faith, must be broken and tamed into God's thinking.

Our series on the Christian disciple began four weeks ago with the miracle of the loaves and fishes, fruits of the earth and sea.

The four actions of Jesus in that miracle anticipated the story of the eucharist as he took the food, recognised the Father in blessing, broke it and gave it out. And these same actions can be applied to the way in which God calls the disciple to follow Jesus. Today's liturgy offers us Jeremiah *(1st Reading)* and Simon Peter as examples of the process.

Those who are taken or called by God are prepared for their task with special blessings. Jesus declared how Simon Peter was specially blessed by the Father with the light of faith. Jeremiah has powerfully described the blessing of God in his life: 'You have seduced me, Lord, and I have let myself be seduced; you have overpowered me: you were the stronger ... Then there seemed to be a fire burning in my heart, imprisoned in my bones.'

How wonderful is the day of blessing! But how mysterious the time of breaking! What did it mean for Jeremiah? Rejection, violence and ruin. 'The word of the Lord has meant for me insult, derision, all day long.'

And for Peter? In this gospel episode the transition from blessing to breaking is very sudden. The word of God was a rude rebuke about his unredeemed thinking. He would be an obstacle in the way rather than a foundation-stone unless he let go of his small-scale thinking. His selfish shell would have to be broken to allow the fulness of Christ's words to be heard. The breaking in of Jeremiah and Peter would have been appreciated by St Teresa of Avila, a woman of wit and wisdom. Thrown from her horse and landing in a river, she complained to God that if this is the way he treats his friends it is no wonder that he has so few of them.

'If anyone wants to be a follower of mine, let him renounce himself and take up his cross and follow me.' We have heard this message before: there is no cheap Christianity: discipleship is very costly.

To renounce oneself is deeper than the annual Lenten challenge to deny oneself a few comforts. It means letting go of any value system, ambition or desire which would be an obstacle to total love of God and one's fellowman.

We must look at what our hearts are set on, at the thoughts which occupy our minds, at the blind stirrings on gut level which excite or paralyse us. If our preoccupations are self-seeking or worldly, these are ideals which must be broken to make space for the one true God.

What is the object of our ambition? Our deepest desire? How do we gauge success in life? How important is power or money if the inner heart is crying in pain because its gasping for eternity is being stifled? 'What will a man gain if he wins the whole world and ruins his life?' If he suffers the loss of all inner meaning?

The old ways of the weary world have to be broken on the cross before the new child of the resurrection reflects the light of God to others. The bread had to be broken before it could be shared with others. The thinking of Simon had to be broken before he could emerge as Peter, a rock for others.

Unless the wheat grain dies it remains only a single grain, but if it dies it yields a rich harvest.

Twenty-Third Sunday

This is the second last of seven Sundays where the focus of Matthew is on life in the community of disciples. Gradually, the picture is clarifying of how the ideal of the kingdom is to be reflected in the church community. Today's reading brings up the very practical matter of how to confront the erring member of the community in Christian charity.

Matthew 18:15-20
If he listens to you, you have won back your brother
Jesus said to his disciples:

"If your brother does something wrong, go and have it out with him alone, between your two selves. If he listens to you, you have won back your brother. If he does not listen, take one or two others along with you: the evidence of two or three witnesses is required to sustain any charge.

"But if he refuses to listen to these, report it to the community and if he refuses to listen to the community, treat him like a pagan or a tax collector.

"I tell you solemnly, whatever you bind on earth shall be considered bound in heaven; whatever you loose on earth shall be considered loosed in heaven.

"I tell you solemnly once again, if two of you on earth agree to ask anything at all, it will be granted to you by my Father in heaven. For where two or three meet in my name, I shall be there with them."

Good News
The Lord promises to be with us (Emmanuel), whenever two or three come together in care and prayer to win back a brother or sister from wrong-doing.

First Reflection
My Brother's Keeper
In the deep folk-wisdom of Genesis the first sin of the human race was the attempt to usurp the moral authority of God to dictate the knowledge of good and evil.

And the second sin was when Cain tried to disown his responsibility for his brother: 'Am I my brother's keeper?' Today's gospel challenges us about the care we keep for our brother or sister who is going astray. On a wider dimension we are challenged about our responsibility for the ways in which our local community ... our government ... the whole of society ... might be doing wrong.

Once upon a time there was a man walking by a river when he saw somebody carried downstream in grave danger of drowning. Bravely the man dived in and pulled the person to the bank. He had just revived the victim when a second person was carried downstream. Again he dived in and performed the rescue. There were onlookers now who admired the man's courage. A third victim came downstream and once again the hero dived in and rescued. Then he gathered his coat and asked the onlookers to save any other victim who might appear. 'But you are such a good swimmer', they said, 'why are you going away?' 'I am going upstream to see where they are falling in.'

It is not sufficient for a Christian life merely to say my prayers and mind my own business. The salvation of others is also my business. And sometimes this demands that I move upstream to confront the social cause of individuals' wrong-doing.

We come from a background of several centuries of privatised spirituality and highly individualistic prayer. We have worked out of the notion that prayer is when I get into my private booth and talk with God on my private hotline. With this sort of background we have great difficulty in grasping the community aspect of sin.

Every sin is a sin against the community of the church. That is one of the reasons why private confessing to God is not sufficient. We owe an apology to the church community. The priest in the role of confessor is regarded as the representative of the church who receives this apology.

In today's first reading, Ezechiel deals with a time when Jerusalem was in danger of invasion from the Babylonian armies. The vigilance of every sentry was vital. Ezechiel extended the sense of responsibility to everybody. Whoever turned a blind eye to the careless sentry was equally responsible and guilty. A chain is only as strong as the weakest link. The weakness of any member of the community affects the whole community. Just as a pain in any part of the body affects the entire body.

Privatised spirituality has left us with an impoverished use

222

of the sacrament of Reconciliation. The traditional dark box, where one whispers to a dimly seen priest, has imprisoned us in that childish conscience which has a tidy little list of sins with no reference whatsoever to social responsibilities. One of the reasons why communal celebration of the sacrament is encouraged is to stir up a greater awareness of the community aspect of sin.

In Christ's great sermon on the last judgment there is no question about having bad thoughts or distractions in your prayers. All the questions from the Judge are about responsibilities towards our brothers and sisters in their needs and pains. The sins that are recognised there are in the neglect or failure to accept responsibility for the neighbour's plight.

Our responsibility to others touches first of all upon the people in our immediate circle of contact – familiy members, associates at work or play. If my care for them is genuine I will be pained if they are going astray. I am failing them if I do not try to win them back.

The circle of our responsibility widens out to the neighourhood I live in. A developed conscience cares about social matters and environmental issues. The challenge today is to move upstream to confront and correct the source of the social pain. It calls for the courage to confront politicians if they are failing in their responsibilities; to oppose those who destroy the environment; to challenge those who manipulate the minds of the young through the media of entertainment.

There is no living in love without pain. The Christian community knows sadness and pain when a brother or sister strays away.But it is consoled and strengthened by the promise of the Lord to be with us when we try to win back the wrong-doer through care and prayer.

The keys to bind and loose were given not to Peter alone, but to the Christian community united in care and prayer.

Second Reflection
The Christian Disciple (6)

A Christian disciple is someone who shares in the loving concern of Jesus Christ to bring back anybody who has strayed from the community.

Today's gospel passage comes immediately after the parable of the shepherd who goes off in search of the one lost sheep. 'It is never the will of your Father in heaven that one of these little ones should be lost.' Kingdom-life is meant to be an earthly reflection of heaven.

Our guiding moral law must always be: 'What does God want in this matter? How did Jesus Christ act or what did he say about it?' The issue of having to confront a person who is doing wrong is perhaps the most delicate challenge of Christian charity.

Far too often we totally shirk the responsibility, or worse, we let the scandal of another's wrong-doing draw out our own negativity.

Instead of facing the person who should be confronted in charity, we are tempted to discuss the matter in uncharitable gossip, criticism, backbiting or name-calling. Instead of drawing back the offender now the gap of alienation is widened. The return of the sinner has been made more difficult. If we could but see it, when we react negatively, it says more about our own dark, repressed life than about the original wrong-doer. The little tyrant or sexual deviant or greedy monster who dwells within us always points the finger of criticism at others. Self-righteousness drives the sinner away. It builds prisons, burned witches and hunted heretics.

The honest person, who is coming to terms with the mixed-up garden in one's own life, is moved to say: 'There go I but for the grace of God.'

The positive reaction of charity asks: 'What would Jesus Christ do?' St Paul outlined the Christian ideal to the Galatians:

'Brothers, if one of you misbehaves, the more spiritual of you who set him right should do so in a spirit of gentleness, not forgetting that you may be tempted yourselves. You should carry each other's troubles and fulfil the law of Christ.' (Gal 6: 1-2)

The issue may be a serious matter such as the abuse of drink or drugs, theft or family betrayal; or it may be a relatively small matter like two people not talking to each other. However, no problem is trivial once it is real. A pebble in the shoe may be very small but it causes real pain.

The first approach, as one brings the care of Jesus Christ to the straying person, is by personal contact. It preserves the atmosphere of maximum confidentiality. As Paul mentioned, gentleness of spirit and the honest remembrance of one's own frailty will give a truly Christian quality to one's effort.

If the one-to-one approach fails then the next step is in shared responsibility. There are people who feel guilty about transgressing the laws of charity if they discuss the faults of another, even out of concern and responsibility. However, it shows a great understanding of human nature to have two or three concerned people confront the straying one. It can be easy to sidestep the evidence of one person. But a small group of caring people, who remain calm and who confront the person with hard evidence, will be very hard to elude.

Whether the approach is made alone or with others, it must all be part of prayer in action. Whoever has to correct another should pray beforehand for the light of truth, for courage of heart and for the tactful gentleness which will heal rather than wound, draw back rather than alienate, and fan the flames of hope rather than of bitterness.

The prayer of others too should be sought, for the reconciliation of a straying member is a community matter. However care must be taken not to breach confidentiality by unnecessarily releasing a person's name.

I remember one occasion when I had to face a rather delicate confrontation. I asked somebody to go in prayer before the Blessed Sacrament to support me. I left the confrontation with the feeling that I had failed to achieve any breakthrough. But when I called to thank the person who had gone to pray, she described how a certain name kept coming vividly to her mind during prayer. It was the name of the person I had been meeting. I knew then that the matter would be alright. And so it proved to be.

We have the Lord's word for it: 'If two of you on earth agree to ask anything at all, it will be granted to you by my Father in heaven. For where two or three meet in my name, I shall be there with them.' The context of these words is correction of a straying community member.

Jesus, Emmanuel, is with the disciples who live in care and prayer.

Twenty-Fourth Sunday

This is our final section from Matthew's life in the community of disciples. Last Sunday's lesson was about winning back a member who had strayed into wrong-doing. Today's question arises from the hurt that one may have received from another. The only true Christian attitude is forgiveness beyond counting.

Matthew 18:21-35

I tell you that you forgive not seven times but seventy-seven times

Peter went up to Jesus and said, "Lord, how often must I forgive my brother if he wrongs me? As often as seven times?" Jesus answered, "Not seven, I tell you, but seventy-seven times.

"And so the kingdom of heaven may be compared to a king who decided to settle his accounts with his servants. When the reckoning began, they brought him a man who owed ten thousand talents; but he had no means of paying, so his master gave orders that he should be sold, together with his wife and children and all his possessions, to meet the debt.

"At this, the servant threw himself down at his master's feet. 'Give me time,' he said, 'and I will pay the whole sum.' And the servant's master felt so sorry for him that he let him go and cancelled the debt.

"Now as this servant went out, he happened to meet a fellow servant who owed him one hundred denarii; and he seized him by the throat and began to throttle him. 'Pay what you owe me,' he said.

"His fellow servant fell at his feet and implored him, saying, 'Give me time and I will pay you.' But the other would not agree; on the contrary, he had him thrown into prison till he should pay the debt. His fellow servants were deeply distressed when they saw what had happened, and they went to their master and reported the whole affair to him. Then the master sent for him. 'You wicked servant,' he said, 'I cancelled all that debt of yours when you appealed to me. Were you not bound, then, to have pity on your fellow servant just as I had pity on you?' And in his anger the master handed him over to the torturers till he should pay all his debt. And that is how my heavenly Father will deal with you unless you each forgive your brother from your heart."

Good News

The Lord is compassion and love, slow to anger and rich in mercy. The experience of his forgiveness enables us to forgive in turn.

First Reflection

From Vengeance to Forgiveness

The bible traces a development from primitive vengeance to the fulness of Christian forgiveness. In early Genesis we come across Lamech, who threatens all and sundry that his policy is to wreak unmitigated revenge on any foe: 'Sevenfold vengeance is taken for Cain, but seventy-sevenfold for Lamech.' *(Gen 4: 24)*

Moses represents a great breakthrough in setting the standard of no more than equal vengeance: an eye for an eye, a tooth for a tooth. While that standard was a great advance in civil relationships, it did not go far enough for the kingom of Jesus. So, in the sermon on the mount he set forth the kingdom ideal: 'You have learnt how it was said: "Eye for eye and tooth for tooth." But I say this to you: offer the wicked man no resistance ... Love your enemies and pray for those who persecute you.' *(Mt 5: 35,43)* But there was still room for misunderstanding and limitation of the ideal. Peter needed a clarification. 'Forgiveness, Master, right! But how often? Seven times?' Surely seven, the holy number, will be the definition of heroic virtue. Nobody could be expected to offer more. 'Not seven, I tell you, but seventy-seven times.'

The wheel of thought has turned full circle from the vengeance of Lamech. Primitive lust for revenge has been replaced by divine compassion now living in our hearts. Divine love will not be stopped by any obstacle, it will not be poisoned by any infection of hatred. How well Peter absorbed the message may be seen in these noble words: 'Never pay back one wrong with another, or any angry word with another one: instead pay back with a blessing ... No one can hurt you if you if you are determined to do only what is right; if you do have to suffer for being good, you will count it a blessing.' *(1 Pet 3: 9, 13-14)*

Christianity is a movement of divine power sweeping through the world. The same power of the Spirit which filled Jesus is the power of the kingdom of heaven upon earth. It is determined to do good and refuses to be infected with the poison of another's evil. It gives one the will to keep on loving even in the face of hurt or wrong. Forgiving means the sort of giving that never ceases, no mat ter what rebuffs it faces.

St Paul describes what a kingdom-person is like: 'Since God loves you, you should be clothed in sincere compassion, in kindness and humility, gentleness and patience. Bear with one another; forgive each other as soon as a quarrel begins. The Lord has forgiven you; now you must do the same.' *(Col 3:12-13)* Paul put his finger on the two secrets of forgiveness: the appreciation of God's compassion towards us and the humble remembrance of our own faults. St John Chrysostom preached that there is nothing that makes the soul so truly wise, so truly gentle and compassionate, as the continuous remembrance of our own sins.

Compassion makes one realise that the wrong-doer is in pain, even if he does not consciously recognise it. He needs our pity and understanding far more than our bitterness. If somebody treats you roughly, you can be sure that you are not his only victim. There is bitterness and hurt inside his soul and the last thing he needs now is another enemy: his own self-hatred is an enemy that accompanies him morning, noon and night. Compassion moves us to pity instead of bitterness. They say that to understand all is to forgive.

The other source of forgiveness is an appreciation of God's compassion towards us. We cannot too often repeat the psalm: 'The Lord is compassion and love, slow to anger and rich in mercy.'

Christian charity is more than a natural, human response to a situation. Charity is a supernatural virtue: that means that it is a gift from God. The charity which can overcome evil is the gift of God's Spirit living within us.

In the Our Father we pray for such a deep experience of God's forgiveness in our own lives that we will be enabled to pass on forgiveness to those who have offended us. When we find it very hard to forgive somebody we must humbly acknowledge that we have reached the limits of our own powers. Our only recourse then is to prayer, to invite God to take over our understanding and our will. We should ask God: "How do you love this erring child of yours, Lord?" For God surely does love the sinner. And we should pray that we might be agents of the creative love of the Father, the redeeming love of the Son, and the sanctifying love of the Holy Spirit.

O divine Creator, love your straying child through me.

O divine Redeemer, reach out your saving hand through me.
O divine Spirit, take me and use me to renew this person
who has hurt me.

Second Reflection
The Christian Disciple (7)

A Christian disciple is someone who forgives much because
he appreciates that he has been forgiven much.

In the immortal words of Alexander Pope: 'to err is human,
to forgive, divine.' Forgiveness of a hurt is part of the victory of divine life over evil. In practice there is no greater test of genuine
Christianity than the willingness to forgive others.

Jesus Christ came on a mission of liberation and reconciliation. He announced that he would open closed eyes and ears,
break open the chains of captives, cleanse the lepers and raise the
dead. It was good news for the poor. His miracles to heal the body
illustrated the healing and liberation that he brought to souls.
When his compassion touched people they were able to let go of
the anger and resentment which had bound them captive.

I remember reading the story told by Martin Buber, a Jewish
philosopher, about his grandfather. Old Grandpa was paralysed.
He was asked to tell about the holy man who was the teacher and
inspiration of his youth. As Grandpa relived his memories he began to imitate the movements and expressions of his teacher of
long ago. All gazed in wonder as the paralysed man moved and
stood and virtually danced through his memories. He was healed
of his paralysis as memory brought him back to the days before
the experiences of life which had caused his ailment.

The story left me wondering how many of the chains that
bind people belong to anger and resentment which they may not
consciously recognise. But the sub-conscious knows with its own
dark way of knowing. Today's first reading begins with the comment: 'Resentment and anger, these are foul things.'

Buried resentment and seething anger bind a person in muscular tension which is very often associated with headache, back
pains, stomach ulcers, asthma, stress on the face and pressure on
the heart. The chains that bind us are often located in areas of unforgiveness in our conscious and unconscious memories. Psycho-
somatic illnesses are seen in the body but are rooted in the mind.
The pain is not the root of the trouble. Treating the ache brings

only temporary relief. Better to regard the pain as a cry from repressed hurt, anger, tiredness or bitterness. This area is coming increasingly to light as attention is given to the victims of rape or child abuse and to the mental stresses inflicted by parents through divorce or alcoholism. When the person who perpetrated the hurt is of close kinship it may be very difficult to admit one's anger. But if there is anger, it must be recognised before one moves towards forgiveness. Forgiveness is very different to turning a blind eye on one's hurt or pretending that nothing has happened. If we do not admit our hurt the danger is that we take it into ourselves and hide it. Then it is dangerous.

The church does not ask us to forget our hurts. On the contrary we are asked to face them, name them and talk them out in the light of confession.

One great obstacle to finding forgiveness is a tendency to self-pity, a sort of martyr complex. People can be in love with their hurts because it makes them feel that they deserve sympathy. You will hear self-pity being expressed in sentiments of vengeance and a certain glee when somebody gets his comeuppance.

St Francis of Assisi had the wisdom of true sanctity when he described anger as a sin against the virtue of poverty: for he saw that there were people who might give up every material possession but hold on to what he called 'the purse of anger.'

One meets people who harbour bitterness about parents, school, the church, the system, the rich, the authorities and that anonymous collection of A.N. Others gathered under 'they'. They did this, they caused that, they ran the system, they made the rules. Mister A or Father B or Sister C may have done me a wrong. If they have sinned then that is their problem. But if I harbour anger and resentment towards them, then I too have a problem. I have been infected by their poison. Now there are two wrongs, a situation which rarely makes a right.

Isn't it significant that when Jesus spoke about the man who would not forgive his fellow servant, the image which dominates the story is prison?

To harbour resentment or to hold on to hurt memories is to be imprisoned: bound in chains and paralysed. But to overcome all bitterness and anger is to be released. It is in pardoning that we are pardoned ... and released ... healed .. and restored.

Twenty-Fifth Sunday

We have entered the fifth and final block of Matthew's construction of the ministry of Jesus. He is on his way to Jerusalem. Clashes with the leading scribes and Pharisees are frequent. Tension fills the air and the tone is argumentative. Through the parable of the workers Jesus unveils the clash between the mind tied to earthly values and the mind that has soared up to God's values. The first reading sets us up for the surprise of the gospel parable by reminding us that God's thoughts are on a different scale from our thoughts.

Matthew 20:1-16
Why are you jealous because I am generous?

Jesus said to his disciples: "Now the kingdom of heaven is like a landowner going out at daybreak to hire workers for his vineyard. He made an agreement with the workers for one denarius a day, and sent them to his vineyard. Going out at about the third hour he saw others standing idle in the market place and said to them, 'You go to my vineyard too and I will give you a fair wage.' So they went. At about the sixth hour and again at about the ninth hour, he went out and did the same.

"Then at about the eleventh hour he went out and found more men standing round, and he said to them, 'Why have you been standing here idle all day?' 'Because no one has hired us,' they answered. He said to them, 'You go into my vineyard too.'

"In the evening, the owner of the vineyard said to his bailiff, 'Call the workers and pay them their wages, starting with the last arrivals and ending with the first.' So those who were hired at about the eleventh hour came forward and received one denarius each. When the first came, they expected to get more, but they too received one denarius each. They took it, but grumbled at the landowner. 'The men who came last,' they said, 'have done only one hour, and you have treated them the same as us, though we have done a heavy day's work in all the heat.'

"He answered one of them and said, 'My friend, I am not being unjust to you; did we not agree on one denarius? Take your earnings and go. I choose to pay the last-comer as much as I pay you. Have I no right to do what I like with my own? Why be envious because I am generous?' Thus the last will be first, and the first, last."

231

Good News

The beautiful news in this story is about the generosity of God, whose gifts are not restricted to our merits and whose call can come at the latest hour.

First Reflection
High Above Our Thoughts

'Yes, the heavens are as high above the earth as my ways are above your ways, my thoughts above your thoughts.' *(Is 55:9)*

The parable of the workers is an instance of how the thoughts of God are on a higher scale than our earthly thoughts. This is what the kingdom of God is like. Our earthly minds respect fair play. We set a just reward for hard work. So does the landowner in this story. God rewards our endeavours. So far there is no leap beyond what the small, earthly mind can grasp.

But the parable is about the great noble mind which makes the landowner generous beyond justice. He chooses to give more than some earned. The calculators come out, sums are done and the small minds start to grumble. The lesson being hit home is not to restrict God to our little calculations. The mind of God works on a greater and more generous scale than we do. And that is something that should gladden our hearts.

As told by Jesus the parable had a lesson for the Pharisees, who were scandalised that Jesus should be associating with the moral riff-raff. But God sees them in a different light. Jesus may well have intended the point for Peter and the apostles too. The story comes immediately after the time when Peter acted like the Union representative to remind Jesus that they had given up everything to follow him: 'What are we to have then?'

Certainly they will get their reward but they must not be so smallminded as to restrict the generosity of God to a sort of wage structure. They, of all people, ought to have realised how, in God's ways, 'the last will be first, and the first last.'

At Matthew's time of writing the parable had a clear lesson for those Jews who were uncomfortable with the practice of taking Gentiles into the church on an equal basis as their own race which had borne the heat of the day in long centuries of service and suffering. The message that God's ways are high above our ways retains its relevance for all who are tempted to restrict God's movements and power to our human calculations.

Jesus once spoke of the impossibility of holding new wine in old sacks. Our tendency may be to restrict the power of the Holy Spirit, who is ever reforming the church, to the structures and traditions we grew up with. Tradition serves religion: but it is a mistake to make religion serve tradition. Then the last line of any argument is: 'But it was always done this way.'

When we hear of a crisis in the church, crisis in a religious congregation, crisis in a parish, it is not necessarily bad news. It represents the challenge to move and calls on our willingness to change, if we discern that the breath of the Spirit is blowing in a different direction.

God's thoughts are on a higher scale and in a wider perspective than our's. We must never underestimate God... that God is present in the church ... that God is in control of the world ... that in his hands all shall be well. The trouble is not with God's thoughts ... but in the smallness of our thoughts.

Second Reflection
Envy or Graciousness

'Why be envious because I am generous?' There's the key to the parable. The most horrible aspect of envy is that it is a negative reaction to some goodness. It is an ugly, poisonous growth which draws its life-blood out of something good and beautiful. Something that we have noted in this book more than once: light hurts the sore eye; and goodness is a threat to the guilty mind.

The goodness of Jesus unveiled a backlash of insane fear and satanic cruelty. Today's parable hints at what was to come as the master's generosity evokes envy and grumbling.

Even within ourselves, every virtue carries the seeds of being a destructive power if it is not held in the proper balance. Our twentieth century audience will be sensitive to equality of rights and likely to react unfavourably to the landowner's policy in paying the same to all, regardless of hours.

The pursuit of justice, concern for fair play and the obtainment of peoples' rights are manifestations of a noble virtue. But justice is blind when the pursuit of one's rights neglects the wider picture of one's responsibilities. Sometimes courts of justice become centres of irresponsibility when they are used to obtain grossly exaggerated sums of compensation: or for sectional pay rises which are to the cost of the common good.

The master of the vineyard was more than just: he was generous and gracious. The small mind of an earthbound life revolves around self. The only goodness that it appreciates is what accrues to self. There is an utter inability to rejoice in another's fortune. By contrast, the Godlike mind of the kingdom-person operates on a much grander scale and views eveything from a higher vantage point.

The kingdom-mind is gracious where the earthbound mind is envious. It rejoices in goodness wherever it is seen. One's own identity is not threatened by another's success, because one is secure in God's love. And love, as Paul tells us 'takes no pleasure in other peoples' sins, but delights in the truth.' *(1 Cor 13:5)*

Another quality of the kingdom-person is being open to surprises. The American storyteller-of-God, John Shea, says that the best preparation for heaven is to develop our capacity for surprise. There is a lovely quality of mind known as serendipity, which is the gift of discovering pleasant or valuable things not directly sought. The word comes from Serendib, a teardrop, the name given by Arabian mariners to the island of Sri Lanka (Ceylon) as this unexpected jewel of an island broke the dry monotony of a long voyage.

The amazing thing is that God strews our path each day with reflections of his creative genius and beauty. If only we had the eyes to see them!

God is the one who makes all things new. There are no stereotypes in God's eyes for the one thing missing from the Creator's equipment is the copying machine.

'The world is charged with the grandeur of God', according to Hopkins. Boredom is an insult to the Creator.

In the lovely lines of e.e. cummings:

I thank You God for most this amazing day ...
(now the ears of my ears awake and
now the eyes of my eyes are opened).

Whoever belongs to the kingdom of God
- has an eye for goodness and no ear for grumbling;
- is constantly amazed and never bored;
- is full of wonder and praise.
'His goodness shall follow me always to the end of my days.'

Twenty-Sixth Sunday

Jesus has entered Jerusalem. The air is crackling with tension like a thunderstorm about to break. The major area of controversy is the authority of Jesus. Who gave this untrained carpenter from Galilee the credentials to teach people? The parable of the two sons is part of the answer of Jesus. By means of the story the Jewish leaders are invited to see themselves: how they may have had the right credentials and all the nice words, but they were not doing what God wanted.

Matthew 21:28-32
He went out moved by regret. The tax collectors and prostitutes will precede you into the kingdom of God

Jesus said to the chief priests and the elders of the people: "What is your opinion? A man had two sons. He went and said to the first, 'My boy, you go and work in the vineyard today.' He answered, 'I will not go,' but afterwards thought better of it and went. The man then went and said the same thing to the second who answered, 'Certainly, sir,' but did not go. Which of the two did the father's will?" "The first," they said. Jesus said to them, "I tell you solemnly, tax collectors and prostitutes are making their way into the kingdom of God before you. For John came to you, a pattern of true righteousness, but you did not believe him, and yet the tax collectors and prostitutes did. Even after seeing that, you refused to think better of it and believe in him."

Good News
God accepts conversion of ways, extends mercy to the repentant sinners and draws them into the kingdom.

First Reflection
Working on God's Farm
There's more trouble down the farm today.

Last Sunday it was grumbling over wages in the vineyard. This week it is a confrontation with the son who said he would do the job but didn't. Conversely, the son who had stamped out in blunt refusal at first, later did the job. If you are asked by God to go work down on his farm, you must be willing to let your hands get dirty. What got into the Pharisees was this fear of dirt or contamination. Their name means the Separated Ones, for they made

235

a religion out of not being contaminated by the wrong-doing of others. Self-preservation became their ideal. They held out no hope to the sinner. And that angered Jesus.

The harvest on God's farm was ripe for the picking. The mission of John the Baptist showed that there were many sinners who were ready to respond to anybody who would give them a second chance in life. John offered them water, washing, renewal, a clean sheet and a fresh page of life.

As John said he would, Jesus came with the Holy Spirit and fire. He reached out to the sick and the sinner, the downgraded and depressed, the marginals and outcasts. He brought healing and uplifting, an end and a beginning, tears of relief and meals of celebration. The self-preserving Pharisees could not take it, for you cannot put new wine into old wineskins. Jesus was a scandal in their eyes.

To be a follower of Jesus Christ one is called to be missionary and apostolic: to work in his fields. He has no time for that privatised spirituality of mind your own business, say your prayers and save your soul. Don't get your hands dirty, don't let your comfortable schedule be upset.

The Christian mission can be described with simplicity: the best way to be a friend of Jesus is to bring a friend to Jesus.

On God's farm today the harvest is huge. Vast numbers of lives which have not been touched by the news of Jesus Christ are wandering down aimless roads of no meaning: they are bored, angry and aggressive: they are jaded and sick from sensuality. They are living without hope. When people are down and depressed, the last thing they want to hear is a sermon of condemnation. What they need is a hand reaching out to pick them up.

One of the great joys of retreat work is the opportunity to help somebody discover the hope and joy that Jesus offers. I recall the man who came to a parish mission and made a much needed confession. He told me what had brought him along. 'I saw you, missioners, having lunch in that hotel yesterday and the way ye were laughing. For seven years I have wanted to laugh like that, so I'm here tonight.' And I thought it was our marvellous preaching which had moved him! It was his hunger for the words of absolution.

It is not as if people today have never heard of Jesus. What happened to many is that the little experience of religion they received was so negative that it merely immunised them from the real thing. The power of the Holy Spirit and the fire of the heart have not reached them. They are left without hope, energy or self-belief. And who can bring them hope? Pray to the Father to send labourers into the harvest. And don't just pray for others to be touched. Don't be afraid to get your own hands dirty. To bring a friend to God you cannot do it from a distance. You too are asked by God to be a living and effective witness to God's love. When you pray 'make me an instrument of your peace', be prepared to get involved, to have your routine disturbed. And if needs be, ready to get your hands dirty.

You will find that farm-earth is clean dirt.

Second Reflection
Hearing and Doing

Many of the parables of Jesus were meant to disturb: not merely to cast light but to burn. How can any teaching penetrate the barriers erected by self-righteousness, smugness and complacency? A simple parable offers a story that cannot be denied: people are made to do their own thinking.

'Which of the two did the father's will?' they know the answer. Jesus confronts the Jewish religious leaders and accuses them of not doing God's will. What a shocker! And he further infuriates them by saying that John the Baptist was an example of true righteousness or conformity with God's will.

The Lord's story is so simple that it belongs to all time. And it continues to probe and find the Pharisee in our hearts today. It is an occupational hazard for all who are professionally dedicated to God that they become so familiar with religion that complacency sets in. The right words are known by rote and the appropriate actions come out in motor response. They are about as spontaneous as a computer. You see it in the sort of liturgy which is no longer a living experience of the risen Lord, but a jaded visit to a musty museum of religious fossils.

Religious communities cease to be centres of prophetic, apostolic response to the needs of the times, and become, instead, middle-class clubs of uncommitted bachelors and neurotic health-watchers. Worst of all is when people are so full of their own righteousness that they think that they, and they alone, represent the voice of God. They are no longer listening to God, to the needs of the times, to the requests of others. In their quest for self-preservation they have ears but they do not hear.

Complacency defends itself by erecting barriers which keep out the harsher sides of reality. The favourite defence system of the Pharisees was the law. Some precept or other could always be found to justify escaping from the painful demands of charity. And who among us can honestly say that he or she has not at times invoked a pharisaical excuse to justify our non-action when charity makes demands of us?

I'm too busy right now ... we are not allowed to do that ... the Superior is out at the moment ... that's not my responsibility ... what would the bishop think? ... this is a dangerous precedent ... we don't know where it will end up. Too often, rules, church laws, bishops or superiors are wrongly blamed for our own lack of initiative or response. Piety has got a bad name from those who use the religious card as a shield from the demands of God. It has been noted that, historically, pentecostal groups have contributed very little in service to others and have offered very little prophetic challenge to society. A true contemplative is missionary and always represents a challenge to the values and lifestyle of the world. But sadly, prayer is sometimes used as an excuse for shirking the painful challenges of charity.

The use of parables in the gospel should prepare us for a God who is never short of surprises. There were many unlikely candidates drawn to John the Baptist: and many who were alienated from practised religion were impressed by the integrity of Jesus Christ. And today there are anonymous Christians who profess membership of no Christian church, but who live according to the light of conscience and are good neighbours: and they are very close to the kingdom of heaven. They may not be saying the right words, nor professing the correct creed, but in their own way they are doing the work on God's farm.

Conversely, there are professed church members whose lives are an utter contradiction to the values of the kingdom. They have all the right prayers and the correct creed, but their actions are a denial.

There are many who are making their way into the kingdom although they are not in the church. And there are many in the church who may not belong to the kingdom.

Twenty-Seventh Sunday

In Jerusalem the conflict between Jesus and the Jewish leaders is reaching a climax. In the parable of the vineyard Jesus tries to open their minds to what they are doing. He reaches back into the preaching of Isaiah (1st Reading) to recall the warning that God would reject the chosen vineyard which was not bearing fruit.

Matthew 21:33-43
He leased his vineyard to other farmers

Jesus said to the chief priests and the elders of the people: "Listen to another parable. There was a man, a landowner, who planted a vineyard; he fenced it round, dug a winepress in it and built a tower; then he leased it to tenants and went abroad. When vintage time drew near he sent his servants to the tenants to collect his produce. But the tenants seized his servants, thrashed one, killed another and stoned a third. Next he sent some more servants, this time a larger number, and they dealt with them in the same way. Finally he sent his son to them. 'They will respect my son,' he said. But when the tenants saw the son, they said to each other, 'This is the heir. Come on, let us kill him and take over his inheritance.' So they seized him and threw him out of the vineyard and killed him. Now when the owner of the vineyard comes, what will he do to those tenants?" They answered, "He will bring those wretches to a wretched end and lease the vineyard to other tenants who will deliver the produce to him when the season arrives." Jesus said to them, "Have you never read in the scriptures: It was the stone rejected by the builders that became the keystone. This was the Lord's doing and it is wonderful to see?

"I tell you, then, that the kingdom of God will be taken from you and given to a people who will produce its fruit."

Good News

The power of God is often seen most clearly in the midst of human failure. He raises up the stone which was cast aside by human assessment.

First Reflection
Anger or apathy?

In the country and time when Jesus lived, people took religious claims so seriously that an issue would provoke extreme anger and the resort to violence: even the ultimate violence of killing.

The Jewish leaders liked to consider themselves as God's chosen vineyard. Jesus used their own favourite image in an appeal to open their eyes to what they were doing. He could see the inevitable eruption of violence. The story he told them was full of violence.

An important point in the story is the ambition of the tenants to gain control of the ownership of the vineyard. If a landowner died intestate, ownership would pass on to the tenants. That explains why they killed the son of the landowner. Jesus confronted the leaders with the unpleasant news that they were trying to take over God's place rather than work in his service. It will always be a temptation to any strong religious group or individual to become so self-righteous in their calling that eventually they appropriate God's position.

They begin to think and act as if they were God. They claim divine rights over people's minds ... and lives ... eventually claiming the right to kill others. By contrast, Jesus let himself be taken and killed.

If Jesus were to walk the roads and preach the kingdom in our time and culture, would he provoke the same anger and opposition? Would he be criminalised today? Would he suffer the equivalent of crucifixion? In our typical western (or more precisely northern) culture, I doubt if he would arouse too much opposition. He would meet with far more apathy and indifference from the ranks of post-Christian secularism.

He would be highlighted as a curiosity for a people whose deepest struggle is with boredom. Admired as an idealist, but utterly naive. He would be invited to the weekend TV chat show, asked questions ranging from the trivial to the most serious, thanked and asked to move over for the next act before the commercial break. The serious business of diversion would continue.

The startling fact is that the Son of God came to earth and was rejected! 'He came unto his own and his own received him not.' (Jn 1:11) Once, the rejection was in anger and violence: today, it is in apathy and indifference.

Anger or apathy? Which is worse? The truth is that either is bad. Whether in anger or apathy, the terrible truth is that we reject him in so many ways.

Second Reflection

The Rejected Stone

Before the availability of concrete blocks and precast cement, the stones of a building had to support one another and they were locked together by the keystone at the apex of an arch. The rejected stone which is later chosen as the keystone is a very consoling image.

It calls to mind the fairytale about the browbeaten housemaid who becomes the beautiful princess after the intervention of the fairy godmother.

Or the boy's comic story in which the fourth division reject is spotted by the shrewd talent-scout who sets him on the way to being the star of the first division.

In Hebrew, the words for stone and son are very similar. Ben means son and eben means stone. It was easy for Jesus as he spoke about the rejected son to switch to the verse of the psalm about the rejected stone, which was later chosen as the important keystone. The early Christian preachers liked to use that verse to explain what happened to Jesus. He was rejected on the cross but vindicated by the Father in his resurrection. *(cf Acts 4:11)*

As the rejected stone, Jesus entered into solidarity with the innocent victims of every age. The parable of the vineyard is a story of terrible violence and bloodshed. Innocent people are beaten and slaughtered by ambitious men. The blood of Jesus, shed upon the cross, became part of the historical current of innocent blood shed in every age. In the twentieth century alone it is estimated that one hundred million people have been killed in world wars, local wars, guerilla wars and gang wars, sabotage, bombings, ideological repression, concentration camps, gulags and assassinations.

When elephants fight the innocent grass is trampled.

Jesus entered into the lot of all the innocent people who suffer as prisoners of conscience, refugees or victims of the suppression of human rights. The world of innocent victims also includes all who are deprived of an equitable share of the world's resources, the victims of monetaristic policies which deprive the poor in order to protect the rich, and the victims of the exploitation of the environment which is harming our air, water and protective ozone layer.

Daily we are the victims of malice or misunderstanding, callousness or carelessness, spite or selfishness. We suffer through the ambition, deceit, vindictiveness, greed and insensitivity of others.

All who are innocent victims can look up at Jesus on the cross, knowing that his extended arms are open to embrace them: for he is the rejected stone, one with all rejects and victims.

On the cross he is a sign of compassion and solidarity. And in his resurrection he is a sign of hope and vindication. The stone rejected by the builders is chosen for the vital job of keystone. 'This is the Lord's doing and it is wonderful to see.'

Jesus is the sign that God is on the side of the innocent victim. God, who raised Jesus from the dead, will vindicate all who suffer in innocence. But they must wait in patience until God's own time of vindication. The day between Good Friday and Easter Sunday is a duration of God's choosing. But the strength to survive with a blessed soul has been promised.

'Happy are you when people abuse you and persecute you and speak all kinds of calumny against you on my account. Rejoice and be glad, for your reward will be great in heaven; this is how they persecuted the prophets before you.' *(Mt 5: 11-12)* Jesus, risen from the dead, is the sign of hope and divine recognition.

'He is the living stone, rejected by men but chosen by God and precious to him; set yourselves close to him so that you too ... may be living stones making a spiritual house.' *(1 Pet 2: 4-5)*

Twenty-Eighth Sunday

In these stories of the wedding feast and the wedding garment the mood is argumentative as Jesus continues his confrontation with the Jewish leaders. God's invitation to salvation met with apathy from some and angry rejection from others. As Matthew relates the stories, their message is not only about Jewish history but contains a warning for the Christian church.

Matthew Mt 22:1-14
Whomsoever you find invite to the wedding

Jesus said to the chief priests and the elders of the people: "The kingdom of heaven may be compared to a king who gave a feast for his son's wedding. He sent his servants to call those who had been invited, but they would not come. Next he sent some more servants. 'Tell those who have been invited,' he said, 'that I have my banquet all prepared, my oxen and fattened cattle have been slaughtered, everything is ready. Come to the wedding.'

"But they were not interested: one went off to his farm, another to his business, and the rest seized his servants, maltreated them and killed them. The king was furious. He despatched his troops, destroyed those murderers and burned their town.

"Then he said to his servants, 'The wedding is ready; but as those who were invited proved to be unworthy, go to the crossroads in the town and invite everyone you can find to the wedding.' So these servants went out on to the roads and collected together everyone they could find, bad and good alike; and the wedding hall was filled with guests. When the king came in to look at the guests he noticed one man who was not wearing a wedding garment, and said to him, 'How did you get in here, my friend, without a wedding garment?' And the man was silent. Then the king said to the attendants, 'Bind him hand and foot and throw him out into the dark, where there will be weeping and grinding of teeth.' For many are called, but few are chosen."

Good News

The wedding is the marriage of heaven and earth in Jesus Christ. All people, good and bad alike, from every point of the cross-roads, are invited to share in the banquet.

First Reflection
Invitation and Response

The story of the royal wedding feast tells of God's invitation to salvation and people's response. The wedding is a very appropriate image of God's invitation for we are called to love God, to be united with him in mind and heart, and to live a life on earth which anticipates heaven. Isaiah, in today's First Reading, promised a banquet of joy and life on God's mountain.

Matthew has skilfully combined the stories of the wedding feast and the wedding garment as a lesson in salvation history for the Christian church at his time of writing.

The first part of this history concerns the Jews as the Chosen People. They are represented by the people who first received the invitation to the royal banquet. But they would not come. Some were more interested in their own affairs. More servants were sent to call them: these were the prophets. But they were scoffed at, persecuted and sometimes put to death. In describing the furious reaction of the king, Matthew is interpreting, as a punishment from God, the destruction of Jerusalem by the Roman armies, which had taken place some years before he was writing.

Then follows the second part of salvation history. The wedding represents the marriage of God with humanity which took place when the Son of God took on our human flesh. We hear, 'the wedding is ready ... go to the crossroads.' The servants at this point in the story represent the Christian apostles who are sent to the crossroads of the world to invite everybody to the wedding. This thought of the Christian mission to the whole world happily coincides with October, the month of the missions.

No longer is the invitation confined to one chosen nation. Nor is it restricted to the uncontaminated or ritually pure. Everybody, good and bad alike, is invited. Many previous lessons of the gospel come back to mind. God, who loves all, makes his sun to shine and rain to fall on good and bad , honest and dishonest, alike. And the kingdom is a field with weeds and wheat, or a net with good and bad fish.

But now there is a warning for the Christian church. Those who accept God's invitation must be seen wearing the wedding garment. In the story this might mean wearing their Sunday best or else some special token for the royal occasion.

In terms of salvation history, failure to wear the wedding garment can be understood in two ways.

Reception into the church through baptism is not sufficient unless one lives up to the Christ-like life that is symbolised in the white garment of the sacrament. 'You have stripped off your old behaviour with your old self, and you have put on a new self ... You should be clothed in sincere compassion, in kindness and humility, gentleness and patience.'*(Col 3:9-12)* A certificate of baptism is of lit tle use without a life showing the fruits of grace.

In the second interpretation of the wedding garment, if we think of it as a special token for the royal occasion, it represents the necessity of divine grace in addition to our human effort. Whoever underestimates the need of divine grace and neglects the ordinary means of grace such as prayer and the sacraments, will be found out as not wearing the royal wedding token.

God sent his Son, Jesus Christ, to embrace the world in the wedding of salvation. The invitation goes out to all people to come and celebrate at the wedding banquet. But the individual's story of salvation is the mysterious interaction of divine invitation and free human response. In order to respond, we must listen to the call, receive it with attention and respect, and not allow our own interests to come in the way. We receive the wedding garment of grace in the sacraments,but we must wear this garment in Christ-like living.

We work hard towards salvation as if it depends on us: but we know that it starts and ends in a gift from God. Salvation is the combination of divine invitation and human effort.

Second Reflection

Amen, Yes, to God

Is it likely that people might receive an invitation to the royal wedding banquet and not come? Is it possible that people might receive an invitation to the banquet of the Lord and not come?

Those who refused to come to the wedding were of two types. The first were not interested: rather, they were more interested in their own business. The second reacted with irrational violence to the invitation: they manhandled the poor messengers and killed them.

This hostile reaction to the good news is a recurring theme in the gospel. The light which came to earth was painful to the sore eyes of those who preferred the ways of darkness. Goodness always threatens those who are insecure in their identity. The hostility of Herod to the rumours of an infant king triggered off an insane massacre of innocent children. We have seen how the preaching of the kingdom provoked hostile opposition and conflict. Should we be surprised when this hostile reaction rears its ugly head today among the post-Christian secularists?

All committed Christians, who are imbued with a sense of their mission, should consider themselves as the servants sent to the crossroads to invite everyone, good and bad, to the Saviour's banquet. But when we meet with an apathetic lack of interest, or an energetic hostility, who is to blame? Is it totally the fault of those who reject the message? Or must the messengers accept responsibility for the poor presentation of the message?

At least it is consoling that the Lord himself met with apathy and hospitality, so why should we imagine that we ought to fare better? The Lord registered surprise when he met someone who believed in him: we are dismayed whenever one does not.

Yet, we must be constantly examining ourselves on whether we are to blame for the poor way that we have presented the Lord's invitation. One remembers Pope Paul VI, at the conclusion of the Second Vatican Council, publicly apologising for the faults of the Catholic church which hindered the mission of the gospel. Ghandi, it is said, was deeply impressed by Christ but not by Christians.

Where we ought to be drawing people to Jesus Christ, are we in fact turning them off? Is it true that in many instances our religious education gives a small and painful dose which immunises people from ever experiencing the real thing? Is it possible that we, preachers, have made God sound boring?

God, the one who makes all things new, the eternal spring to satisfy our deepest thirst, the life beyond all time and limitation, the love that heals, uplifts and offers hope! This God... boring?

That religion might prove difficult to understand is understandable: but that religion should be boring is inexcusable.

Is our liturgy so verbal, dull and flat that it offers no mountains of vision, no invitations to wonder? So we keep an eye on the clock and have the carpark cleared in time. Is all our theological energy spent in tilting against the windmills of ancient heresies so that the exciting story of God's love is no longer told?

I like the words of the American poet e.e.cummings:

'I'd rather learn from one bird how to sing than teach a thousand stars how not to dance.'

Have we become so depressed by the bad news that we are forgetting to tell the good news? Are our Christian lives so pampered and protected that we are more like blocks of dead wood than fruitful branches envigorated by the sap of the Holy Spirit?

The liturgical word for yes to the invitation of God is Amen.

Christ is the Word of the Father, the perfect Amen of God.

In Jesus of Nazareth we recognise a life of total Yes to God.

'The Son of God, the Christ Jesus that we proclaimed among you ... was never *Yes* and *No*: with him it was always *Yes*, and how ever many the promises God made, the *Yes* to them all is in him. That is why it is 'through him' that we answer *Amen* to the praise of God.' *(2 Cor 1: 19-20)*

As his followers, we are invited to come to his banquet and join in his unconditional *Yes, Amen,* to the Father.

Twenty-Ninth Sunday

Today's readings open up the relationship between religion and politics, between the sacred and the secular areas of life. In today's 1st Reading, the political decision of Cyrus unwittingly serves the plan of God for the release of the captives in Babylon. In the gospel, the enemies of Jesus try to trap him in the political minefield of the question of paying taxes to the Romans.

Matthew 22:15-21
Give to Caesar the things that belong to Caesar and to God the things that are God's

The Pharisees went away to work out between them how to trap Jesus in what he said. And they sent their disciples to him, together with the Herodians, to say, "Master, we know that you are an honest man and teach the way of God in an honest way, and that you are not afraid of anyone, because a man's rank means nothing to you. Tell us your opinion, then. Is it permissible to pay taxes to Caesar or not?" But Jesus was aware of their malice and replied, "You hypocrites! Why do you set this trap for me? Let me see the money you pay the tax with." They handed him a denarius, and he said, "Whose head is this? Whose name?" "Caesar's," they replied. He then said to them, "Very well, give back to Caesar what belongs to Caesar – and to God what belongs to God."

Good News
The news of God here is the reminder about the absolute dominion of God in all areas of life. There is no part of life from which God should be excluded.

First Reflection
Show Me Your Coin

History tells of many odd marriages of convenience between the proponents of opposing ideologies in order to confront a common enemy. The Pharisees had reached such a state of desperation that they formed an alliance with their political adversaries, the Herodians. Pharisees were, by definition, the Separate Ones who were totally against Roman influence or domination. The friends of Herod, by contrast, operated totally under Roman patronage. But the two parties were prepared to bury their differences in an attempt to discredit Jesus.

If he is against paying taxes to the Romans they will make a political case against him in the civil court. But if he favours payment, then he will lose all popular support. Either way it seems that Jesus is in a no-win situation.

Jesus, however, was a step ahead of their clever conspiracy. He did not directly answer the specific question. Rather, he sprung the trap back on the trappers by making them find the answers. And they found their answer in a most surprising place ... in their own pockets.

Jesus knew that where your coins are, that's where your heart is too. Each coin was like a mirror of their lives. If they chose to accept the advantages of the Empire in better roads, commercial opportunities and international protection, then they should be prepared to pay for them.

Give your rightful return to the secular power, yes! But absolute worship is to be given to God alone: not to Caesar, as the Romans demanded when they raised their emperors to the level of gods. Jesus not only eluded the trap but used the occasion to reaffirm the absolute dominion of God in all areas of life.

'Show me a coin,' he said. 'Whose image is this? Whose name?' We can take these words as a continuing challenge to our lives. Reach into the pockets of how you live and reflect on the coins you find there. The coins represent the talents you are gifted with: and the payment you have received for your work. The coins in your hand are the means for paying your way and acquiring what you need. They represent your security.

But the question behind the reflection is: 'Whose image do they bear?' Is your life a reflection of values which seem to be divorced from God? Values like material prosperity as an end in itself, prestige, power and pleasure.

The best advertisement for God and true religion is the face of a person who is living a full life in both secular and sacred area. Somebody who is prayerful, emotionally integrated, intellectually stimulated, physically fit, socially sensitive, environmentally alert and politically responsible. There is somebody whose life is a coin that bears God's image: somebody who is using all the talents or coins of life to make profit unto the glory of God.

As St Irenaeus put it: 'The glory of God is best seen in a person who is fully alive.'

Second Reflection
The Sacred and the Secular

This is the age of the Christian lay faithful, who are called to be bright witnesses to Christian values in a world where many are trying to make God redundant by separating the secular world from the sacred.

The opponents of Jesus knew that when politics and religion overlap, the mixture is potentially explosive and clever minds can exploit the tension. But Jesus used the occasion to reaffirm the absolute dominion of God in all areas of life. In today's world this dominion of God is obscured by the concerted efforts to have the secular area of life stand on its own without any recognition of the sacred: it wants politics with no religious dimension; the state as an entity totally separate from God.

Secularism is a movement of thought, attitude and behaviour which seeks to render God irrelevant to the way we live as individuals or in society. It spawns a type of humanism which is not fully human since it disregards the restless thirsting of the soul for God. It sets human life as the centre of the universe. It repeats the mistake of Adam, who was beguiled by the tempter's promise of moral autonomy and divine status: 'On the day you eat it your eyes will be opened and you will be like God, knowing good and evil.' *(Gen 3:5)*

The recognition of God's place in life, that is the sense of the sacred, is under constant attack today. There is perhaps more danger from hidden propaganda than from open conflict. The secularistic culture which is beamed into our homes from television, magazines, newspapers and fiction will inevitably erode all sense of the sacred if allowed unchecked access.

What is as soft as a drop of water? Yet a constant flow of drops can wear away and crack open a hard rock if given time. In the average viewer's quota of TV over a year, how many deaths are seen with no reference to one's entry into eternity? How many acts of adultery, violence or theft are portrayed as if there were no moral implications? Immorality is bad enough: but what is more dangerous is amorality, or the attitude that moral principles are utterly irrelevant. There is no such word as sin in the vocabulary of secularism. Little wonder then if the sacredness of conceived life and the sanctity of marriage vows are not appreciated. Nor is there any clear belief in life after death, or any understanding of the ultimate failure of suffering the loss of one's soul.

Secularism, when it totally disregards the sacred dimensions of life, is a crude and unsophisticated form of atheism.

The secular and sacred dimensions of life necessarily overlap because they are parts of the one life. True religion cannot be confined to a sort of prayer that is separated from what goes on in the rest of life. The Holy Spirit is leading the church to recognise that today's area of conflict is the secular world and that the troops in this area are the laity.

For centuries past the principal area of conflict was the field of doctrinal heresy. Since the Council of Trent the church has been well served by a strong clerical leadership and expertise in matters of doctrine. But the principal area of conflict has now shifted and this is the age when the church depends more on dedicated lay faithful. The light that is needed for today's world must shine especially in those areas of life which belong to the laity. They are to uphold a Christian conscience in politics: preserve healthy moral standards in entertainment: and serve the truth in charity through the news media.

They are called to be images of God's unchanging love by their fidelity in marriage. They show the sacredness of life by maintaining the sacred dignity of procreation. They use their talents by developing the world's resources through science and technology. They are generous with their possessions, and wherever possible, seek to generate employment. They reflect the beauty of God by enriching the world through art and works of adornment.

The gospel images of salt, light and yeast apply in a particular way to the role of lay Christians in the midst of secular society. They are the salt which preserves what is good and adds the sharp taste of Christian challenge in society. They are the light which brings the teaching of Christian morality in the confused judgments of conscience. They are the leaven or yeast which gives the lift of hope to the depressing pessimism of the age.

'Give back to God what belongs to God.' We must answer to God in every area of life ... for where can we go from his spirit or where can we flee from his face? In all things we must give back to God the world that belongs to God.

Thirtieth Sunday

The hostile reaction to Jesus in Jerusalem persists and another trap is set for him. Last Sunday's gospel on the question of paying taxes to Caesar was a political minefield. The question today about the greatest commandment was an attempt to entangle him in a web of sterile debate.

Matthew 22:34-40
You shall love the Lord your God and your neighbour as yourself

When the Pharisees heard that Jesus had silenced the Sadducees they got together and, to disconcert him, one of them put a question, "Master, which is the greatest commandment of the Law?" Jesus said, "You must love the Lord your God with all your heart, with all your soul, and with all your mind. This is the greatest and the first commandment. The second resembles it: You must love your neighbour as yourself. On these two commandments hang the whole law, and the Prophets also."

Good News
The ultimate purpose of God's law and revelation is to point the way to love of God and neighbour. On this twofold precept hangs the whole law and all religious teaching.

First Reflection
A Religion of Love

Juan Arias, a Spanish priest, wrote a book entitled 'The God I Don't Believe In.' His catchy title came from a remark made by a bishop on television. It was a panel discussion. This bishop sat there in silence as the church and religion in general were attacked. Eventually the TV host asked the bishop to reply to the points made. He began by saying: 'The God I have heard about here tonight is the God I do not believe in.'

In Jesus' day, long before TV panels, there was no shortage of religious debate. There were many who put all their heart, all their energy and all their mind into talk about religion. One of these debaters now attempted to draw Jesus into the confusing mist of words and the tangled web of argument.

'Which is the greatest commandment of the Law?'

They had 613 precepts: 365 prohibitions, corresponding to the days of the year; and 248 laws of direction, one for every bone in the body. Was there one in particular which was the key to all the others? It was a question which had supplied endless hours of debaters' thrust and parry.

Jesus cut through the web of opinions and commentaries in a simple and challenging answer. Religious laws and prophets' sermons mean nothing if they are not pointed towards total love of God and love of one's neighbour as oneself. Love of God and love of neighbour were not new precepts. But Jesus emphasised the necessary connection between the two as no one had ever done before. You cannot have one without the other. Love of God, whom we cannot see, is bogus if it is not expressed in love of the people whom we do see. And love of people is incomplete unless it is infused by love of God. In the strength of his answer Jesus was more or less saying, like the bishop on TV, 'Yours is the God I do not believe in ... yours is the religion I have no time for.'

Jesus had no time for the religion of barren debate and unproductive words. Nor did St Paul have time for such empty discussion: 'Have nothing to do with pointless philosophical discussions – they only lead further and further away from true religion. Talk of this kind corrodes like gangrene.' (2 Tim 2: 16-17) When talk becomes an end in itself we settle for a sitting theology.

Sitting theologians are to be found behind a desk-top mountain of books out of which they draw learned theses and are awarded degrees and doctorates. But ask them to face a class of school-children to share with them the story of God, and they will run a mile. Panellists sit in an animated TV discussion about social injustice or world hunger: after which they drive off in very expensive cars to their very luxurious homes.

Jesus had no time for the sitting theology which never drives one to fall on one's knees in humble adoration of God: which never makes one stand up in the shoes of the poor to challenge the rich and greedy: which never makes one walk with the zeal of a missionary to share the word with others. Sitting theology is sterile unless it also makes one kneel, stand and walk for God.

Jesus had no time for the religion of casuistry ... playing around with laws and commentaries. We can be so intent about the rubrics of worship that we squeeze out all joy and celebration from the service. For too long we have so burdened confession with lists of sins and penances that we forgot how to celebrate reconciliation.

Jesus had no time for that hyprocrisy where the mouth has all the nice words about God, heaven, grace, prayer, sacraments, fasting, novenas ... but the heart harbours bitterness, retains barriers between people and remains socially insensitive.

Nor did Jesus have time for that substitute religion which makes man the centre of the universe. It neglects God and expends all energy in trying to build a better social order here. Lenin and Stalin wanted a social order without God. To achieve this they deliberately planned an agricultural catastrophe, a famine and the extermination of millions.

The religion Jesus did favour totally hung together on love. The laws, the sermons, theologies, liturgies, institutions and social plans have lost their direction if they are not helping us towards loving God with our total energy of heart, soul and mind: and loving our neighbour with an extension of the love which we ourselves have received from God.

Second Reflection
As You Love Yourself

Jesus asks us to love our neighbour as we love ourselves. Too many people cannot even start on that programme because basically they do not love themselves. You cannot love another if you do not first love yourself: you will project all your own self-hatred and guilt on to the other.

Sad to admit, but in many cases religion has contributed greatly to the burden of self-hatred which oppresses them. One person carries the legacy of strict childhood correction which blocked the growth of self-worth. Another is burdened with such unreal perfectionism that he cannot tolerate any spot on the page of life: there is always a pain on his face: if things are going well it is too good to last: and it is doubtful if heaven itself will please him. Another carries a load of shame and guilt which he cannot cast off, because, to him, God is still a Holy Terror . He has never come to know that Jesus who said to Peter: 'If I do not wash you, you can have nothing in common with me.' (*Jn 13:8*)

And there are many who concentrate so much on the 'Thou shalt not' signs on the road of life that they see nothing of God's beautiful scenery all about. They have no problems about loving God: all their problems are about liking God ... and being comfortable with God.

There are three reasons why I should love myself ... the Father, the Son and the Holy Spirit.

God the Father has loved me into being. I was first a thought in the beautiful mind of God before ever I was spoken into life. God, who loved me before I arrived, still loves me and always will. This loving God has gifted me with my unique composition of talents. and God wants to see me grow and develop these talents so that his glory may be reflected in my life. The catechism defined the purpose of life as 'to know, love and serve God here in this life: and to see and enjoy him in the next.' Perhaps it would have been better if it read: 'to know that I am loved by God.'

The second reason why I should love myself is that God the Son loves me. 'I came down from heaven to save you,' he says. 'I have lived for you, suffered and died for you. I rose again for you. I substituted myself for you and bore the spits and blows, mocking and rejection for you. Look at my cross and know how much I love you.'

The third reason is the Holy Spirit. In the gift of God's Spirit the spark of God's love has been lit in my heart. If I let the wind of the Spirit fan this spark it will become a passionate fire of love which will burn away all vestiges of hatred and negativity.

If I love myself for these three divine reasons, it will follow that I will love others for the same reasons.

I will share in the love of the Father for all his children.

I will share in the love of Jesus Christ who deliberately sought out those whom others despised and whose self-esteem was low. His pity was immense, his compassion was wide and his understanding was divine. When I know how much I am loved by Jesus I will want others to know that love in their lives too.

The Spirit's love in me will want to tear down any barriers or blockages which are preventing growth. Whenever my sinful eyes focus on how unloveable the other person is, then I must beg the Holy Spirit to overcome my sin and to grant me divine eyes to see with understanding.

Love of God and love of others cannot be separated. They spring from the one source ... God's love for us, known and appreciated.

'Let us love one another since love comes from God and everyone who loves is begotten by God and knows God.' *(1 Jn 3:7)*

Thirty-First Sunday

Today's gospel, along with the reading from the prophet Malachi, is a light of judgment on the religious leaders of every time and place. It will always be a temptation for religious leaders to siphon off for themselves much of the honour and respect due to God alone.

Matthew 23:1-12
They do not practice what they preach

Addressing the people and his disciples Jesus said, "The scribes and the Pharisees occupy the chair of Moses. You must therefore do what they tell you and listen to what they say; but do not be guided by what they do: since they do not practice what they preach. They tie up heavy burdens and lay them on men's shoulders, but will they lift a finger to move them? Not they! Everything they do is done to attract attention, like wearing broader phylacteries and longer tassels, like wanting to take the place of honour at banquets and the front seats in the synagogues, being greeted obsequiously in the market squares and having people call them Rabbi.

"You, however, must not allow yourselves to be called Rabbi, since you have only one Master, and you are all brothers. You must call no one on earth your father, since you have only one Father, and he is in heaven. Nor must you allow yourselves to be called teachers, for you have only one Teacher, the Christ. The greatest among you must be your servant. Anyone who exalts himself will be humbled, and anyone who humbles himself will be exalted."

Good News

God alone is the Master of all authority, the Father of all life and the Teacher of all wisdom. To serve God humbly is the greatest of all callings.

First Reflection
On Religious Leadership

Matthew clearly had a bee in his bonnet about the scribes and Pharisees. The entire twenty-third chapter of his gospel is a vehement indictment of these religious leaders and their abuse of power and prestige.

Biblical scholars tell us that the vehemence of this chapter is due more to Matthew's editing than to any great hostility on the part of Jesus towards the scribes and Pharisees. An overall view of the gospels shows that some of the Pharisees were on friendly terms with Jesus, though he did condemn the Pharisaical tendency to exaggerate outward observance of the law while being blind to its inner spirit or meaning.

Matthew had his own reasons for using his editorial role to highlight the condemnatory words of Jesus and to caricature the scribes and Pharisees. By the time Matthew was writing, the Christian community had suffered at the hands of the Pharisees. The final expulsion of Jewish Christians from temple and synagogue was still a fresh memory.

Furthermore, Matthew was aware of emerging divisions within the christian community as their leaders were taking on titles of self-importance which were contrary to the teaching of Jesus. But one would miss Matthew's message by restricting its lesson to the religious leadership of the first century. The message of the gospel is a living word for every age.

In recent times the conscience of the Catholic church has been uneasy over the show of ecclesial pomp and prestige quite at variance with the spirit of the gospel. Indeed, at the collective examination of conscience which developed at the Second Vatican Council, it was admitted that triumphalism and clericalism were prominent among the sins of the church. Recent popes have been distinctly unhappy with some of the historical trappings of worldly authority which survived from past centuries. They have led the way by their own example of leadership as service to God's people.

Speaking to priests Paul VI said: 'Each of you will have to repeat to himself: I am destined to the service of the church, to the service of the people. The priesthood is charity. Woe to him who considers that he can put it to his own selfish use.' In these words he returned to the gospel insight that it is an occupational hazard for all ministers of religion to think that the honours due to God alone are due also to those who serve in his name.

An idea that is dear to the heart of Pope John Paul II is the consideration of a vocation to the priesthood or religius life as a grace given to the community. 'The sacramental priesthood is from Christ himself and is a gift to the community.' (*Letter to Priests, 8-4-79*) The call is not to a position of social prestige but to a life of serving the Christian community with the message of the gospel.

Jesus Christ was compassionate to the sinner and gentle with the fallen. But he was openly angry with those who would use religious leadership for their own advancement. Religious exploitation usurps God's place ... God's titles ... and God's honour.

Second Reflection
Hypocrisy and Humility

Matthew's caricature of the Pharisees was so powerful that ever since then the name Pharisee has become a proverbial catchword for hypocrisy. The word hypocrite comes from the Greek word for an actor playing a role on stage. Hypocrisy has come to have special associations with acting an exterior role of piety and goodness which one does not match up to interiorly.

Jesus put his finger on three areas of hypocrisy where the Pharisee in each one of us tries to cover up the hollowness of our deep personal insecurity.

First is the tendency not to practise what we preach. We are very quick to point out the faults of others while we have excuses ready for our own failures. We forget that when the one finger of criticism points at another person, there are three fingers pointing back at ourselves. We criticise the splinter in our brother's eye and fail to notice the plank in our own. But persistent condemnation of others is usually a sign of deep personal insecurity.

Whoever is humbly facing up to his or her own faults will be very slow to preach at others. For those of us who must preach, it is a harrowing but ultimately enriching experience to feel this huge gap between the fine words we use before others and the truth of our own sinful lives. The preacher who comes through this crisis has a new tone of compassion in his voice every time he speaks. People will listen to this voice which speaks with them. But an audience is alienated by the hard voice that preaches at them.

The second tendency of hypocrisy is to lay heavy burdens on others while not attempting to lift them ourselves. It is said that every loudmouthed fanatic is deeply insecure: too insecure to negotiate with enemy or opponent, for if one stone of the defensive wall is taken away, all might collapse. The motto of the fanatic is: argument weak, shout for effect. Whoever has not negotiated with his or her own shadow or negative side will be full of deep prejudices. They frequently utter angry, broadside condemnations. They make dishonest demands on others, far in excess of what they themselves produce.

The third weakness of the hypocrite is to depend on marks of honour and people's attention. The person who is hollow within has to bolster up self-esteem by outward pomposity and prestige. If we are very weak in this regard we cannot function for long without constant strokes of affirmation. Self-doubt and fatigue set in if words of praise or tokens of affirmation are not forthcoming. Quite often, situations are so manipulated as to make oneself seem indispensable to others. Being needed is then a tremendous stroke of affirmation.

The basic mistake of all hypocrites is to expect to find their security through their own merits. It is significant that, immediately after speaking about hypocrisy, Jesus went on to talk about humility . Humility is precisely what the hypocrite needs to discover. Humility comes from the Latin word for the earth. As a virtue it means having your feet set honestly in the bedrock of truth. It brings us to admit our own faults. But it does not stop there: it leads us on to cast our cares upon God and trust that he will be our hope and protection.

In that way, as Jesus said: 'Anyone who humbles himself will be exalted.'

Today's responsorial psalm portrays the humble soul which is totally secure in God:
'O Lord, my heart is not proud
nor haughty my eyes ...
Truly I have set my soul
in silence and peace.
A weaned child on its mother's breast,
even so is my soul.'

Gospel greatness begins in the humble recognition of our own faults and failures: then it learns that the true source of security is not what we might merit but what God's mercy offers us. The soul then delights in following the example of Jesus Christ who made himself the servant of all.

Thirty-Second Sunday

The parable of the ten bridesmaids is part of the last of Matthew's five great semons on the kingdom which are the pillars of his construction. This final sermon is about the ending of our earthly experiment with the kingdom, when the Lord will come again to bring about the heavenly perfection of the kingdom. At the moment of death, the door is closed on further experimentation and the Lord will shine his light of judgment to test our readiness. This reminder about death and judgment is in keeping with the mood of November, the month of the departed.

Matthew 25:1-13
Look, the bridegroom comes. Go out to meet him

Jesus told this parable to his disciples: "The kingdom of heaven will be like this. Ten bridesmaids took their lamps and went to meet the bridegroom. Five of them were foolish and five were sensible: the foolish ones did take their lamps, but they brought no oil, whereas the sensible ones took flasks of oil as well as their lamps. The bridegroom was late, and they all grew drowsy and fell asleep. But at midnight there was a cry, 'The bridegroom is here! Go out and meet him.' At this, all those bridesmaids woke up and trimmed their lamps, and the foolish ones said to the sensible ones, 'Give us some of your oil: our lamps are going out.' But they replied, 'There may not be enough for us and for you; you had better go to those who sell it and buy some for yourselves.' They had gone off to buy it when the bridegroom arrived. Those who were ready went in with him to the wedding hall and the door was closed. The other bridesmaids arrived later. 'Lord, Lord,' they said, 'open the door for us.' But he replied, 'I tell you solemnly, I do not know you.' So stay awake, because you do not know either the day or the hour."

Good News
The Lord will return to open the door for us and invite us to come to the Father.

First Reflection
Be Ready Today

The message of the parable is very clear: be ready for the coming of the Lord.

Yet we have an amazing capacity for complicating what is simple and for casting a fog of confusion over what should be perfectly clear.

Nothing is more obvious about human life than the fact that everybody must die some time. Yet our confused minds make us think and act as if we had the right to live on here for ever. As secularistic thinking takes more of a grip in people's mind, death is becoming a taboo subject. The inevitability of death is not being honestly faced. Coping with bereavement is becoming a widespread problem. People are tending to live with no thought of where the journey of life is going to.

There is a sharp ray of wisdom in the story about the three devils who were planning a strategy to confuse our thinking and lead us astray. The first said: 'Tell them there is no hell, so there is nothing to be afraid of.' The second disagreed: 'No, that's not enough. Some of them fancy that they act for more noble motives than fear. Why not tell them that there is no heaven . Take away all hope, take away a future to look forward to. ' The third spoke out of the experience of his years: 'Forget about this heaven or hell tactic. That is all too unreal for them. I know how they live and how they think. You must meet them where they are. Don't bother telling them there is no hell. Don't tell them there is no heaven. Just tell them there is no hurry.'

The story of the ten bridesmaids reaches its climactic moment when the heavy crossbar falls into place and the door is closed. The heavy oriental door was a complicated affair. So, from that moment on, there was a clear separation of the wise, who were inside the door, from the unwise, who were outside. It was the end of the time of waiting and the beginning of the festivities.

One of our central beliefs in Christianity is about facing the light of judgment when we die. The doctrine that developed in the growth of Sacred Scripture maintains that there is life after death: and that it is either a life of glory and reward or a life of damnation and punishment.

Earlier in Matthew we came across the mixture of good and bad in the earthly kingdom: wheat and weeds in the one field, good fish and useless in the one net. The sorting out would not take place until the final day of judgment and separation. The moment of death is when the door is closed. The time of experimentation with the kingdom is over. The examination has started and it is too late for cramming: you have signed your name to the document and it is too late to pull back from the contract.

When we wonder about our readiness for that final examination, the best indicator is our readiness to answer the call today. The past is gone. The future has not come back to meet us. Each present day is all we have to cope with. 'If you hear his voice today, harden not your heart', said the psalmist. Today is the day you are to hear the call of the bridegroom, and bear his light, and be ready to follow him.

Second Reflection
The Inner Light

Some people get a bit sore over this parable of the foolish and sensible bridesmaids. They feel that the sensible ones acted in a mean and selfish way. They should have taken a chance and shared their oil in the spirit of one for all and all for one. Those who are uncomfortable with the story probably feel that sensible people are far too sensible anyway! You know, all that caution and planning and saving instead of letting go and having a ball!

There was not enough oil to share because the story is really about a light that cannot be borrowed. There are some tasks you have to do for yourself ... believing, hoping and loving. Nobody can do your believing for you ... or hoping ... or loving. Faith, hope and charity, the three theological gifts, are three flames in the candle we receive at baptism. We must protect these flames from extinction and provide the oil of prayer, study and action to keep them burning ever more brightly.

The flame of faith helps us to see everything in life in the light of God's love. The flame of hope gives us unsinkable confidence in God's goodness, support and protection. The flame of charity enlivens our loving with divine understanding and compassion.

I once heard somebody commenting on this parable who said that the presence of Christ is recognised, not discovered. It was a subtle distinction: recognition is of something already present; discovery is of something not present until it is found or uncovered.

The point being made is that God is everywhere present even though we do not always recognise him. It is not as if we have to discover God: we are to recognise him, already present. It is only the divine inner light of faith, hope and charity which enables us to make that recognition of him.

There are other texts in today's liturgy which link up with this theme of the inner light which recognises God. In our extract from the Book of Wisdom we read:

Wisdom is bright and does not grow dim.
By those who see her she is readily seen,
and found by those who look for her. *(Wis 6:12)*

Wisdom is the inner light given by God. The reading makes the point that, while it is a divine gift, it is given only to those who thirst for it, seek it, love it and carefully nurture it when received.

It is like what St John Damascene said of the gift of prayer: 'Prayer is a gift that God gives to those who pray.'

The inner light which recognises the presence of God and hears his voice is a combination of divine gift and human response: just as prayer is a combination of divine gift and human response.

Today's responsorial psalm offers a portrait of the faithful soul who is responding to God from morning rising to sleeping at night:

'My body pines for you ... I gaze on you in the sanctuary ... I will bless you all my life ... on my bed I remember you, on you I muse through the night.'

The lamp in that soul was ready for God's coming at any hour ... sometimes thirsting for God, or gazing in the holy sanctuary, or returning thanks and blessing throughout the day's activities, or closing the day in the remembrance of God.

The inner light which recognises God is divine wisdom. How sad to see people living as if the externals of life matter more than the inner light! How much fretting and energy are put into the outside fittings of the lamp while the inner oil of wisdom is neglected! What good is it to have the most expensive lamp, or the latest fashion, or the most clever piece of modern technology, if the inner light is lacking?

When midnight comes, and the call is heard, it is the light from within which alone prevails in the darkness.

And that is a light which cannot be borrowed.

It must be your own.

Thirty-third Sunday

The liturgy is attuned to the mood of our northern November. Trees have shed their leafy adornment and now stand as stark skeletons against grey skies. The liturgical readings for the month reveal the unadorned shape of life. It is the month when we think of the judgment we must face to render an account of our lives.

Matthew 25: 14-30

Because you have been faithful over a few things, enter into the joy of the Lord.

Jesus spoke this parable to his disciples: "The kingdom of heaven is like a man on his way abroad who summoned his servants and entrusted his property to them. To one he gave five talents, to another two, to a third one; each in proportion to his ability. Then he set out. Now a long time after, the master of those servants came back and went through his accounts with them. The man who had received the five talents came forward bringing five more. 'Sir,' he said, 'you entrusted me with five talents; here are five more that I have made.' His master said to him, 'Well done, good and faithful servant; you have shown you can be faithful in small things, I will trust you with greater; come and join in your master's happiness.' Next the man with two talents came forward. 'Sir,' he said, 'you entrusted me with two talents; here are two more that I have made.' His master said to him, 'Well done, good and faithful servant; you have shown you can be faithful in small things, I will trust you with greater; come and join in your master's happiness.' Last came forward the man who had one talent. 'Sir,' he said, 'I had heard you were a hard man, reaping where you have not sown and gathering where you have not scattered; so I was afraid, and I went off and hid your talent in the ground. Here it is; it was yours, you have it back.' But his master answered him, 'You wicked and lazy servant! So you knew that I reap where I have not sown and gather where I have not scattered? Well then, you should have deposited my money with the bankers, and on my return I would have recovered my capital with interest. So now, take the talent from him and give it to the man who has the five talents. For to everyone who has will be given more, and he will have more than enough; but from the man who has not, even what he has will be taken away. As for this good-for-nothing servant, throw him out into the dark, where there will be weeping and grinding of teeth.'"

Good News

God has invested in our lives and trusts us to make a profitable return. If our testing shows us faithful in small things he will trust us with more and invite us to share in the master's happiness.

First Reflection
Judgment and Accountability

This is a story about our accountability fo God. There is a very serious sense of personal responsibility in the story which runs counter to the fashion of thinking today.

We have come from an age when many people were weighed down by an excessively strict concept of God. Theology was far more concerned with the defence of orthodoxy than with savouring the delight of God: like somebody at a sumptuous meal who is so concerned about the possibility of harmful additives in the food that he cannot enjoy the taste of anything. Fear of God paralysed many people in their creativity and stunted their initiative. Many consciences were damaged for life.

From the extreme of strictness we have swung to the opposite extreme of leniency. Authority is rejected: discipline is not in favour: the need for punishment is not understood: correction is not accepted. As a result, we have a generation with no backbone, when people are incapable of making a firm commitment or of sticking faithfully to a promise.

It has led to a very feeble sort of religious thought and produces wishy-washy statements like: 'All Jesus really asked for was love, but all the church gives us is laws.'

But where is the strongminded Jesus who preached the need for repentance: who was angry with the money-changers and hypocrites: who forgave the adulterous woman but told her to sin no more: who asked his followers to take up their crosses and follow him? This feeble thinking picks and chooses what one likes from religion and dis-regards what does not appeal.

The existence and influence of the devil are not taken seriously. Hell is denied. And having to face the light of judgment and render an account of life is totally forgotten. At the old extreme, justice untempered by mercy produced a servile fear of God. 'Sir, ... I was afraid ... so I hid your talent in the ground.' But at the present extreme, a religion which stresses mercy but disregards God's justice is producing serious moral irresponsibility.

The parable of the talents makes the point that God has invested in us and expects to make a profit on each investment. The return that God expects is that the divine love which we have received would be spread out on earth by us.

St John seems to suggest that God's love is incomplete until we pass it on. 'As long as we love one another God will live in us and his love will be complete in us.' *(1 Jn 4:12)* God's love does not come to perfection on earth until we accept it and pass it on to others. God's investment is to be turned to profit, not to be buried in the ground.

The mistake being made by our contemporary feeble thinking is in underestimating how firm and tough Christian love must be.

Love is firm in its obedience to the commandments: in its faithfulness until death: and in its stubborn refusal to be turned aside by hurt or malice. Love is tough in its willingness to confront, to challenge and to correct. Love is the courage to take up the cross and the loyalty to stay with Jesus. Love is being faithful to God in every small moment and in every small encounter, for the small moments accumulate and give the overall shape to life.

In the parable, the master congratulates and rewards those who were faithful and productive in the small affairs. And when we render an account for our lives, it will be according to these everyday uses of God's talents in us.

'Well done, good and faithful servant; you have shown you can be faithful in small things, I will trust you with greater; come and join in your master's happiness.'

Second Reflection
He Dug a Hole

The servant who dug a hole to hide his talent offers a very true to life picture of how undeveloped talent makes a person very negative. Not alone does he return no profit to the master but he manages to shift the blame from himself to the master. 'I had heard that you were a hard man...' He so twists the situation about that he forgets how the master trusted in him and invested in him: all he chooses to remember are the bad things that others were saying about him.

We dig a hole and try to bury part of ourselves whenever we do not come to terms with our failings, or accept our experiences truthfully or when bitterness distorts our memories. The repressed or buried part of us turns foul and comes up in various forms of negativity.

One common form of negative energy is the tendency to off-load our personal responsibility by shifting the blame to others; like that servant trying to blame the master for his own lack of profit.

Another form of negative energy is cynicism. Cynicism flows out of a stagnant pool of life. Waters stagnate when there is no fresh inflow and no corresponding outflow. A stagnant life results when there is no healthy intellectual stimulation or spiritual inspiration. Yet there can be hours spent every day in television passivity or waste of brain power on useless curiosities and vapid reading. The master rightly accused his unprofitable servant of laziness. The unproductive life and stagnant mind have already begun to experience that hell where all is dark and there are tears of frustration and the angry sound of grinding teeth.

This darkened mind is unreceptive to new initiatives or words of light but it avidly absorbs every tatty little detail of scandal: just like the way the unprofitable servant latched on to the bad things that were being said about his superior. As we have noted more than once, light hurts the sore eye and goodness is very threatening to those who are insecure in their identity.

You will hear the grinding of teeth in that voice which acquires new energy only to scoff at the efforts of others or to gloat over any failure or departure from the ministry.

The angry mind digs a hole which becomes a cesspool of stagnant water. Not only does it do no good itself but it will poison all that drink of it.

But whenever the lake of life is stimulated by a healthy inflow and expressed in a productive outflow, the waters are life-giving. Good investments produce more. 'To everyone who has will be given more, and he will have more than enough.'

That's the way it is in life. The batteries of life are charged by being used: they lose the charge if the generator is not switched on. Physical exercise increases our capacity to take on more. The jogger is prepared to suffer momentary tiredness for he knows that by this effort he is generating more energy. By contrast, lack of physical exercise causes muscular atrophy, principally of the vital heart muscle.

Intellectual stimulation does not exhaust the mind but produces a person who is alert and attentive in all spheres of life. The stimulated mind never experiences the heavy hand of boredom which is an off-shoot of television passivity.

The same principle of growth applies to the spiritual life. 'Train yourself spiritually,' wrote Paul to Timothy. 'Physical exercises are useful enough, but the usefulness of spirituality is unlimited, since it holds out the reward of life here and now and of the future life as well.' *(1 Tim.4:7)*

Paul holds out the promise of full living here in the present as well as in the future: just as the profitable servants were productive in the present and promised reward in the future.

God invests in us, not to see his talent buried, not to hear us off-loading our own responsibility by blaming others, not to see us cringe helplessly and uselessly in fear.

His desire is to be able one day to congratulate us on a job well done and to reward us with the happiness of heaven.

Our Lord Jesus Christ, Universal King

Many of the themes of the year of Matthew come together in today's recognition of Jesus Christ as King. His style of kingship is very close to the role of a shepherd, a point that is recognised in the choice of texts for the first reading and responsorial psalm. Above all else, the criterion for belonging to his kingdom is the practical, everyday love which attends to those in need.

Matthew 25:31-46
He will sit upon his seat of glory and he will separate men one from another

Jesus said to his disciples: "When the Son of Man comes in his glory, escorted by all the angels, then he will take his seat on his throne of glory. All the nations will be assembled before him and he will separate men one from another as the shepherd separates sheep from goats. He will place the sheep on his right hand and the goats on his left. Then the King will say to those on his right hand: 'Come, you whom my Father has blessed, take for your heritage the kingdom prepared for you since the foundation of the world. For I was hungry and you gave me food; I was thirsty and you gave me drink; I was a stranger and you made me welcome; naked and you clothed me, sick and you visited me, in prison and you came to see me.' Then the virtuous will say to him in reply, 'Lord, when did we see you hungry and feed you; or thirsty and give you drink? When did we see you a stranger and make you welcome; naked and clothe you; sick or in prison and go to see you?' And the King will answer, 'I tell you solemnly, in so far as you did this to one of the least of these brothers of mine, you did it to me.' Next he will say to those on his left hand, 'Go away from me, with your curse upon you, to the eternal fire prepared for the devil and his angels. For I was hungry and you never gave me food; I was thirsty and you never gave me anything to drink; I was a stranger and you never made me welcome, naked and you never clothed me, sick and in prison and you never visited me.' Then it will be their turn to ask, 'Lord, when did we see you hungry or thirsty, a stranger or naked, sick or in prison, and did not come to your help?'

"Then he will answer, 'I tell you solemnly, in so far as you neglected to do this to one of the least of these, you neglected to do it to me.' And they will go away to eternal punishment, and the virtuous to eternal life."

Good News
Jesus Christ is the King of the Universe and the true shepherd of all people. He will come again to vindicate and reward all those who live according to the ideals of the kingdom.

First Reflection
The shepherd-King
David was the shepherd boy chosen to be king. His name became a symbol of the hope that God would raise up a new shepherd to lead the people to the ways of justice and love. It was important in Matthew's eyes that the conception of Jesus in Mary's womb should be announced to Joseph, who was of the descendants of David. Furthermore, the birth of Jesus took place in Bethlehem, the town of David. David was the shepherd who was chosen to be king, but Jesus was the king who chose to be a shepherd.

His style of kingship avoided all the pompous circumstances associated with worldly royalty. Jesus was born, not in a palace,but in a cave borrowed from the animals. The royal birth was announced, not to the royal courts of the world, but to the shepherds on the hillside and to some wise men who read the signs in the stars. From Bethlehem he was taken to Nazareth, a town so unpretentious that nobody expected anything good to come from it.

When Jesus began to preach to the people it was about the kingdom of heaven to be set up on earth. His dream was to have people living in such perfect accord with the plan of the loving creator that society on earth would be the mirror of heaven. Heavenly happiness would begin on earth. But this kingdom ideal would mean reversing many of the principles upon which life was commonly operated. The sermon on the mount reversed the principles of this world. The blessed were the people-of-no-power.

At one stage people were so impressed with his miracles that they wanted to make him their king. But he avoided their move, because they misunderstood his notion of kingship. When the time came for him to acknowledge his kingship, the crown he received was of thorns, and his throne was the cross. As he had said, the good shepherd lays down his life for the flock. So identified was he with his sheep that later writers called him the Paschal Lamb, whose blood was shed to release his people from their sins.

Jesus was not a power-hungry king, but one who took on the role of shepherd to his people. 'I shall look for the lost one, bring back the stray, bandage the wounded and make the weak strong.' *(Ezek 34:16)*

In baptism we are united with Christ in his kingship. 'He loves us and has washed away our sins in his blood, and made us a line of kings, priests to serve his God and Father.' *(Rev 1:6)* If we belong to Christ's kingly line, then we must live in imitation of his kingly way. We are the people of the king only if we have the loving heart of the king.

On our knees we pray 'Thy kingdom come.' And on our feet we go to work for that kingdom in the very practical, everyday work of attending to the needs of our brothers and sisters. The kingdom is about food and clothing, welcoming and visiting.

Matthew, at the beginning of the gospel referred to Jesus as Emmanuel, God-with-us. At the end of the gospel, Jesus is again Emmanuel: 'know that I am with you always; yes, to the end of time.' Between the first coming and the last coming in glory, he is with us. And he awaits our daily attention. Where? In the blessed ones who are poor in spirit, gentle, mourning or hungering for justice. 'In so far as you did this to one of the least of these brothers of mine, you did it to me.'

Second Reflection
The Kingdom of the King

The introduction to Matthew's gospel in the Jerusalem Bible calls it 'the great charter of the new order which, in Christ, completes God's plan.' The feast of Christ the King is an opportunity to recap on how we saw the theme of the kingdom developing.

When Jesus began to preach his initial message was: 'Repent, for the kingdom of heaven is close at hand.'*(Mt 4:17)* Immediately after announcing the kingdom, Jesus called the first disciples. He was recruiting the community who would be the taskforce of the kingdom. This community of disciples is later identified as the church.

In the sermon on the mount Jesus proclaimed the ideals of

271

the kingdom. The beatitudes portray the attitudes and actions of kingdom-people. Virtue in the kingdom must be more sincere than what has previously posed for virtue. The inner heart must be renewed. Our great passions must be redeemed and the energies which have been destructive must be harnessed for good.

The focus of Christ's attention then narrowed down to the special training of the twelve apostles. They are repeatedly told of their need for courage. There will be no cheap way of following Jesus. The cost will be the cross.

The focus then broadens out to address the whole crowd. The kingdom will have to grow in a hostile climate. In spite of all opposition it will grow, as wheat in the midst of weeds.

The attention is transferred back again to the disciples as Jesus trains the community who will continue his work when he is gone. Peter is singled out as the rock of the foundation. Jesus must face Jerusalem, where death and resurrection will be his destiny. Over the course of seven Sundays we heard many lessons about life in the community of disciples – about compassion, courage, faith, taking up the cross, dying to self, supporting the erring brother and offering forgiveness. The final section on the kingdom began when Jesus reached Jerusalem. The brewing hositility erupts into open confrontation. In this context of confrontation Jesus develops the theme of the vindication of the kingdom-people in the final judgment. The harvest will see the separation of those who have their lamps ready from those who have not: of those who use their talents profitably from those who did not.

The ultimate criterion of kingdom-people occurs in today's gospel. The kingdom of heaven-on-earth essentially means that our love of God is to be shown by attending to the daily needs of others.

When Jesus comes in final glory, the true kingdom-people will be vindicated. They will be rewarded for they noticed the needs of others and came to their help. Those who did not notice, much less helped, will be duly punished.

The response to God is given in the ordinary, everyday affairs of life. One need not even be aware of their eternal value.

The kingdom of heaven is close at hand.

As close, in fact, as the hand that serves.